Advance Praise

"Stephen Porges cracked the code with his Polyvagal Theory for the physiological mechanism of the human socio–emotional exchange system upon which we build our emotional landscapes. *Our Polyvagal World* reviews the theory and reminds us that the importance of others is baked into the human genome. When we look at the effects of traumatic events, we must recognize how our nervous system responds and changes, and impacts how we react to stress long after a traumatic incident. Finally, the authors show us that the solutions lay in the interpersonal deployment of the vagal exchange."

—**Drew Pinsky, MD,** FACP, Board Certified Internal Medicine/
Addiction Medicine

"This wonderfully useful book combines the groundbreaking power of Polyvagal Theory with penetrating clinical insights and warmhearted practical tools—all for greater healing, resilience, and well-being in a stressful world. You can feel the kindness of its authors on every page, with candor about their own father–son relationship and what they've learned inside of it. The scientific aspects are explained with masterful clarity. With applications to couples, families, education, and institutions such as prisons, there is value here for every kind of reader. And so timely as we recover from past social disruptions and face new ones. Truly a gem."

—**Rick Hanson, PhD,** author of *Resilient: How to Grow an
Unshakable Core of Calm, Strength, and Happiness*

"*Our Polyvagal World* is an awesome book. It is readable and written in plain language so that it is easy to understand. This book will help you comprehend your trauma and help you live a better life. In addition to breathing optimally (super important), yoga (also cool), the bottom line of this book—and of the Polyvagal Theory—is that human relatedness matters: Nothing is more profoundly beneficial to our health and the health of our nervous system than relational connection with people we love and trust, i.e., those people with whom we feel safe. A good conversation, all the more so over a meal, can reverse eons of evolution; we can get our nervous system in its most engaged and evolutionarily advanced form. I highly recommend this book to anyone interested in the science of safety and to anyone interested in living a better and healthier life without having to commit to extreme measures. And if both apply to you, this book is a must."

—**Diana Fosha, PhD,** developer of AEDP, founder of the AEDP Institute,
and editor of *Undoing Aloneness & the Transformation of
Suffering Into Flourishing: AEDP 2.0*

T0246702

"At last, a simple, eloquently straightforward, and comprehensive rendition of one of the most important recent advances in psychology and physiology, by its pioneer. Stephen Porges, ably assisted here by his son Seth, places his indispensable Polyvagal Theory into the context of our present-day frantic, post-pandemic, complicated lives and thereby guides us toward the safety on which our well-being, personal and social, depends. Essential reading; this book leaves me filled with appreciation."

—**Gabor Maté MD,** CM, author of *The Myth of Normal: Trauma, Illness and Healing in a Toxic Culture*

"The great challenges in understanding ourselves is how minds, bodies, and brains work together. In this excellent book, written for the layperson, Porges and Porges outline their important and internationally acclaimed concepts of Polyvagal Theory; on how the autonomic nervous system is fundamental to how we experience threat and safety. Polyvagal Theory has made major contributions to our understanding of how stress and trauma changes our bodies and also how, by working with the autonomic nervous system, we can find balance again. As such, it has made major contributions to psychotherapy and the importance of social connectedness in our lives. A must-read for anyone who wants to understand how the autonomic system regulates emotional states and what they can do to cultivate well-being."

—**Paul Gilbert, PhD,** OBE, author of *The Compassionate Mind*

"In this book, the authors explain the Polyvagal Theory in a simple, relatable way that is easy to absorb and understand. Illustrated with real-life examples, *Our Polyvagal World* convinces us that that how we feel depends upon our physiological state, showing us why a felt sense of safety is essential for a rich, fulfilling life. Reading it inspires moments of personal recognition and life-changing understanding, but it goes one step further to give us the practical tools we need to deepen our social bonds and sense of safety in this stressful modern world. It's an empowering, hopeful book that you will be glad you read!"

—**Pat Ogden, PhD,** founder of Sensorimotor Psychotherapy Institute and author of *Body of Knowledge Card Deck: Sensorimotor Practices for Awareness, Regulation, and Expansion*

OUR POLYVAGAL WORLD

OUR POLYVAGAL WORLD

How Safety and Trauma Change Us

Stephen W. Porges and Seth Porges

W. W. NORTON & COMPANY
Celebrating a Century of Independent Publishing

For information about permission to reproduce selections from this book,
write to Permissions, W. W. Norton & Company, Inc.,
500 Fifth Avenue, New York, NY 10110

For information about special discounts for bulk purchases, please contact
W. W. Norton Special Sales at specialsales@wwnorton.com or
800-233-4830

Manufacturing by Lakeside Book Company
Book design by Anna Knighton
Production manager: Gwen Cullen

"The Polyvagal Theory" chart designed by Lauren Graessle

ISBN: 978-1-324-03025-6 (pbk)

W. W. Norton & Company, Inc., 500 Fifth Avenue, New York, NY 10110
www.wwnorton.com

W. W. Norton & Company Ltd., 15 Carlisle Street, London W1D 3BS

10 9 8 7 6 5 4

For Sue Carter, who gave us oxytocin

Contents

Introduction: What Is the Polyvagal Theory?   *xiii*

PART 1: IN YOU

1 The *Automatic* Nervous System   5
2 Neuroception: Our Body's Surveillance System   18
3 The Vagus Nerve   45
4 The Evolution of the Polyvagal Theory   68
5 Connectedness and Co-Regulation: A Biological Imperative   77
6 Trauma and Addiction   92

PART 2: IN THE WORLD

7   The Pandemic Paradox   125
8   The Polyvagal Theory at Work   135
9   Education   154
10 Incarceration   164

Epilogue: The Polyvagal Life   177
Acknowledgments   183
Glossary   189
References   209
Notes   217
Index   221

"I think, therefore I am."

—DESCARTES

"I *feel myself*, therefore I am."

—THE POLYVAGAL THEORY

Introduction: What Is the Polyvagal Theory?

Good question!

We can summarize the Polyvagal Theory, and this entire book, in one sentence:

> *How safe we feel is crucial to our physical*
> *and mental health and happiness.*

It really is that simple.

When we *feel* safe (notice it says "feel" safe and not that we actually *are* safe—this is an important distinction we'll come back to repeatedly), our nervous systems and entire bodies undergo a massive physiological shift that primes us to be healthier, happier, and smarter; to be better learners and problem solvers; to have more fun; to heal faster; and generally to feel more alive.

(Pretty neat, right?)

As you may have figured out, key to all this is the vagus nerve. It's right there in the title: "Poly" means multiple, and "vagal" means . . . well . . . vagus.

If you opened up an anatomy textbook, you'd see that the vagus is a cranial nerve. That is, it is one of precisely 12 special nerves that originate in the brainstem and offer direct lines between the brainstem and key parts of our body.

What makes the vagus special is that, unlike the other cranial nerves, it doesn't have just one primary destination in the body. As an example, the optic nerve (which is responsible for eyesight) runs from the brainstem to the eyes—and pretty much nowhere else.

Instead, the vagus winds its way down from the brainstem and weaves through almost the entire body, all the way down to the gut. Because this wandering nerve (literally: The name "vagus" comes from the Latin word for "wandering," similar to the word "vagabond") touches so much of our body and so many of our organs, the vagus serves as a sort of shared connection that allows our numerous bodily systems and organs to communicate with one another and act in concert.

If the body is a symphony, full of discrete systems and sections charged with fulfilling specific functions, then the vagus is the conductor: the shared link that allows the body to work together as a cohesive unit.

It is through the vagus that feelings of safety and threat bounce up and down through our entire bodies, changing our emotions and the ways we feel—as well as how our bodies, organs, and senses operate on a physical level.

Which brings us to the topic of trauma: perhaps the defining health threat of the 21st century.

We live in a world in which trauma is endemic but rarely understood. All around us: millions of people silently suffering on their own, often unable to explain bizarre changes that traumatic experiences seem to have caused in their bodies.

When people discuss what they feel post-trauma, they often describe it with an air of mystery. As if their experiences are unique and unexplainable (or perhaps unscientific) phenomena:

I left my own body. Floated above it and looked
down at somebody else who looked like me.

Ask a trauma survivor to recount their experience and how it changed them.

Rather than a cohesive story, you're likely to hear them recount an abstract collage of visceral feelings and sensations. For trauma survivors, memories are often encoded in body parts or sensory experiences that light up and shut down in ways that feel new and foreign. Flashes of sights and sounds and colors amid a complex patchwork of memories and feelings and dissociative out-of-body experiences. A body and brain wired into a new existence.

> *A car horn resonates as a brain-crushing din. It's like there's*
> *a selective megaphone in my ear. Some sounds fade into*
> *the background. Others overwhelm and consume me and*
> *turn me into a rabid monster that I don't recognize.*

It can come from sexual assault or surviving a war. From one awful experience, years of torment and abuse, or a parade of small daily stressors that slowly eat away at us. But what makes trauma *trauma* is that it changes us in ways that are new and frightening and rarely understood. And because these changes are largely invisible, they are often left to gnaw away at our insides over time. An unseen shadow that many live with and either accept as normal or dismiss as abnormal.

> *Everything I thought of as me was gone. I'm*
> *not sure who this person is anymore.*

To most people, trauma remains a misunderstood metamorphosis—and one that is often taboo to talk about. It's a strange trip, and mere words are often not enough. Sounds sound different. Tastes taste different. Things that once excited or caused joy are experienced through a muted fog. Breathing and digestion and countless other bodily processes shift in their function.

> *Nobody understands just how abstract it all is. Like it isn't even real.*

Trauma is often treated (or dismissed) as a purely psychological issue that is literally all in our heads. But trauma is not merely a psychological phenomenon—it's also a physiological one.

What we mean by that: The impact of trauma is not isolated to our brains, but stretches through our nervous system to virtually every part of our body, changing how our senses sense, how our organs operate, and just about every aspect of our physical and mental health.

In other words: Trauma changes our bodies, in addition to our brains. The Polyvagal Theory offers an explanation for how these changes occur—and how we can deal with them.

The Polyvagal Theory shifts our discussion of trauma away from the actual event, and toward the way it transforms and becomes embedded in our bodies. These changes may be drastically different for different people who experience the same traumatic incident, and can come from truly shocking experiences or the sorts of mundane pressures that few people associate with the word "trauma."

It is through the vagus that these changes occur.

It is through the vagus that trauma and pervasive stress effectively act as preexisting conditions, making us more susceptible to almost every physical or psychological ailment.

And it is through the vagus that we might find a way out of such an existence. A light at the end of trauma's tunnel, and a pathway toward healing and happiness in a world that seems designed to threaten and traumatize us at every turn.

———

Our goal with this book is not just to show how feelings of safety, threat, and trauma change us from a scientific and evolutionary perspective but also to offer practical information for living our safest—and therefore best—lives.

This is a book that we hope gives you a series of *aha!* realizations about your own experiences, while also providing practical techniques for being happier, healthier, and generally more together in a world that seems increasingly determined to make all of us stressed, scared, and anxious.

To be clear, this is not an anatomy class, nor a book about nitty-gritty science. It *is*, however, the story of our nervous system and our bodies told through real-world examples and relatable experiences that we hope will bring it all to life in a way that is simple, accessible, and shareable.

With that caveat out of the way, we'll offer a slightly more academic framing of what the Polyvagal Theory is:

The Polyvagal Theory is a new model for how our
nervous system and entire body responds to, and changes
with, how safe or threatening the world feels to us.

What do we mean by that?

Well, let's say we're calm and in a blissful state of relaxation. In that case, all our internal machineries operate in a way that is supportive of health, growth, and restoration. Scared to death? Our innards and organs switch gears so as to operate with the laser-focused goal of temporary survival.

At the core of the Polyvagal Theory (we'll occasionally call it PVT for short) is the idea that these shifts in how our bodies operate come with wide-ranging and perhaps surprising consequences when it comes to our health, our mental state, how others respond to our presence, and how we experience the world on a sensory level.

The Polyvagal Theory also offers us a way of approaching the world that allows us to understand human nature on a profound, empathetic, and satisfying level. It provides an explanation for what our chronically unsafe, traumatic, and anxiety-filled world does to our health—and how we can reclaim our bodies and brains from the grips of a world that seems designed to scare and hurt us.

Viewing the world through a polyvagal lens allows us to make sense of behaviors we may loathe in ourselves and others, and to see below the surface of seemingly irrational or aggressive actions and see them as a natural response to the world we're all living in. One filled with endless threats and fears and anxieties that conspire to trigger survival instincts that have been baked into our bodies through millennia of evolution.

PVT also offers a sense of understanding for those visceral moments when our bodies feel driven by instincts outside our conscious control, or act in ways our brains would rather they didn't.

To the countless people who suffer from trauma or chronic anxiety, their experiences are often clouded by a sense of confusion and doubt. What is actually happening to them and their bodies is treated as a mystery.

The Polyvagal Theory sheds light on that mystery.

We live in a world that is designed to scare us.

Politicians and talking heads fomenting outrage and fear. Digital algorithms that make visits to cyberspace feel like glimpses into end times. Hours straight spent sitting in anger-fueling traffic or thinking about work deadlines. Employers who use spreadsheets full of numbers to rate and rank us. Everything that comes with surviving a global pandemic.

Be they incidental or (as is sadly often the case) intentional, we are inundated with a barrage of signals and signs that our bodies and brains funnel through the same neural pathways that were once reserved for rare life-threatening events.

So while we evolved to be occasional tourists to the state of fear
and alarm, many of us have become full-time residents.

The unfortunate truth is that many of us now live with pervasive fear, chronic anxiety, and trauma that isn't just inconvenient on a superficial level but also carries very real consequences for our health and quality of life. For many (and perhaps most) of us, trauma has become a way of life—even if we don't recognize it. Some people confidently state that trauma is something that only war veterans or assault victims experience. This is simply not the case.

Think of our bodily systems and organs as engines that can be overloaded to the point of being flooded or stalled. When this becomes the norm, we become anxious, overwhelmed, and burned out. We also become less healthy in a very real sense, and more likely to fall prey to virtually every physical or mental health malady there is.

To live in a state of fear is to live a life in a body that is tuned away from health, growth, restoration, happiness, and sociality. Life is shorter and harder. This state is a slow-motion killing machine that eats away at our bodies and spirits, causing real damage to our organs while acting as a numbing or dissociative depressant that keeps us from enjoying life.

It also changes the way we experience the world—and usually not for the better. When we feel unsafe, our very senses change. Things taste, look, smell, and sound different. Experiences we once loved lose their luster. Our ability to live, learn, and think critically evaporates in favor of an immediate need for survival. We become easy to manipulate and susceptible to following the direction of our most craven and cynical peers.

In short: When we never feel safe, everything is simply *worse* than it could be. Our physical and mental health suffers, and a numbing fog becomes the norm.

But there's a flip side to this doom and gloom!

Just as a constant feeling of threat transforms our bodies, there's a sort of magic that occurs when we feel safe.

Our bodies and brains operate better. Our organs and anatomical systems enter a physiological state of healing that primes us to recuperate from just about every physical or mental ailment better and faster. Our ability to live, laugh, and love (to borrow a phrase from trite motivational posters) is just sort of turned on. We become more creative, curious, intelligent, social, and fun.

With the wrappers of defense removed, the brilliance of our compassionate, benevolent, creative, and loving core is capable of shining through. **A safe life is a good life—and makes the lives of those around us better.**

The Polyvagal Theory explains the healing and transformative power of simply *feeling* safe—and the dangerous and traumatic power of constantly feeling like we're under threat. It also offers meaning to the many mysteries of trauma and explains how fleeting incidents can stick with us and transform our bodies in ways that many experience but few understand.

What emerges from this new understanding is a worldview filled with optimism and hope.

Apologies to the philosophers of yore who spent centuries debating whether humans are innately good or bad. The polyvagal answer to this question is actually quite simple:

> *When we feel safe, we are capable of generosity,*
> *empathy, altruism, growth, and compassion.*

When we don't (or perhaps never) feel safe, our sense of self-preservation trumps all else, and selfish, desperate, and aggressive behaviors are all but inevitable for most people.

On a macro scale, this understanding offers a clear road away from a divided world in which we look at our sisters and brothers as others, and toward one based on empathy and a realization that many actions or traits we may dislike, dismiss, or fear in others are simply the natural responses of a scared person (or scared group of people) desperate to feel safe. And that, given the same circumstances, many of us would act the same way.

And on an individual level, the Polyvagal Theory doesn't just demystify the mysteries of how trauma changes us. It also offers fixes that are currently revolutionizing the clinical world and leading to new treatments and techniques that anybody can take advantage of—either with the help of a professional, or while sitting at home reading this book.

To that end, this book is designed to be readable, shareable, and accessible. It is not a science textbook, and we may gloss over details that require a PhD to understand. If you feel like digging deeper, you can check out our other books and papers on the subject.[*] And while the text is meant to be read in order, it's divided into chapters that offer a bit of browsability.

The first part of this book outlines what the Polyvagal Theory is, and breaks down the science into what we hope are understandable terms. You'll want to read this part in order, as subsequent chapters build off of one another.

The second part dives into specific applications of PVT in our world and explains how its principles apply to circumstances and settings such as the pandemic, the workplace, schools, and prison. While we hope you read it all and in order, these chapters can be browsed or read selectively to suit your interests.

---

[*] There's a handy list of these at the end of this book (see "Other Resources" in the References section).

There's also a glossary in the back, just in case you forget what a certain word means or how it fits into the bigger picture.* There will be no quiz at the end, and if you need to gloss over some of the more technical sections, we get it.

And with that, our journey begins.

---

* The glossary offers more detailed and technical information about many of the topics at hand.

OUR POLYVAGAL WORLD

PART 1

IN YOU

1

The *Automatic* Nervous System

To understand the Polyvagal Theory, we first need to understand the autonomic nervous system (or ANS, as we'll sometimes call it).

Let's just make it simple: The word "auto**nomic**" means "auto**matic**." So the autonomic* nervous system might as well be called the *automatic* nervous system.

Think of the ANS as our body's autopilot system that allows our heart to beat, our lungs to breathe, and our pupils to dilate without our having to think about it. It is effectively the control hub for all bodily functions that operate without our conscious control.

This is important! Without the ANS taking control, we'd have to consciously think about every little thing our body did—down to our individual sweat glands. And while this might seem like some mind-over-body fantasy, it would also be incredibly exhausting and more or less impossible. For those of us who struggle to walk and chew gum at the same time, can you imagine having to also juggle the functions of dozens of discrete organs at any given time? We wouldn't be able to go to sleep without our hearts and lungs stopping. And the less we have to think about taking control of the messy business of digestion, the better.

We like to think of ourselves as being in control of our faculties,

---

* The very similar word "automaton" refers to self-operating machines such as robots. Same concept here.

but our ANS autopilot controls the vast majority of our bodily functions.

Let's use the trite trope of an iceberg. That little bit jutting above the water in plain sight? That's all the stuff in our body that is controlled by conscious thoughts. By thinking about it, we can wag our tongue to say a specific word or move our legs to run or dance. But beneath these consciously controlled functions lies a vast and complex network of interwoven bodily systems that just sort of tick along, keeping us alive and as healthy and happy as they can, without our having to manually pull the levers or divert attention.

And good thing too! Attention is a precious resource. If we were consumed with consciously operating every bit of our body, we couldn't enjoy a movie, have a conversation, swing a baseball bat, eat a nice meal, write down our thoughts, or look after loved ones.

By taking this load off our conscious selves, our ANS frees us up to actually *live*.

It's important to point out that, for most people, there is one major bodily function that can be controlled *both* by the ANS *and* by our conscious thought: breathing.

Just by thinking about it, we can choose to hold our breath or blow out air with the precision required to play the clarinet. But if we ignore or forget about breathing, our lungs still do their thing without our permission. Otherwise, we'd have a hard time sleeping through the night.

Breathing's unique presence as an ANS-autopiloted system that we can *also* commandeer at will makes it very special. Like a heroic character that finds itself drawn between two worlds, this dual citizenship makes it uniquely suited to bridge the gap between our brains and bodies, and offers a salve for when our bodies act in ways that our brains would rather they didn't.

Therapists and yogis spend a lot of time talking about the healing and restorative power of controlled breathing. And while breathing's power is often couched in New Age or religious language that can inspire skepticism in the empirically minded among us, its effects are very much rooted in basic anatomy and the ANS. Keep reading and you'll understand how.

The Lens Through Which We Experience the World

The ANS is not a monolithic system, and it doesn't always operate the same way.

In fact, our ANS is constantly engaged in an invisible game of budgeting and economics. Our bodies have a vast array of functions at their disposal but have limited resources when it comes to precious attention and energy.

The imperative to conserve resources is a metabolic one. These days, access to food is almost too easy for many of us. But for the vast majority of our species' evolution and existence, we dealt with—and had to adapt to—times when food (and thus energy) was scarce. It was necessary for our survival that our bodies be capable of funneling attention and resources to specific systems and functions at specific times. We have only so much fuel to throw in the tank, and our bodies need to use it wisely.

Running from a saber-toothed tiger? Our ANS wants to make sure we have the blood flow and adrenaline spike necessary to get away and will distribute resources and activate systems accordingly to survive this fleeting danger.

Sitting by a campfire and enjoying a meal with trusted friends? Entirely different bodily systems will be engaged to help us laugh, sing, eat, socialize, make others feel safe, and heal our own bodies during these times of safety.

Let's continue with the "autopilot" metaphor. Depending on the circumstance, imagine this system is controlled by a different software program—each with a unique personality and purpose.

One of these autopilot programs acts angry, aggressive, and on alert; while another is cool, calm, and collected.

Each of these autopilot programs (or subsystems of the ANS, if we drop the metaphor) is activated at different times and serves a different function. And even if you don't know their names, you certainly feel their effects every single day.

Sympathetic Nervous System (SNS)

This system mobilizes our bodies and supports "fight-or-flight" behaviors. It is activated when our bodies sense danger or need a burst of energy, allowing us to rev up and be ready for action.

But while its "fight-or-flight" reputation (and association with stress and turmoil) often gives the SNS a bad rap, its ability to mobilize our bodies can also come in handy for positive experiences such as exercising, dancing, and playing.

Parasympathetic Nervous System (PNS)

This system immobilizes and slows down our bodies, and is our "rest-and-relax" system. It is activated when our bodies feel safe, causing us to remain calm, collected, and social. The vagus nerve is an important component of the PNS, and is key to the body's ability to activate this system and experience its healthful benefits.

And while the PNS (and its ability to calm us down) is often viewed as *always* good, we will soon learn that the truth is more complex, as the PNS features neural pathways that may also immobilize us and shut us down when we experience danger or trauma.

Depending on whether the SNS or PNS is in control of our body, we enter a different "**autonomic state.**"

Our autonomic state is effectively a reorienting of the entire body's operation around either the SNS or PNS.* So at any given moment, our autonomic nervous system, and thus our entire body, might be dominated by one system or the other. At their extremes, this would be experienced as either "fight-or-flight" or "rest-and-relax."

One of the key tenets of the Polyvagal Theory is that our autonomic state is effectively the lens through which we perceive and experience the world. Our autonomic state doesn't just change how our organs and bodily functions operate, it also transforms our sensory experience.

---

* If you happen to be an expert on neuroanatomy, you'll understand this is an oversimplification. But we'll get to that soon enough.

Things look, smell, sound, and feel different when we are in a sympathetic "fight-or-flight" state versus a parasympathetic "rest-and-relax" state.

In other words, the result of switching into a specific autonomic state (or autopilot program for our ANS, if you find that framing helpful) is that virtually every fiber of our bodies transforms their function, and even physical form at times, in a rather stark and amazing way.

When doctors and science students are taught about the nervous system, the SNS and PNS are typically described as being in discrete control of different functions in our body, and engaged in a sort of internal tug-of-war that determines our "autonomic balance." So some bodily functions are viewed as entirely driven by the SNS, while others are controlled by the PNS, with these systems battling for control of our bodies.*

So what determines whether the SNS or PNS is in control of our body at any given moment, and thus which bodily systems will be activated or suppressed? How does our body choose which autopilot program to load at any given moment?

The answer comes down to one simple question: **How safe do we feel?**

Notice that it says "How safe do we *feel*" as opposed to how safe we actually are. This is crucial for everything that is to follow.

The nervous system doesn't particularly care, or have any real way of knowing, how much actual danger we're in. What matters to the nervous system is merely how safe we *feel*. And depending on the answer to that question, virtually every function in our body acts very differently.

We all sort of understand this on a basic level. Just about everybody has heard of the concept of "fight-or-flight," and how a sense of danger can rev up our heart rate and prime us to run away or fight like hell. But few understand just how deeply a sense of danger or safety impacts how our body operates.

---

* This traditional "SNS vs. PNS" model for the ANS is incomplete and is effectively replaced by the Polyvagal Theory. But to understand what's new and interesting about PVT, we first need to understand the old thinking that it builds upon and replaces.

When the SNS is activated in moments of perceived danger, we get ready to fight or flee:

- Our heart rate speeds up, allowing us to run or fight.

- Our pain tolerance goes up, making it easier to stand our ground against an adversary.

- Our facial affect goes flat.

- Our middle-ear muscles are disengaged, making it easier to hear extremely low-frequency sounds associated with danger and predators.

When the PNS is activated in times of perceived safety, other systems are engaged in service of our ability to rest, relax, heal, and be social:

- Our heart rate slows, allowing us to sit or stand still.

- Saliva and digestive systems are stimulated to help process food.

- Facial muscles are activated so we can better convey emotional nuance through our face.

- We have increased vocal prosody (that is, a more singsongy and less monotone way of speaking) and eye contact.

- Our middle-ear muscles shift position to better hear the sounds of the human voice.

We can think of it like the Marvel character the Hulk, who is actually a rather apt physical representation of the ANS. Depending on how angry or scared the character feels, he might manifest as the smash-happy giant Hulk—or the thoughtful, contemplative, and sometimes romantic Bruce Banner.

We may not grow larger or change colors like the Hulk, but the changes that occur within our bodies when we face a feeling of threat are no less dramatic. During these times of sympathetic (again: that's *fight-or-flight*) activation, our entire body transforms to meet the moment.

Likewise, when we feel safe enough for the PNS to take over, the Hulk within us melts away for a deeply human state of rest, relaxation, healing, growth, ingestion,* and sociability. Yes, the bodily functions involved with eating food and with socializing with others are closely linked from a physiological perspective—which is probably why meals are so closely associated with times of bonding, friends, and fun. From a bodily perspective, conversation and food go well together!†

Again: It all comes down to resource distribution. Our bodies use our level of perceived safety as an internal gauge for which bodily functions are necessary at any given time. And while the functions associated with surviving immediate danger are important mechanisms that have helped ensure humanity's survival for thousands of years, they take a lot of energy. This makes them extremely costly to engage from a sheer metabolic and energy perspective—which is why they were designed to be activated for only short and temporary bursts.

Likewise, when we feel safe, our bodies revert to a state of healing called "homeostasis." Imagine lying on a hammock in the shade without a worry in the world. No predators chasing after you, and no bosses calling you about deadlines. When we are in this state, our body transforms and simply *feels* different.

This homeostasis is our ideal baseline state, and it is necessary for our bodies to properly heal and recuperate.

It's important to understand that our bodies *want* to (and in many ways, need to) revert to homeostasis. With that comes the understanding that prolonged exposure to our danger systems and time away from homeostasis may have very real (and very negative) effects when it comes to our health and ability to function.

Of course, we now live in a world in which too many people spend far too much time in autonomic states that evolved to temporarily help us survive fleeting danger—and far too little time feeling safe and achieving homeostasis. Even when we do get those

---

* What scientists call eating.

† This is also part of why people experiencing trauma often deal with digestion and gut issues. More on that later.

rare moments of reprieve, it often takes little more than a vibrating phone to rile us out of them.

In this crazy and stressed-out world, we're too often left flooding our engine, burning the candle at both ends, and otherwise engaging in all the colorful metaphors we use to describe the state of *overdoing it*. In this modern world, we're too often the Hulk and not enough Bruce Banner.

The cost of this imbalance is our health, happiness, and sanity. Overusing these danger systems makes us more susceptible to almost any illness,* damages our organs, and wrecks our mental health.

After all, what is anxiety if not the constant feeling of threat and danger—even when none is truly there?

Our autonomic state also transforms the way we experience the world on a sensory level. Depending on whether we're in a sympathetic or parasympathetic state, things taste, look, smell, sound, and seem different. People, places, or things we once loved might lose their luster, or take on a new light—all because of how safe we feel.

Ever find yourself, in times of stress or anxiety, unable to enjoy things you once loved? This could be why.

This also raises an important question that we will come back to later: What happens to our bodies when we *never* feel safe? The answer to this question has enormous implications for understanding the nature of (and how we treat) trauma, chronic pain, and other such conditions that impact our bodies and our lives.

After all, what is trauma if not the inability to ever feel truly safe—and the effects such an existence has on our bodies?

---

* Trauma, adversity history, and pervasive stress are effectively preexisting conditions that make us more vulnerable to almost every health condition there is, including viruses like COVID-19.

AN INTERVENING VARIABLE

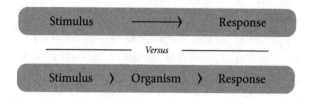

When I (Stephen) began my academic career in the 1970s, human behavior was viewed as being the product of a "stimulus–response" (or S–R) model. In that model, our behavior can be viewed as a somewhat predictable machine, in which a stimulus (basically, anything you encounter or experience in the world) goes in, and a specific behavior comes out as the response.

I saw things differently and proposed that human behavior was actually the result of a "stimulus-organism-response" (or S–O–R) model. With an S–O–R model, the organism itself (that's you, or me, or anybody, really) is a key variable that sits in the middle of this machine and influences how we respond to the world around us.

An S–O–R model posits that all humans are different from one another—and differ among ourselves at different times—and that these individual differences (basically what makes us *us*) can influence how we respond to different stimuli or scenarios. So the same experience might be pleasant to one person and frightening to another. And depending on how we feel or what autonomic state we're in, the same thing might bring us joy in some circumstances, and grief in others.

If you've ever felt your mood influence how you respond to something, this should seem obvious. But what's obvious to us today was anything but for rigid-minded researchers 50 years ago, when I started my scientific journey.

I was far from the first person to propose an S–O–R model; the concept dates back to the early psychological theories.* What *was*

---

* (e.g., Woodworth, 1929)

new was the idea that our physiological or autonomic state—that is, how we *feel* at any given moment, and whether we are in a sympathetic state of danger or parasympathetic state of safety—can change how we respond to the world around us.

In other words: Our physiological state and how we *feel* are intervening variables in how we experience the world, and can change just about everything related to the experience of being alive.

If you've ever felt your emotions overtake you, this idea should be perfectly obvious. But then again, so should a lot of concepts that past generations failed to grasp.

Key to this model is the idea that our conscious intent (what we think) and bodily state (what we feel) are often at odds with each other. So our higher thinking might *want* to respond to something one way, while our body pushes us in a different direction.

To me, this is all only logical. When we're angry or hungry or both (and who hasn't been "hangry" on occasion), we're apt to respond differently to things than when we're calm, cool, and well fed.

The Polyvagal Theory offers a scientific and neurophysiological explanation for this process.

Before we move on, it should also be noted that our autonomic state is not our fate. Just because we're riled up or relaxed, it does not mean we will *definitely* respond to something in a particular way. Rather, changes in our state shift the *likelihood* that certain behaviors or feelings will occur.

Let's put it this way: If you're angry or irritable, that doesn't mean you are certainly going to raise your voice at somebody. But you sure are more likely to do so than if you are feeling calm and relaxed.

The Freeze Effect

Earlier, we wrote that this dichotomy between the sympathetic and parasympathetic nervous systems is how the ANS has been *traditionally* modeled, with our bodies presented as being engaged in a constant tug-of-war between "calm" and "activated."

The Polyvagal Theory proposes that this model is incomplete and, in some ways, inaccurate.

The traditional model of the ANS, in which the SNS supports fight-or-flight defense and the PNS supports calmness and health, has at least one crucial flaw: It suggests that the *only* way our bodies respond to threats is to rev up to run or fight. And while it is often true that we fight or flee from threats, this is not *always* true.

The truth is that when we are under severe duress—not just minor threats, but the sorts of experiences that make us feel like we might die—we often do not run or fight. Instead, our bodies might freeze, dissociate, or even shut down to the point of losing consciousness.

The traditional model for the ANS, which the Polyvagal Theory effectively replaces, does not account for these natural and common immobilization responses.

This is important! When people undergo severely traumatic instances that result in a "freeze" or "shutdown" response, they and those around them are often left questioning these experiences and responding in ways that lack compassion, empathy, or understanding.

Because we are taught to assume that people who are threatened will naturally run or fight (or imagine that is what we would do if faced with a dire circumstance), it confuses us to hear that somebody might instead freeze, dissociate, or shut down.

In our imagination, we're all cowboys or action heroes. And it's a natural tendency to say to ourselves things like "Well, I would have run" or "I would have fought."

The truth is, the ANS doesn't care what you think you would have done. Our response to threat is an autonomic—meaning *automatic*—one that is largely separate from our conscious thinking and decision-making process.

Our consciousness has one narrative about who we are and how we'd rise to an occasion, and our unconscious nervous system just sort of ignores it. Freezing under threat is not a sign of weakness or complacency, but a natural and common bodily response that is completely outside of our control.

Unfortunately, few people understand this.

Because we assume that the inevitable response to a threat is to run or fight, assault victims who fail to respond this way are often doubted by judges, juries, legal systems, peers, and a press that assumes dire circumstances such as physical assault must logically be met with signs of struggle. After all, isn't that what *you* imagine you would do?

This thought process even torments victims, who are often left questioning their own experiences:

> *"Maybe I wasn't actually assaulted? Maybe part of*
> *me wanted it? Why else didn't I fight back?"*

This results in a compounding of trauma that can make the worst day of your life even worse. When victims lack support or begin to doubt their own experiences, it can lead to a dark path of depression, self-medication, and even suicide.

We will explain more about this freeze response later, and add some nuance to it, since there is a real difference between freezing, dissociating, and fully fainting. For now, it is just important to know that a key tenet of the Polyvagal Theory is to challenge the traditional model of how our ANS responds to the world.

It isn't just about the sympathetic nervous system versus the parasympathetic nervous system (that's SNS "fight-or-flight" vs. PNS "rest-and-relax"). Rather, there are other possible responses to threats—including a natural and common dissociative state of freezing or shutting down, as well as a possibility that a victim might display fawning or appeasement behaviors toward a perpetrator. Understanding this changes the way we conceptualize, talk about, and treat trauma.

If readers of this book walk away with just one takeaway, let it be this: **To freeze, shut down, dissociate, or even pass out is a natural (and often inescapable) response to moments of severe duress.**

We don't always fight or run, and just because there's no sign of a struggle doesn't mean somebody was any less a victim. Quite the contrary: A shutdown response typically means an event was *especially* terrifying, traumatic, and possibly even life-threatening—or at least interpreted by the unconscious recesses of our nervous system as being so.

We hope that merely learning about this simple concept can result in real change.

Just imagine a world in which every seated member of a jury knows that somebody can be a victim of assault and not also have shown signs of a struggle. The personal trauma that comes from surviving danger or tragedy is multiplied when victims feel like nobody is offering belief or compassion—or when victims cannot offer it to themselves because they are left doubting their own experiences.

One more time: Just because you might imagine that you would have transformed into an action hero in certain circumstances doesn't mean a thing. Our nervous systems are in charge, and until you've been in a situation where you've lost control of your body, you simply have no idea. Unfortunately, many people require personal hardship to feel true empathy.

And if you're reading this and nodding your head in recognition of your own traumatic experiences, now is a good time to pause and reflect on the fact that your conscious self had nothing to do with your body shutting down or not fighting back. It simply wasn't up to this part of you, which was relegated to the passenger seat of your own body, cut off from conscious control. And if you feel a sense of shame or confusion at how you behaved in the moment of duress, know that no matter how much you wish you could have been a hero, your nervous system had another plan.

If you have shut down in the face of danger, you experienced a natural and common survival reflex that has been experienced and shared by millions upon millions of others.

It wasn't your decision, or your fault. And you are not alone.

Lastly, we acknowledge that many people may be socialized to believe that inaction or silence can be construed as consent—and that people will speak up and let it be known if they are in an uncomfortable situation. The hope is that, by understanding how our bodies work, at least some people might also avoid inadvertently traumatizing others in the first place by misreading these cues.

2

Neuroception: Our Body's Surveillance System

In the last chapter, we learned that the primary variable that determines our autonomic state (and thus the lens through which we experience the world) is how safe we feel at any given moment.

But how exactly does our nervous system gauge this seemingly abstract concept of "safety"?

To understand this mechanism, we're going to introduce a process I (Stephen) have termed "neuroception." That's "neuro" for the brain or nervous system, and "ception" as in "perception" or "detection."*

Let's walk through this together.

If we come into contact with a possible threat, we may not have the time or capability to consciously think through the scenario and come to a plan. We often operate viscerally, and at a gut level.

Let's place ourselves in the shoeless feet of our prehistoric ancestors, perhaps roaming an ancient prairie. If we see a strange person or animal in the distance, we might question whether this stranger is a friend or foe or—

Oops. Too late. By the time you've come to a thoughtful decision, the spear or teeth could already be in your neck.

When it comes to assessing possible threats, time is of the

---

* When naming this mechanism, my (Stephen's) first instinct was to simply use the word "perception." However, that word implies a level of conscious awareness. Neuroception is an unconscious process handled by our brain and nervous system. Hence the "neuro" prefix—and the need for a new word.

essence, and our bodies need to effectively determine how safe any given circumstance is as close to instantly as possible.

Neuroception can be viewed as a sort of invisible sense or radar system that constantly scans the world for any and all external signs and signals that might help us determine how safe we are at any given moment.

Think of it like a black-box computer algorithm that is embedded in our nervous system. This algorithm uses our senses and past experiences to take in data points from the world around us and then uses that information to spit out a reading: *Safety* or *Danger*.

When we feel pain, we react to it before we can identify the source or even have a conscious awareness of the injury. When we accidentally touch a hot pan while cooking, we instinctively draw our hands away. This is our unconscious neuroception at work.

Sights, smells, sounds, colors, tastes. Our senses inform our conscious existence, but they also funnel information to the unconscious and automatic recesses of our ANS without our ever being fully aware.

Here's one example of how our senses influence our ANS in hidden ways: Right next to the rods and cones that allow our eyes to bring the world around us to life in vivid color are light-sensitive cells* that have nothing to do with actual eyesight. Instead, these cells scan the world for light so as to shift our alertness level up during the day, and then back down at night.

Other senses act similarly, with both a conscious component (*"I hear somebody talking to me"*) and an unconscious one (*"Those sounds make me feel unsafe"*).

Our eyes, nose, ears, and skin constantly take in the world around us and pull out key bits of data that allow us to instantly and (hopefully, though not always) accurately determine how much danger we're in at any given moment. To fall back on yet another comic-book reference, neuroception is our Spider-Sense, searching our environment for subtle signs of danger that may escape our conscious realization.

---

* These cells are called "intrinsically photosensitive retinal ganglion cells," and they were not fully identified until 2002.

If something or somebody just feels *off* to you, it's not your imagination; it's your neuroception.

Depending on the answer to the safety question (that is: "*How safe does my neuroception think I am?*"), our autonomic state changes to best handle the situation. And with that, the entire body shifts its orientation and function toward one of peace, relaxation, and sociability on one hand—or fear, defensiveness, and aggression on the other.

This process happens nearly instantly, and is outside of our conscious control. We don't think to ourselves, "Better turn on that fight-or-flight!" It just happens. And it happens very quickly.

At times, neuroception can feel like a bit of a magic trick, with subtle sounds, sights, and social cues causing our nervous system to ebb and flow between different autonomic states, transforming our bodies in both form and function. We'll talk more about this later, but this idea holds enormous implications when it comes to designing physical environments and spaces that are conducive to learning (such as schools), relaxation (such as spas), or rehabilitation (such as prisons or drug-treatment centers).

It is through neuroception that our physical environment can cause real shifts in our health, well-being, and productivity.

What many of us write off as mere aesthetic preferences for things such as lighting and acoustics can have very real impacts on our nervous systems and how our bodies operate. When we feel especially at peace or productive in one place, or amped up and uneasy in another, that's our neuroception at work.

Our neuroception is why some of us like to light candles or dim the lights or play soothing music or sit by the ocean. Quite simply: The environment we are in changes the way we feel, and how our bodies operate.

The neuroception system is also self-reinforcing. Depending on which autonomic state we are in, our nervous systems and entire bodies shift their orientation and bias to better pick up signals that further reinforce the existing notion that we're in a state of safety or danger.

In other words, when we sense danger, our bodies become primed to pick up more signs of danger. Likewise, when we sense safety, our bodies are better able to pick up more signs of safety. So to a scared person, the world tends to feel scary. And to somebody who already feels safe, the world tends to feel safe.

This priming process isn't just in our heads. Rather, it's a real physiological and sensory change and comes from actual shifts in our anatomy that occur when our ANS changes states.

We may not turn big and change colors like the Hulk when we are scared or angry, but virtually every part of our body transforms to meet the perceived threat in front of us.

Here's another example of this bodily shift, which we're going to come back to repeatedly in this book:

Our middle ears feature tiny muscles that evolved to filter incoming sounds and pick up the mid-frequency waves associated with the human voice. If you're ever able to have a conversation with somebody in the middle of a loud concert or crowded bar, you have these muscles to thank. The sound of human speech is special to our brains and instantly gets our attention.

The ability of our middle-ear muscles to pull off this trick of extracting the sound of speech from a loud environment is controlled by nerves that sprout out of our brainstem. Depending on how safe we feel, these nerves toggle this ability on or off.

So when we are in a parasympathetic state of rest and relaxation, these ear muscles are primed to pick up the sound of speech. After all, our nervous system thinks we're safe and ready to be social and have a conversation.

However, if our neuroception detects danger and slides our ANS into a sympathetic fight-or-flight state, these middle-ear muscles shift position so as to adjust the tension of our eardrums so they can focus on low-frequency sounds that the body associates with predators and danger.

If that last bit sounds confusing, here's all you need to know: Our audiology readouts—that is, the literal sound waves we pick up and process—actually change depending on how safe we feel. So while the sound of the human voice is indeed unique and special to our ears and brains and something we can easily pick out of a crowded cacophony, this is *only* the case when we feel safe.

When we don't feel safe, the very sounds we hear and process in our brain shift so that speech sounds are muffled and depressed, and we instead pick up the very low frequencies that our nervous system associates with predators and threats. The growl of a tiger in the bush, for example.

This can become a vicious cycle. Low-frequency sounds both make us feel unsafe and transform our middle-ear muscles to pick up even more low-frequency sounds, which make us feel even more unsafe.

And while the ear example is a simple and concrete one, a similar process occurs with a whole host of other bodily systems as a sense of danger primes our very anatomy and senses to pick up more signs of danger. When we feel unsafe, our pupils dilate, making our eyes more sensitive to light. Our skin becomes more sensitive to being touched. We become newly keyed into the ways the world around us might cause us harm. With the body retuned to support defense, our behavior might shift away from seeking novelty in favor of experiences that are predictable and less risky. This change stretches down to our ingestive and digestive systems, which may shift their bias toward bland or familiar foods.

Feeling threatened retunes our nervous system to respond to *everything* as if it is a threat. Just think about the many instances of road rage, in which a stressful situation can cause minor grievances to quickly and tragically escalate.

Of course, the flip side is true as well. When we feel safe, these systems are actively seeking and registering additional signs of safety. We are better able to see, hear, and experience things as they truly are on a human level.

Those middle-ear muscles are also one reason why a large number of trauma survivors (not to mention people with autism and various psychiatric diagnoses) are hypersensitive to sound and suffer from auditory processing disorders that include difficulties understanding human voices in crowded and noisy environments such as shopping malls, restaurants, or parties.

You may have heard or experienced yourself the fact that first responders or veterans coming home from war often have a hard time with loud noises or have difficulties extracting specific words from conversations. This is part of the reason why.

When we feel unsafe, we hear sounds differently. And what is trauma if not being stuck in a state of never feeling safe?

This brings us to another major takeaway from this book: **Trauma is not merely psychological but also physiological.***

We often treat trauma as if it is a psychiatric issue that can only be met with talk therapy or perhaps drugs targeted at specific areas of the brain. But the truth is that trauma (and its flip side of feeling safe) literally changes the way countless systems in our bodies operate on a physiological level, down to the sounds our ears pick up. You may have heard that trauma embeds itself in the body (or that "the body keeps the score," as my colleague Bessel van der Kolk called his best-selling book about trauma). This is part of what we mean by that.

Trauma also reprograms our neuroception system so it is primed to pick up more signs of threat, at the expense of feeling safe. This "reprogramming" manifests in how our nervous system interprets the world around us (so things that once felt safe may now feel threatening), as well as in our sensory experience (so that senses such as hearing are shifted to pick up the sounds of potential predators, at the expense of understanding human speech).

This book's authors have met countless traumatized individuals who have endured strange and mysterious changes in their bodies. As their sensory experiences transform, these people may suddenly suffer from sensory hypersensitivities or auditory processing disorders. When trauma patients attempt to bring these issues to their doctors, it is common for these individuals to have the issues met with disbelief or even derision. Other times, patients are prescribed drugs aimed at fixing individual symptoms, without the doctor or patient understanding that there is an underlying autonomic issue.

This book is not a screed against modern medicine (quite the contrary), but it should be noted that all medicines and drugs have side effects and come with consequences, and relying solely on medication might numb a symptom but do nothing to fix the underlying issue if somebody doesn't feel safe.

---

* In other words: Trauma is not only in our mind but also in our body. (See van der Kolk, 2014.)

Understanding this basic idea—*that trauma is physiological*—doesn't just open the door to understanding why your friend or loved one might have trouble with hearing or digestion issues (another immensely common bodily occurrence with trauma patients). It also opens up new frontiers in research and treatment that are currently changing the way we approach healing trauma—while also perhaps lifting the sense of shame and guilt many traumatized people feel for being unable to understand what is happening to their bodies.

With this, the Polyvagal Theory helps us reframe a lot of big and complex issues—such as trauma, general health, and even the goals of fields such as architecture and business management—in very basic terms: *"If people who feel safe are healthier and happier, what can we do to make people feel safe?"*

This is why we wrote earlier that the Polyvagal Theory potentially offers a new way of seeing the world: one in which making people *feel* safe is paramount when it comes to human health, happiness, communication, productivity, quality of life . . . and so many other things that we value as individuals and as a society.

We'll come back to this later, but it's also important to note that determining whether a situation is dangerous is about as primal an instinct as one can imagine, and pretty much every vertebrate has some level of threat detection built into it. After all, evolution favors organisms that manage to live. "Survival of the fittest" and all that.

But detecting threats is one thing, and detecting *safety* is something entirely different—and far rarer within the animal kingdom.

Neuroception as a system for detecting safety is part of what distinguishes humans and other evolutionarily modern and social mammals* from our asocial reptile ancestors.

If we were capable of seeing the world around us only in terms of threats, we'd be like reptiles that sit in isolation, waiting to eat or be eaten.

It is through the detection and seeking of *safety* that we have

---

* And likely many birds, though that veers a bit away from the domain of the Polyvagal Theory, which is solely focused on mammals.

evolved into a social species that can trust and love and build cities and societies.

Everything we cherish as humans comes from the evolutionary transition that allowed us to detect not just danger—but *also* safety. And neuroception enables us to do this.

Trigger Warnings

We're admittedly describing neuroception in broad strokes. So before we move on, let's pause for a few quick notes on how neuroception might operate differently with different people.

1. Our neuroception is both hardwired and adjusts based on our previous experiences or conditioning.

Our past experiences—and traumatic ones in particular—can reprogram our neuroception.

A particular color, location, voice, or smell might make us feel calm and safe—until it is experienced alongside a life-threatening event. From that moment on, these environmental cues might take on new meanings to our nervous system.

It's easy to dismiss or even make fun of people who put caveats such as "trigger warning" in front of graphic material or articles that discuss traumatic experiences. But the truth is that simply seeing or reading things that we associate with past traumatic events is capable of causing a shift in our nervous system and bodies that can be enormously painful, stressful, and even bad for our health.

It's also important to note that repeatedly experiencing signs of danger (especially ones our nervous system views as truly life-threatening or traumatic) can change the way we respond to them.

The first time we have a traumatic encounter, we might completely shut down. However, if it happens again, we may stay alert but in a dissociative state. And if it happens again and again (as is common with people who live in war-torn regions or abusive homes, for example), such feelings of dissociation can completely take over our existence.

Dissociation is often treated as a form of psychosis. The Polyvagal

Theory posits that it is an adaptive process that evolved to keep us safe and sane so that the individual is capable of mobilizing to survive a dangerous scenario, while the consciousness is effectively sent elsewhere to insulate it from the horror.

Dissociation is frightening and damaging, but it comes from the body's need to protect itself. Understanding this is key to trauma-informed approaches to therapy, and to removing a sense of shame and mystery from the reality of living with trauma.

2. Our neuroception acts differently based on our current autonomic state.

If we already feel threatened and are in a state of fight-or-flight, we'll be predisposed to interpret things around us as threats. Just think about how abused dogs snarl or snap at anybody and anything.*

Likewise, if a traumatic existence trains our nervous system to believe that everything can be a threat, then that is going to change how you respond to everything. And, like a wounded dog, you'll be much more likely to growl or display aggression to the world.

3. Neuroception comes hardwired and ready to work without prior learning.

While neuroception certainly comes baked in with a degree of innate variance (with different environmental cues impacting different people in different ways or to different degrees), these differences are surprisingly minimal.

Loud noises startle just about everybody, and we all respond to signs of safety in similar ways. So while there may be individual differences in how reactive our neuroception is to the world around us (and prior experiences can certainly transform the way we respond to just about anything), people have a lot more in common in this department than one might think. As a result, the

* How dogs act will be our go-to example for a lot of things addressed in this book.

concept of "safety" is surprisingly universal—at least as far as our nervous systems are concerned.

We'll cover this more in the second half of the book, but this is important when you think about how places, spaces, and therapeutic interventions can be designed to elicit feelings of safety.

If everybody's nervous system and neuroception system randomly interpreted different environmental cues as "safe" or "dangerous," it would be impossible to come up with any sort of unifying ideas about what makes a person or place pleasant or threatening. However, because our neuroception systems come hardwired so similarly, it is indeed very possible to discern exactly what cues and design decisions generally make people feel good versus bad.

Whether or not it comes as a surprise, many features of our world that purport to keep us safe might actually make us feel very unsafe.

We like to cast people and entire groups as "good" or "bad." As if certain people are more deserving of punishment or suffering than others. But inside, our nervous systems are all essentially the same. We all need safety, and suffer and express anger and possibly aggression when we are deprived of it.

What We Mean by "Safety"

This is, if nothing else, a book about safety—and that's a word we're going to use a lot.

But what exactly is "safety"?

Most of us treat the concept of safety as the removal of a threat. In this context, metal detectors keep us safe from guns. TSA security lines keep us safe from bombs. And so on.

The Polyvagal Theory proposes that what is important is *feeling* safe, at least as far as the nervous system is concerned. That's not to say that our actual physical safety isn't important, but that when it comes to our nervous system, autonomic state, neuroception, and the impact of all those things on our health and happiness, our body's *detection* and *feelings* of safety are what matters.

Perversely, many things that are designed on the surface to keep us physically safe also make us *feel* unsafe—and thus come with a very real price that is too often ignored.

Take the aforementioned metal detectors. These are tools designed to suss out the presence of weapons. However, kids who go through them every day on their way into school are being barraged with signals and signs that the world around them is a dangerous place. That they *should* be afraid. From a bodily perspective, this has real implications for our health, happiness, and ability to thrive in environments such as schools (see Chapter 9 for more on this).

There's a brutal irony to the fact that many of the features of our built world that are billed as keeping us safe also make us feel unsafe. If one wanted to take a cynical point of view, one might posit that, at times, this is an intended outcome. And that certain individuals or institutions may want us to feel unsafe for their own selfish ends.

But why would anybody actively want to make us feel unsafe?

The Polyvagal Theory offers a simple explanation: When we feel unsafe, our bodies shut down our ability to critically think or learn in favor of a need for immediate survival.

This change is not hypothetical but, rather, occurs on a very real anatomical and neurophysiological level, with certain circuits in our nervous system shutting down or turning on, depending on how safe we feel. When we feel chronically threatened, our worst and most tribalistic tendencies surface. Like a scared dog, we see others as threats, and perhaps act threatening ourselves.

For an authoritarian or would-be strongman, convincing a large number of people that they are under threat is basically required to maintain power. You see this when political actors don't just civilly disagree with their opponents or with entire groups of people but cast them as outsiders and subhuman bogeymen.

If your constituents are made to fear that somebody or some group is an existential threat to their way of life or might replace them in some way (unfortunately, we've seen the word "replacement" used a lot in this context in recent times), then these constituents may let you get away with nearly anything. It becomes "us versus them." It is through this playbook that tyranny, extreme nationalism, and political violence thrive.

Making us feel unsafe can also lead to big profits. Nothing keeps you staring at cable news or clickbait Facebook posts like a feeling of threat. For social media companies that funnel information to us based purely on data-driven metrics of engagement, it is nearly inevitable that content that scares us will bubble to the top until it overwhelms almost everything else. When we're scared, we are activated, engaged, and will continue to stare at our screens.

These cynical motives can easily conspire to create a world in which the messaging and media around us—in effect, the entire reality we experience—are entirely driven by a sense of existential dread. Needless to say, to our health and happiness, this is a disaster. But to those people and institutions who benefit from controlling people or keeping us engaged with content for power and profit, that is often the point.

A lot of us feel stressed and anxious and threatened pretty much around the clock. One of the big questions we hope readers ask themselves upon completion of this book is: "*Who or what is sending me messages that make me feel unsafe, and who or what benefits when I feel this way?*"

There's an old maxim in tabloid journalism: "If it bleeds it leads." In other words: We are drawn to stories and imagery that frighten us and confirm our worst fears. When our bodies are scared, we enter states of arousal, attention, and focus. When our bodies feel that survival is at stake, we become willing to follow the lead of anybody or anything that offers us salvation from a threat—even if that threat is manufactured or exaggerated. Outrage is both easy to incite and a powerful tool for bad actors.

So next time you turn on the TV and see a story where some person or group is presented as a monstrous villain, we encourage you to question the true motivation behind the narrative— especially if it feels like a narrative that certain voices are repeating ad infinitum as if they all were reading from the same memo.*

Given this perspective, it's hard not to feel that many of our feelings of danger, anger, outrage, and anxiety are cynically and intentionally engineered—at the cost of our personal health and

---

* In many cases, they literally are all reading talking points from the same memo.

happiness as well as our ability to find common ground across seemingly uncrossable ideological, ethnic, or cultural gulfs.

We are sure that some people reading this are nodding their heads and feeling validated in their preexisting hatred of the media, certain politicians, or groups that they feel may be particularly villainous.

What we're encouraging you to do instead is to look a level deeper and ask yourself: *Who is making me fear and loathe these people in the first place?* And by that, we mean: Who in the public sphere is stoking your fears and pushing these messages that fill your TV sets and social media feeds? Who is telling you to be angry? Which politician is tossing you the red meat that tells you that it's okay to hate or even harm others whom they are casting as rivals?

In effect: Who is exploiting your nervous system to make you physically and mentally unhealthy for their own cynical ends? Whether it's to hold on to power or simply to keep you focused and engaged through the commercial break.

By making you feel this way, they are using you, harming your health in a very real way, while also depriving you of the sense of safety that might allow your nervous system to second-guess their messaging and motives.

The Search for Safety

The Polyvagal Theory posits that the search for safety can be viewed as the primary organizing principle behind human evolution and human society. The need for safety is so central to our survival that virtually everything we are drawn to or enjoy is, in some way, a reflection of this need.

The search for safety is why we build cities, form relationships, and *like* almost anything that we as people tend to like.

But why is this? What is it about the human species that made this idea of "safety" such an important driver of our evolution? And how does this separate us from our reptile ancestors?

Being able to sense safety is uniquely important to us as humans and mammals for numerous reasons. Let's break some of them down:

1. Unlike most reptiles, all mammal newborns require care from their mothers after they are born. From the moment we are born, it is thus essential to interpret some behaviors as safe and nurturing.[1]

2. Many mammals (including humans) require long-term social relationships to physically survive. Deprived of social contact, we suffer. This is why social isolation inspires the unpleasant feeling of "loneliness," and why long-term social isolation can be truly traumatic and severely compromise our health.

   To accomplish these safe social relationships, our bodies must have a system for detecting which members of our own species are likely to be safe.

3. Our nervous system requires that we be in safe physical spaces in order to perform key biological and behavioral functions, including reproduction, nursing, sleep, and digestion.

   Our bodies are simply incapable of properly completing these tasks when we are on the run or in a threatened state. This biological need for safe spaces is especially true during periods when we are highly vulnerable, such as when we are pregnant or very young.

   A lot of this need for safe physical spaces comes from the fact that humans have such large and resource-hungry brains. That big mass of gray matter under our skull requires a ton of energy and a ton of oxygen. When we are on the run from a predator, our bodies are busy using that energy and oxygen for immediate survival or escape, rather than giving it to our brains. Only when we are calm and immobilized in a safe space can our brains get the resources they need to fully function, think critically or creatively, and otherwise offer us their peak performance.

Put all these points together, and it's clear why our bodies needed to develop a system for gauging which people and environments are actually safe and will help, rather than hurt, our chances of survival.

This is why, unlike with ancient reptiles, our human neuroception can detect safety in addition to danger, and why our need for safety can be viewed as nothing short of the driving force behind the development of almost every feature of our bodies and brains—as well as our societies and cultures.

As the Polyvagal Theory developed, I (Stephen) began to view it as the story of how, through evolution, mammals departed from our vertebrate relatives with new neural pathways that allowed us to seek safety for ourselves, signal safety to others, and provide feelings of safety to them through the process of co-regulation (see Chapter 4).

Without the ability to seek, sense, and provide feelings of safety, humans simply wouldn't have made it this long on this planet.

Red Light, Green Light

Time for a quick refresher. As we've already discussed:

- Our autonomic nervous system (or ANS) is our body's autopilot, allowing countless organs and systems to operate without our conscious control.

- Our neuroception scans the world around us looking for signs of safety and danger and uses this information to transform how our ANS—and thus our entire body—operates. The result here is our autonomic state.

- Our autonomic state is the lens through which we experience the world, transforming our bodies and brains in ways both big and small. This includes our sensory experiences and our ability to physically heal and to think critically or creatively.

Now that we have a handle on all this—and how our sense of safety or danger transforms our bodies—let's introduce a simple way of visualizing these different autonomic states.

To do this, let's once again go back in time and place ourselves in the shoeless feet of a prehistoric ancestor roaming a great prairie.

Up on the hilltop, we see a strange figure or mysterious beast. Faster than we can even think about it, our neuroception system takes in all available sights, sounds, and smells (and any other sensory data points it can get its hands on) in order to decide just how safe the situation is.

To visualize this process, let's imagine our neuroception system as a common traffic signal with three lights: green, yellow, and red.

Depending on how safe our neuroception deems the situation, one of those three colored lights will turn on—each corresponding to a different autonomic state:

- the "Green" system for when we feel safe

- the "Yellow" system for when we feel in danger

- the "Red" system for when our bodies feel like we are about to die

This traffic-light metaphor is one we'll use repeatedly throughout the book, so it can't hurt to bookmark this page or the diagram following page 42.

The Green System: Safety

If our neuroception deems the situation safe, it can relax and turn down defensive and aggressive behaviors so as to conserve resources. Instead, it turns on the systems that are conducive to being social, trusting, and communicative to others. It also optimizes the perfusion of oxygen into our blood.

This on switch for social behavior and health manifests by engaging our "Social Engagement System." We'll dive deeper into this concept in Chapter 5, but this system encompasses the muscles and functions in our face and head that allow us to be expressive and social creatures. This includes muscles in our face that allow us to express emotion, ear muscles that allow us to hear and process speech, and the muscles in our larynx and pharynx that let us intone with singsongy prosody.* When these systems are engaged,

---

* Prosodic vocalizations are surprisingly important to the polyvagal story, and are something we'll come back to repeatedly.

our heart rate also slows down to rest, relax, and stay calm for social interactions.*

The Green system is basically our entire body saying that, in the absence of imminent danger, it's okay to relax, recuperate, have a good time, and build trust with others. To that end, our bodies transform so as to facilitate these very functions.

The Green system is also key to the brain's ability to learn and think, as well as the body's ability to physically heal. Only in the absence of threats can our bodies afford to spend the resources to fully recuperate—not to mention share jokes with friends or do anything involving compassion or creativity.

The Yellow System: Danger

Let's say our neuroception has sniffed out the situation and determined that the strange figure on the hypothetical horizon is a threat. Well, it's time to trigger the danger zone and the Yellow state.

In this case, our sympathetic nervous system—or fight-or-flight system—takes hold. Our expressive facial muscles give way to a flat facial affect. Our prosodic and singsongy voices transform into a more monotone timbre. Our tolerance for pain increases, adrenaline spikes, and heart rate accelerates to give us the energy and blood flow needed to throw fists or make a quick escape.

To call back to our earlier metaphor: We transform from Bruce Banner into the Hulk.

But something else happens to the body and brain when the Yellow mode is activated. Since our metabolic resources are diverted to defend, our ability to physically heal is diminished in favor of a need to immediately survive (literally: wounds heal more slowly), as is our ability to think critically or creatively. What's more, our

---

* Interestingly, there are two reciprocal relationships when these small muscles become activated and express positive feelings: One is the reduction of the metabolically costly activation of the skeletal spinal muscles that require sympathetic excitation, and the other is the enhanced oxygenation of blood and the optimized regulation of cardiac and smooth muscles. Thus, feelings of safety and happiness are linked to optimizing the homeostatic functions of health, growth, and restoration.

neuroception is primed so that everything around us begins to feel like a threat. Our capacity for seeing nuance and feeling empathy evaporates. If you've ever tried to approach an abused dog who growls at everybody, this is what's happening.

As humans, we act rashly and impulsively when we feel threatened. Our bodies suffer, along with our ability to enjoy life, be creatively productive, and otherwise project warmth to those around us.

The Red System: Life Threat

Now, here's where the Polyvagal Theory drifts away from the traditional model for the ANS. The scientific community has long recognized the Green (parasympathetic/rest-and-relax) and Yellow (sympathetic/fight-or-flight) systems. But what happens when we encounter a situation so seemingly dire that our neuroception believes that our life is truly and immediately threatened?

In these situations, our bodies often do not fight or flee; rather, they shut down, dissociate, and possibly even pass out. While this "freeze" or "shutdown" response is common, the traditional scientific narrative does not account for it, and our society largely does not acknowledge its existence.

This reality creates pain and confusion for millions. Our failure to grasp that a shutdown response is a common and natural reaction to danger has very real consequences, as assault victims and others who have endured trauma are often doubted if they didn't show signs of struggle—and often doubt themselves.

The Polyvagal Theory doesn't just account for the existence of this "Red" state, it also explains how and why it occurs from an anatomical and evolutionary perspective.

Evolution in Reverse

The traditional model of the ANS proposes that there are two basic subsystems, perpetually locked in a battle for control of our body.

The Polyvagal Theory updates this model in several important ways. First is the very existence of the Red state, where severe duress causes our bodies to freeze, dissociate, or shut down.

The Polyvagal Theory also posits that, rather than rolling the dice among each of these states, our nervous system actually approaches them in a specific hierarchical order. This is a reverse evolutionary order that takes us further back in time to our asocial reptilian ancestors as the level of perceived threat increases.

Our ANS is a time machine. The more threatened our bodies feel, the more evolutionarily ancient our response.

What's that mean exactly?

To understand, let's introduce the concept of "dissolution," which was first proposed in this context by English neurologist John Hughlings Jackson in the 19th century.[2] Jackson observed that the higher brain structures that are involved in functions such as cognition and deep thinking actually inhibit more primitive and instinctive ones. Likewise, when our higher brain functions shut down, the vacuum is filled by visceral and gut instincts that go back to our reptile ancestors and beyond.

To put it another way: When we use our heads, we're less likely to act instinctively and rashly. According to Jackson, our bodies turn to the more evolutionarily modern processes first, before going back in time to more ancient systems.

The Polyvagal Theory applies this idea to how we as humans handle possible threats.

How this plays out: When we come into contact with that strange and possibly dangerous figure on the hypothetical horizon, our neuroception scans the situation and first tries to deal with it by turning to the most modern solution, before going back in time and eventually landing on the Red system that we inherited and repurposed from our asocial reptile ancestors.*

One more time: The more threatened our nervous system feels, the more primitive our response.

As we get more defensive and fearful, the higher thinking that is unique to (and in many ways makes us) humans is bypassed in favor of reactionary gut instincts. When we feel unsafe, we effectively

---

* In truth, this Red response is even more ancient than our reptile ancestors, who themselves inherited it from very ancient vertebrates that included primitive, jawless fish.

devolve back in time from freethinking modern humans to savage and scared vertebrates—and possibly even immobilized lizards.

This is important! A recurring theme of this book is how feeling safe helps our bodies stay healthy and happy. When we feel safe and have access to safe others as a way of regulating our bodily state through co-regulation (more on that in Chapter 5), our bodies elevate sociality and cooperation as a tool for survival. In doing so, our bodies downshift our threat responses, allowing us to stay calm and to access the homeostatic functions of health, growth, and restoration (the Green).

However, when we feel threatened, this dissolution process places immediate survival and ancient threat responses (Yellow and Red) above social functionality or the ability for the body to heal itself.

In short: Only when we are feeling safe can we properly access all of our body's social functions, and fully heal and restore our bodies.

Think of this dissolution process like a flow chart. Our neuroception first asks: "*Should I switch on the Green zone?*" If the answer to that question is yes, then it stops there. However, if the answer is no, it then asks if it should go to Yellow. If things are so dangerous or dire that not even the Yellow mode will do, it's then on to the Red.

The Green system, which allows us to deal with situations via sociability and diplomacy, is present only in evolutionarily modern mammals. Humans, dogs—creatures like that.

Just a small fraction of the animal kingdom is capable of tapping into the evolutionarily modern Green state to handle problems via social solutions. On the other hand, the Yellow ability to rev up into a fight-or-flight state is much older than the Green system, and many, many more species—including ones far more evolutionarily ancient than humans and other mammals—are capable of these aggressive and defensive behaviors.

The Red system, which causes us to shut down in the face of threats, is even older, and dates back to ancient primitive vertebrates, who responded to dire circumstances by shutting down to minimize the use of bodily resources and play dead. This is an adaptation that popped up hundreds of millions of years ago and

stuck around to the point that it is now present in virtually all vertebrates, including us humans.

You might hear scientists or performance gurus talk about
your "reptile brain." This Red system is often what they mean, in
the sense that its activation occurs outside our conscious thought
and control.*

People don't think to themselves that they want their bodies to
shut down or dissociate. Rather, it is an unconscious and often
unwanted reflex, and the autonomic (meaning *automatic*) nervous
system makes it so.

It's important to note that this process is different for everybody.
No two people's neuroception is exactly the same. We all have different levels of resilience, and a similar traumatic situation could
prove debilitating to some—while barely impacting others.

The Importance of Play

The traditional model of the autonomic nervous systems presents
the parasympathetic nervous system (or Green system) and sympathetic nervous system (or Yellow system) as being two opposing systems, effectively locked in a battle for control of our bodies.
According to this model, we feel either safe (in which case the Green
takes over) or threatened (when it's Yellow fight-or-flight time).

Another way the Polyvagal Theory deviates from this old ANS
model is by acknowledging that our bodies are often not strictly
controlled by just a single Green, Yellow, or (as the Polyvagal Theory adds to the mix) Red state at any one time.

Rather, our bodies are capable of mixing and matching features
of each of these systems to create autonomic cocktails that serve
very specific functions. For example, the Yellow system isn't just
for fighting or fleeing threats. Its ability to mobilize us is utilized
almost anytime we need a boost of energy—something that often
comes in handy during moments of safety or even fun.

---

* A deeper dive into comparative neuroanatomy would revise the idea of "reptile
brain" so it includes other evolutionarily antecedent species, including fish and
amphibians.

Let's take somebody playing a game of basketball. They are running and jumping and guarding and posting and hopefully working up a sweat. In other words, they are tapping into exactly the kind of physical exertion that we commonly associate with the fight-or-flight Yellow system.

Of course, playing basketball is not the same as running for your life. And unless something goes horribly wrong on the court, the player shouldn't feel like they are in any real danger.

Which begs the question: Is somebody playing a physically exhausting game of basketball with friends using their fight-or-flight Yellow system, or their social Green system?

It turns out, they are using both.

The same goes for dancing, running, exercising—basically any activity that requires physical intensity but is *not* perceived by our bodies as dangerous (especially if it's done socially with other people, such as playing a team sport or dancing at a club).

While the Yellow system is certainly a key part of how we respond to danger, there are countless nonthreatening scenarios in which its ability to activate our body in this manner can come in handy.

When this happens, the safe social context is functionally inviting the Social Engagement System to take over control of the autonomic nervous system, and to effectively repurpose our evolutionarily ancient fight-or-flight mobilization system into something that can be used for enjoyable activities.

Situations like this are why it's a bit of an oversimplification to say that we are controlled by just our Green, Yellow, or Red state at any given time. Often, more than one of these states has something to offer, and healthy individuals are perfectly capable of mixing and matching them as needed.

This is especially important to understand because the academic community has long cast the Green parasympathetic state as "good" and the Yellow sympathetic state as "bad."

In truth, *none* of our body's states (and that includes the Red) are innately bad, as they all offer us important and adaptive functions that were honed by millions of years of evolution to help keep us alive. The problems tend to come when our Yellow and Red systems are overused in the service of defense (as is endemic to our stressful modern world), or when we become effectively trapped in them and shut out of access to the restorative and healing Green state (as is common with those who suffer from trauma).

The aforementioned hybrid state of the Yellow and Green systems—meaning we're physically mobilized and socially functional at the same time—is one that is particularly near and dear to all of us. This is, quite literally, the autonomic state of play.

Play is really important to the nervous system!

Take dogs as an example.* When dogs play with one another, they engage in an amazing ballet that shares numerous features with actual defensive fighting but is clearly something different. Even as they run around the dog park nipping at one another's heels (that's the Yellow system at play), they also maintain eye contact, pull back if their partner seems legitimately in trouble, and frequently trade positions between submission and dominance. All that stuff comes from the Green system, which fuses with the energizing Yellow to create a highly physical game where it is clear to all participants that they aren't actually trying to hurt the other.

Again: None of the three primary states (Green, Yellow, and Red) is innately "bad." The problems come when we're *stuck* in states of danger and are consequently shut out of the restorative and healing abilities that come from Green.

Our bodies rely on the Yellow system for survival. But tapping into it is metabolically costly, and keeps us from properly healing and restoring our bodies—not to mention properly enjoying our lives. In an ideal world, we'd be able to turn this system on when needed, and then immediately jump back to the safe space of Green a minute later.

Play can be viewed as a neural exercise that allows our nervous systems to practice this switch between Green and Yellow so that we can utilize the mobilizing Yellow system when needed, without getting stuck there.

This ability to utilize the Green and Yellow systems without get-

---

* If you notice we keep mentioning dogs, it's not just because they are awesome. Rather, it's because they are modern mammals whose nervous systems operate in a way that is very similar to our own.

ting locked into one is crucial to our sense of resilience and our ability to withstand hardship without it completely overtaking our lives.

With apologies to readers who may actively avoid the dance floor, this is also an explanation for why dancing is generally viewed as a fun, pleasurable activity. It allows us to tap into our Yellow system safely while also exercising our nervous system's ability to balance and bounce between the Green and Yellow systems. Sure, you can dance by yourself, but doing it with others—an innately social act that is the underlying premise behind the entire nightclub industry—only increases the integration of the Green system into this exercise.

And while the *need* for play is driven by our nervous system and hardwired into children and animals (who do it instinctively), our culture has long been dismissive of its importance, and even viewed it as frivolous. The Polyvagal Theory forces us to reevaluate this notion.

Once you begin to understand just how important the act of play is to our nervous systems and our health, it emerges as a real argument for the value of recess and team sports in developing children—and nights out with friends for adults.

Rather than viewing these activities as simple physical exercises or pointless distractions, they can and should be viewed as opportunities to exercise our nervous systems—not to mention our bodies—to develop the resilience required to stay sane, happy, healthy, and (especially for younger children) well adjusted.

Intimacy

Before we move on, let's quickly address some other "hybrid" autonomic states that call upon multiple color-coded autonomic systems at the same time.

When we are in a state of danger, our Red system can cause us to freeze, shut down, and dissociate. But the same neural pathways that cause immobilization in times of perceived danger are crucial to our ability to immobilize when we feel safe and are around trusted loved ones.

When the Red system (which is used for immobilization) is activated along with the Green (meaning we feel safe), these circuits take on a whole new, and usually much more welcome, purpose: the deeply restorative state of intimacy.

Like play, intimacy, in effect, has its own autonomic signature and can be viewed as a unique autonomic state.

With these hybrid states, it's clear that a sense of safety—as determined by our neuroception—radically recontextualizes the Yellow and Red systems: from ones of danger that are actively harmful to our body when overutilized, into ones of pleasure, health, healing, fun, attachment, and co-regulation (see Chapter 5).

Fawning and Appeasement

When faced with a threat, we sometimes fight or flee. Other times we freeze or shut down. But for some of us, the nervous system tries to navigate the treacherous journey from danger to safety with yet another strategy: an attempt to support, and even soothe, a perpetrator who means us harm.

These responses are most common when somebody is surrounded by a pervasive and nearly nonstop threat, as is the case with those who have been abducted or who live in a chronically abusive environment.

These seemingly supportive behaviors are often observed as "fawning" or "appeasement," two terms that are frequently used on social media to describe the seemingly paradoxical behaviors of survivors who appear to exhibit caring behaviors toward a perpetrator. Although fawning and appeasement are frequently lumped together, the Polyvagal Theory attempts to distinguish between them as separate survival strategies with their own autonomic signatures.

Fawning is an attempt to please the perpetrator through compliance, with the pragmatic expectation that such compliance will diminish aggression and reduce the threat.

Appeasement, on the other hand, can be viewed as an attempt to convince the perpetrator's nervous system that the victim is actually on their side.

When people freeze or shut down in the face of a threat, they

THE POLYVAGAL THEORY

WHEN WE FEEL
SAFETY
(Parasympathetic Nervous System—Ventral Vagal Complex)

THE GREEN SYSTEM

Social Engagement/Health, Growth, Restoration

BEHAVIORS
Optimizes social behavior, compassion, mental and physiological calmness, critical thinking, the neurophysiological foundation for mental and physical health, and an ability to be an effective co-regulator.

INCREASES
The body's ability to physically heal, think critically and creatively, digest food, recuperate, socially connect, hear and listen to voices, and transmit feelings of safety to others.

DECREASES
Defensive systems that mobilize the body.

WHEN WE FEEL
DANGER
(Sympathetic Nervous System)

THE YELLOW SYSTEM

Mobilization

BEHAVIORS
Physical activation, fight-or-flight, panic, restlessness, reactivity, rage, and anxiety.

INCREASES
Physical mobility and defensive systems, blood pressure, heart rate, adrenaline, pain tolerance and reactivity, and ability to hear and process ultra low-frequency sounds.

DECREASES
Social behaviors, the ability to accurately detect the feelings of others, facial affect and vocal prosody, physical and mental health, digestive systems, and the ability to hear and process human speech and co-regulate with others.

WHEN WE FEEL
LIFE-THREAT
(Parasympathetic Nervous System—Dorsal Vagal Complex)

THE RED SYSTEM

Immobilization

BEHAVIORS
Bodily shutdown, blacking out, dissociation, numbness, depression, hopelessness, helplessness, and an inability to socially engage and communicate with others.

INCREASES
Immobilization and pain tolerance.

DECREASES
Heart rate, blood pressure, depth of breathing, body awareness, awareness of others, and the ability to socially engage and communicate.

are often met with a lack of understanding as to how or why they responded the way they did. The same sense of disbelief and dismissal often meets those who demonstrate fawning or appeasement behavior. After all: Why would anybody try to please or send signals of support to somebody who is hurting them?

It is our belief that we should reframe these behaviors as bodily survival strategies and remove conscious intent from our judgment of such situations. And while understanding fawning and appeasement as a response to trauma is an evolving topic within the Polyvagal Theory, we feel it is likely that these behaviors come from unique autonomic states that are a part of our body's mission to keep us alive.

As a defensive state that is called upon in times of severe duress, fawning may involve activation of the Red and Yellow systems. When we are dominated by these systems, our Social Engagement System and capacity for co-regulation are effectively disengaged. Without positive social cues to accompany the compliant behavior, a perpetrator may read this behavior as disinterested, disconnected, or dishonest, which can lead to further aggression and danger.

What makes appeasement different is that it also involves an activated Social Engagement System, which allows the victim to project signals of safety and co-regulation to their assailant. This allows the victim to functionally convince the assailant's nervous system that the victim is on their side, increasing the chances of survival.

It is possible that this appeasement behavior involves the recruitment of a unique autonomic state that combines elements of the Green, Yellow, and Red systems at the same time. So the threat is detected, but the Social Engagement System is still sufficiently resourced to send cues of safety, sociability, and co-regulation to the perpetrator in order to help the assailed survive the ordeal.[3]

Not everybody responds to trauma or abuse in this way. But rather than casting shame or doubt over those who do respond in such a manner, a more compassionate approach would be to view these behaviors as the result of a nervous system that has developed a remarkable ability to adapt and survive through challenging or life-threatening times.

Three Circuits, Several States

With our new "hybrid" states added to our list of autonomic states, we're up to seven in total. Our initial three color-coded states, plus four additional hybrid states that draw from more than one system:

Hybrid Systems:

Three circuits, several states

	State(s):	Behavior:
Social Communication	Green	Social Engagement
Play/Dance	Green, Yellow	Social Engagement & Mobilization
Fight/Flight	Yellow	Mobilization
Intimacy	Green, Red	Social Engagement & Immobilization
Appeasement	Green, Yellow, Red	Social Engagement & Threat Detection
Fawning	Yellow, Red	Compliance Without Co-Regulation
Shutdown/ Dissociation	Red	Immobilization

Now that we have a sense of the ANS and how it transforms us, it's time to look at how this occurs on an anatomical level. And with that, we return to the "vagal" part of the Polyvagal Theory and the star of our show: the vagus nerve.

3

The Vagus Nerve

At long last, it's time to turn the spotlight to the vagus. The protagonist of our story, somewhat hidden in the margins up until now.

The vagus nerve is a binding bundle of fibers that weaves its way through almost the entire body, from our brainstems down to the gut, touching countless organs and bodily systems along the way.

In doing so, it serves as a shared connection that allows the autonomic nervous system to exist as a cohesive entity, capable of coordinating so many discrete bodily functions. So if we're in a Yellow fight-or-flight state, our heart doesn't speed up while our breathing slows down. Because the vagus connects our heart to our lungs (and many other organs as well), they rev up together.

The vagus is also unique in how it interacts with other cranial nerves, particularly the ones that facilitate face and head movements that are key to social behavior, including ingestion, facial expressions, and speech.

As we go deeper into this book, we're going to repeatedly reference the idea that social behavior can transform our nervous system and physiological state. The connection between the vagus and the nerves and muscles that allow us to be expressive and socialize with others is key to this magic.[1]

To pull a page from modern technology, you can think of the vagus as a neural fiber-optic cable that sends signals up and down the entire body. The key signal at play here: how safe our neuroception determines us to be.

Feel safe? The vagus spreads the good news from our brainstem and down throughout our entire body so that our heart, lungs, and all the rest of our organs respond appropriately and respond together.

Feel threatened? The vagus acts as a signal fire on top of a mountain, sending the message from our brainstem to the rest of our body and giving permission to our neural circuits of defense to take control.

It is through the vagus that our neuroception and autonomic state impact our entire body—and not just a single discrete part of it. If our bodies are an orchestra that consists of a multitude of different organs and systems, then the vagus is the conductor, raising the baton so they all can join together into a shared symphony.

The vagus doesn't just serve as a passive messenger. When activated, it also acts as a braking mechanism that reduces our arousal, slows us down, and enables us to feel calm.

It is through this braking mechanism that the vagus downshifts us away from Yellow states of defense and functionally opens the portal to the Green state. This ability of the vagus to calm us down and relax us is why so many people in the wellness world are so obsessed with activating it.

Activities such as some forms of yoga and breathing exercises calm us down because they directly send signals through the vagus to slow our heart rate. Many activities or sensory experiences that we view as pleasant or calming—singing, laughing, and playing music, for example—are actually triggering the vagus, causing that nerve to send its soothing signals up and down between our body and brainstem. In doing so, these activities literally make us feel safe, which is probably why we tend to enjoy them and seek them out.

If you've ever seen studies suggesting that music education makes students perform better at subjects such as math, this is likely why. The acts of listening to and making music help us activate the vagus and access the Green state, which enables our bodies to better access neural pathways that are conducive to all types of learning, problem-solving, and creative thinking.

———

The vagus's ability to send signals of safety and danger is not a one-way street. Rather, it's a bidirectional neural superhighway.

In other words, it can send signals of safety or danger from our brain (and conscious realization) down to our body, *or* it can take signals from our body and senses, and pass them up to our brain.

This bidirectionality allows the vagus to shuttle these signals up and down between our brain and viscera until an overall sense of safety or threat takes over and manifests itself across our entire body. The result here is our autonomic state and the process through which our entire body is thrown into the Green, Yellow, or Red zone.

These signals are managed and interpreted by the brainstem, but it is through the vagus that they bounce up and down our bodies.

So to recap:

- *Our senses and bodily systems are constantly scanning the environment for signs of safety or danger, via the process of neuroception.*

- *Any signals of safety or danger we pick up are then sent up and down our vagus, resulting in an autonomic state that effectively transforms how the entire body functions.*

However, like a highway that features express lanes in only one direction, the vagal pathways between our body and brain are not equal. Approximately 80% of the vagus's fibers go from the body up to the brain, while only about 20% go from the brain down to the body.

Because of this mismatch, our visceral sensory experiences may be far more important than conscious thought when it comes to determining our autonomic state. This is why, as far as our nervous system is concerned, *feeling* safe is much more important than consciously *thinking* we are safe.

We are body-first organisms, and our bodies truly are oriented to feel the world, rather than to think about it. This book began with the famous Descartes quote: "I think, therefore I am." While that is true at times, the more accurate expression might be a polyvagal twist on it: "I *feel myself*, therefore I am."

Simply *feeling* safe or threatened does indeed transform our bodies, our health, and the way we live our lives. And in a world that now seems consciously designed to scare us through a never-ending barrage of threats, news alerts, and anxieties, it's no wonder so many of us feel so stressed and unhealthy so often. You do. We do. We all do.

The good news: It's not our fault, and there are things we can do about it.

The Power of Breath

"Just breathe." "Take a deep breath." "Inhale . . . now exhale."

While we've all heard these words in some capacity, few people understand just *why* breathing is such a powerful tool for maintaining calm, staying cool, and living in the Green. If you've read this far, the answer should come off as surprisingly tidy and logical. Needless to say, it all comes down to the vagus.

As we've just learned, the vagus acts as a bidirectional neural highway, sending signals of safety or danger up and down our body, so that the whole thing acts in synchrony. So if you feel scared or safe, our entire body responds by activating the Yellow or Red systems—or downshifting into the Green.

This process is driven by the body and is largely automatic and unconscious. As a result, when we are pushed into an undesirable autonomic state it can feel like we are losing control of our body. We may desperately *want* to calm down (or perhaps snap back at somebody who insists we relax with a clichéd "*Don't tell me to calm down!*") but feel helpless as these feelings overwhelm us.

This is particularly present in people who suffer from anxiety (and really, who doesn't to some degree these days?). We may consciously know that there is no reason to be anxious or worried, but the body has a way of taking over. And as the signal runs up and down the vagus, it manifests in the entire body, from head to toes.

So what does this have to do with breathing?

Our autonomic (one more time: that means "automatic") systems operate on an unconscious level that is outside of our conscious control, meaning we can't will our heart into slowing down or our sweat into stopping. However, for most people, there is one major exception to this rule, and one key autonomic function that we can also control at will when needed: our breathing.

We can choose to hold our breath while underwater, breathe out slowly to play an instrument, or use all the air in our lungs to fill a balloon. Alternatively, we can simply go about our day or go to sleep and let our lungs do their thing without our needing to think about it.

Because breathing is the unique autonomic process that we can also take control of at will, slowing it down sends a powerful signal to the rest of the ANS:

"If I have the time to breathe slowly, I'm probably not actually running for my life. Maybe I am safe, and we can turn things down a little, autonomically speaking."

To accomplish this, deep and slow exhalations activate sensors in our respiratory system that serve as vagal triggers, causing us to downshift our autonomic state. This message of safety then proceeds to bounce up and down our vagus until it reaches the rest of our body, making breathing an incredibly powerful tool for keeping our entire body calm and cool.

Long *exhalations*, in particular, are key to this process. The opposite type of breathing, with short exhalations and long inhalations, effectively mimics the act of hyperventilation and can have the opposite effect, revving up our ANS into a state of danger.

The calming effects of breath have been known for thousands of years. Controlled breathing that uses slow exhalations is an important component of many ancient traditions and several forms of yoga, and its power has long been couched in spiritual or religious language. We do not mean to be dismissive of these traditions (which can be viewed as powerful tools for passing on this knowledge through millennia of ancient, prescientific, and even preliterate times), but adding an anatomical understanding to the process might make it more accessible to the science-minded among us, and to the millions of people who may cringe at the idea of doing anything related to yoga.*

So next time you feel anxious or overly activated, do yourself a favor and take that deep breath, hold it for a moment, and then breathe out very slowly. If it helps to think about it in spiritual or religious terms, so be it. But to throw some science behind the magic, you are activating your vagus and effectively telling your body that, by virtue of having the time to slow down and take this breath, you are actually safe and not running for your life.

Your body will get the message.

STIMULATING THE VAGUS

On June 2, 2022, *The New York Times* ran a story with the provocative headline "This Nerve Influences Nearly Every Internal Organ. Can It Improve Our Mental State, Too?"

The nerve in question is, of course, the vagus, which the article correctly calls an "information superhighway" that runs from the brainstem and connects to virtually every organ in the body.

What the article goes on to discuss, and what I (Stephen) could have never predicted when I began studying the vagus in the early 1970s, is that finding ways to "activate," "tone," or "hack" the vagus has become something of a social media obsession. The article mentions that, as of its publication, TikTok videos with the hashtag #vagusnerve have been viewed more than 64 million times. On Instagram, the hashtag has accompanied some 70,000 posts.

The reason for this obsession is simple: The idea of activating the vagus has entered the conversation as a sort of catch-all salve for all sorts of conditions related to both physical and mental health. PTSD, diabetes, depression, epilepsy, long COVID. The list goes on.

"It can sound sort of magical with all the things it does," Eric Porges, PhD, an insightful researcher in the department of clinical and health psychology at the University of Florida, told the *Times*.

---

* Their loss.

If you think seeing the vagus enter the big time like this is weird for me, you're right. Of course, the strangeness of the experience is only amplified by the fact that the above-quoted Dr. Porges is, in fact, my son (and my coauthor's brother). Apples falling near trees and all that.

So what's the deal with stimulating or activating the vagus? And can it really help with this laundry list of conditions?

In short: yes.

Approximately 80% of the nerve fibers that make up the vagus are sensory. Meaning that they take information from our organs about how we are feeling, and send that information up to the brainstem.

It has been known for decades that stimulating these sensory fibers can have health-enhancing effects. As is mentioned in the *Times* story, researchers first looked into the vagus as a way of treating epilepsy as far back as the late 1800s, and soon discovered that activating it also seemed to help with mood and mental state. Stimulating the vagus is now an accepted treatment to reduce epileptic seizures, as well as treatment-resistant depression.

Vagal nerve stimulation (or VNS) devices work by sending electronic pulses to the brain through the sensory portals of the vagus. The brain then interprets these pulses and reacts to them by sending calming signals through the vagus back down to various organs. These signals appear to channel a sense of safety to the body, which helps free our organs from the demands of being in a defensive state and supports our ability to enter the healing Green state of homeostasis.

The challenge with most VNS devices is that they are implanted via invasive surgery, with the nerve being accessed through an incision in the lower region of the neck. All surgeries come with risks and costs. These are not casual treatments, but last-ditch (and sometimes even lifesaving) options for people who need them to manage conditions that severely impact their quality of life.

The reason that social media has recently become obsessed with the vagus likely stems from the increasing awareness that we don't necessarily need a surgical operation to take advantage of the nerve's power to shift our bodily state, calm us down, and heal us.

In fact, we can stimulate the vagus without directly touching it. Certain mundane actions such as applying pressure to a certain part of the body or breathing in a certain way also stimulate the vagus, which features sensory portals that can be found in easily accessible areas on the external ear, eardrum, and face.

We'll explain why this matters later on in this chapter, but it's no accident that many of these vagal activation points are found on parts of the body involved with social interaction. **The Polyvagal Theory suggests that merely engaging in safe social interactions serves as itself a form of vagal stimulation, capable of rehabilitating and optimizing many of our bodily systems without resorting to social media "hacks."**

Even electrical vagal nerve stimulation is now accessible without invasive surgery,* which is paving the way for it to serve as a useful treatment for additional conditions, including PTSD and gut issues such as irritable bowel syndrome.[2]

The hope is that, by removing the need for surgical implantation, the benefits of electrical vagal nerve stimulation devices might be accessible to far more people.

And in the meantime, the rest of us can activate our vagus simply by having a nice conversation with somebody near and dear to us.

Back to Breathing

Let's dive a bit deeper into breathing, and the science behind how it triggers the calming mechanisms of the vagus—and how these same effects might be felt through actions such as singing, smiling, and listening to or playing music.

With the Polyvagal Theory as our guide, along with a smidge of neural anatomy, the answer becomes clear.

In the brainstem, there is an area that functions as what scientists call a "common cardiorespiratory oscillator."[3] This basically means that this area provides signals that tell the heart and respiratory system to work in synchrony. We can actually see this effect in real time by measuring somebody's heart-rate patterns while they are breathing, as changes in breath also shift heart rate.

---

* (e.g., gammaCore, https://www.gammacore.com/)

The link between our heart rate and respiration makes sense when you think about the primary purpose of the heart, which is to pump oxygenated blood throughout the body. When we inhale (which brings oxygen into our body), our heart increases its speed to deliver that extra oxygen throughout our circulatory system. So deeper breathing gets us more oxygen, which is then pumped throughout our body by a sped-up heart.

The physical process that links our respiration and heart rate largely happens through our bronchi. If you've ever heard of bronchitis, the word should be a familiar one. Bronchi are tubes that transport air from the windpipe to the lungs. Once our oxygen is inhaled and then moved to the lungs, the bronchi tubes lead to a network of even smaller tubes called bronchioles. At the end of these small tubes are tiny air sacs known as alveoli. The alveoli are where our lungs and blood exchange oxygen and carbon dioxide during the process of breathing in and breathing out. The oxygen we breathe in passes through the alveoli and into the blood and then travels to the tissues throughout the body. Meanwhile, carbon dioxide travels in our blood from our tissues and eventually passes through the alveoli to be breathed out when we exhale.

To aid in this oxygenation process, our bronchi oscillate their diameter to create pressure that pushes oxygen through the alveoli into the blood. These oscillations in both the bronchi and heart rate are synchronized with the respiratory changes in our heart rate. This synchronization is made possible by the vagus, which sends a "respiratory signal" (think of this as a bit of data that has our breathing pattern embedded in it) from our brainstem to both the bronchi and heart. This allows the bronchi and heart to synchronize and optimize the diffusion of oxygen into the blood.

The vagus contains cardioinhibitory fibers (as the name suggests, these help slow the heart) that calm and reduce our metabolic load and allow us to conserve energy. It is through the activation of these vagal fibers that slowing and extending the duration of our exhalations also slows down the heart and calms the body.

The magic of breathing comes from the fact that this synchronization between our breath and our heart rate can occur either through natural, unconscious breathing or through deliberate, voluntary breathing. So by consciously changing our breathing patterns, we can also influence how fast our heart is beating. And the vagus is the neural pathway that makes this happen.

This idea isn't some new breakthrough. As far back as 1910, physiologist Heinrich Hering[4] documented that he could identify cardioinhibitory fibers traveling from the brainstem down to the heart, through the vagus. As he so succinctly put it: *"It is known with breathing that a demonstrable lowering of heart rate . . . is indicative of the function of the vagi."*

Hering's observation that breathing lowers our heart rate, and that the vagus is behind this slowdown, was hugely foundational for the development of the Polyvagal Theory. It also gave me (Stephen) a neurophysiological basis to develop a noninvasive method for measuring vagal activity using a component of heart-rate variability called respiratory sinus arrhythmia (or RSA).

With this ability to easily measure vagal activity (or "vagal tone," as we sometimes call it), I could objectively test various hypotheses derived from the Polyvagal Theory.

To sum up, what's important for now are two basic points:

1. Changing our breathing will change our heart rate. This synchronization between our breathing and our heart rate is driven by the vagus.
2. We can test whether anything—including stress or voluntary changes in our breathing—causes changes in vagal activity via a noninvasive measurement called respiratory sinus arrhythmia (RSA) that can be derived from heart-rate variability. This is essentially the measurable amplitude of the respiratory rhythm in the beat-to-beat heart-rate pattern.

Anyway, back to Hering and the question of how breathing slows down our hearts and calms us down.

More than 100 years ago, Hering noted that the ability of the vagus to influence the heart was effectively switched off and on by breathing. Specifically, he saw that heart rate increases during inhalation, and decreases during exhalation.

What this means: In general, the vagus is efficiently calming the heart and decreasing arousal *only* during the exhalation phase of breathing—and not during inhalation. With this knowledge, we suddenly have an anatomical understanding of how deep breaths, specifically deep breaths with short inhalations and long, slow exhalations, are calming.

The reverse is true as well. Breathing with long inhalations and short exhalations tends to dampen the vagus's ability to calm us down, increasing our heart rate and arousal. This type of breathing is likely to activate our Yellow sympathetic nervous system and rev us up. You often see this huffing-and-puffing breathing pattern when somebody is anxious or hyperventilating.

To quickly summarize all that:

- Extending the duration of exhalations calms us down and activates our Green parasympathetic nervous system.

- Extending the duration of inhalations revs us up and activates our Yellow sympathetic nervous system.

Understanding these mechanisms means that we are suddenly equipped with the ability to manipulate our physiological state, and either calm down or amp up, through little more than a slight shift in how we breathe. This magic trick is the basis for ancient traditions that emphasize breathing (such as yoga), and is also why activities such as singing, vocalizing, or blowing into a wind instrument can serve as vagal triggers that calm us down: They all involve long, slow exhalations.

Many musicians and singers describe making music as an ethereal or calming experience. Something that keeps them cool and collected, when nothing else will. They likely have the vagus to thank for this.

The Vagus as a Neural Brake

Activating our vagus and breathing with slow exhalations calms us down because the vagus acts as a powerful neural brake, capable of downshifting our entire physiology.

At first blush, one might assume that this braking mechanism is beneficial. And, in fact, it often is. This slowdown is what allows us to be cool and collected. It is through this mechanism that we can be around others and be social without being aggressive or defensive. It is through this mechanism that we can engage the Green system.

However, although the Polyvagal Theory emphasizes the positive attributes of a ventral vagal brake (we'll get to the "ventral" part of that shortly), there is another side to the vagus and its ability to downshift our physiology.

Vagal braking isn't just about slowing us down to make us happy, healthy, and social. The Red system—the one that causes us to freeze, shut down, and dissociate in the face of severe duress— also involves the body slowing down, through a different and much more evolutionarily ancient branch of the vagus.

The Polyvagal Theory posits that the vagus has two braking mechanisms—one that slows us down to be happy and social creatures; and a separate one that contributes to immobilizing in defense, which might be experienced as freezing, shutting down, dissociating, collapsing, and even passing out.

To understand these two very different slowdown responses— one for the Green system and one for the Red—we finally get to the "poly" part of "polyvagal."

But first, let's go back a beat to the origins of the Polyvagal Theory, and how it came about in the first place.

The Dark Side of the Vagus

Before the development of the Polyvagal Theory, the autonomic nervous system was viewed as being composed of two diametrically opposing subsystems. You have the parasympathetic nervous system (which allows us to rest and relax) and the sympathetic nervous system (which activates us into a fight-or-flight state).

When I (Stephen) was in graduate school, the SNS was viewed as the system of stress, and thus our "mortal enemy" (I remember being taught those words in particular), while the PNS was viewed as having the capacity to counter and inhibit the debilitating influences of this "enemy." The net result was thought to be a "balance" between these two antagonistic autonomic systems, which were stuck in an eternal battle for our bodies.

In other words: We were all taught that the Yellow sympathetic state meant stress, and was always bad, while the Green parasympathetic state meant relaxation, and was always good.

I was taught that the vagus nerve is a major part of the parasympathetic nervous system and that activating it is key to our body's ability to relieve stress.

Because the vagus activates our relaxing PNS, I was taught that vagal activation was *always* good.

This prevalent model, which had been taught by schools and passed around as scientific orthodoxy since the early 1900s, began to break down for me in the early 1990s.

At the time, I was conducting research with newborn babies and focused on developing new methodologies to measure vagal activity. Since the vagus was part of the "good" parasympathetic system, I assumed that vagal activity would act as a protective feature that could help predict positive clinical outcomes for newborns.

Basically: If vagal activation was viewed as always healthy and protective, I wanted to measure it.

In 1992, I published a paper on the subject in the journal *Pediatrics*[5] and soon received a puzzling letter that would change my life.

A neonatologist who had read the paper wrote to me to counter the idea that vagal tone was protective. While I had been taught that the vagus was there to help us, his medical training had taught him that the vagus could actually *kill* us.

I immediately knew what he was talking about. In the neonatal intensive care unit, vagal activation is associated with bradycardia and apnea—conditions that are characterized by massive slowing of the heart rate and inability to breathe. For some preterm infants, these conditions can prove fatal. As a result, doctors that work with newborns were taught to view vagal activity not as protective but as a warning sign.

"Perhaps too much of a good thing was bad," the neonatologist suggested.

For months, I carried the neonatologist's letter in my briefcase, and I began to wonder: How could the same nerve facilitate our body's ability to withstand stress *and* slow our heart and breathing to a lethal degree?

How can the vagus be both protective and life-threatening?

I called this question "the vagal paradox," and my desire to solve it led directly to the Polyvagal Theory.

———

In search of an answer to the vagal paradox, I looked to the literature, our anatomy, and our evolutionary history.

I observed that the vagus nerve is composed of multiple discrete motor branches. One system that slows us down to counter stress and heal us, and one that also slows us down but might do so in a way that resulted in the life-threatening states of bradycardia and apnea.

Through my study of comparative anatomy,* it was clear to me that these discrete circuits evolved sequentially. The life-threatening branch of the vagus is found in our ancient asocial reptile ancestors, while the de-stressing branch appears only in relatively modern mammals. This, of course, includes humans.

So we have two vagal motor branches. One very ancient and potentially debilitating. One relatively modern and restorative.†

It is these multiple branches that give us the "poly" in "polyvagal." And depending on which of them is in play, the vagus's ability to act as a neural brake can shuttle us into either the Green (for safety and restoration) or the Red system (for freezing and shutting down).

To understand how these motor branches differ in function, let's first go over how they differ in their physical forms.

———

* More on this in the next chapter.

† While there are two motor branches to the vagus, there are three branches in total. The third is the sensory branch, which contains the majority of the vagus's total fibers.

Difference #1: The Myelinated Sheath

The first major difference between these two vagal pathways is that only the modern vagus, as found in mammals, is myelinated—meaning it comes contained in a fatty sheath called myelin.

To get back into modern technospeak, you can think of this sheath like the rubber coating that can be found on the sort of coaxial cable that you might find at Best Buy. On such a cable, this outer insulation helps improve the transmission speed and the clarity of its signal. With the modern vagus, the fatty myelin sheath does essentially the same thing. It is through this increased signal speed and clarity that the modern vagus can rapidly activate our Green system—and our ability to be calm and socialize.

Difference #2: Where They Sprout From

The second difference between the modern and ancient vagus is where they physically originate in our brainstem, with each of the two branches plugging into different areas of the brainstem that are involved with very different functions.

The ancient (or "dorsal," if we're getting technical) vagus plugs into the back (or "dorsal" side, if we remember our high school biology) of the brainstem. Whereas the modern (or "ventral") vagus hangs out of the front (or "ventral") side of the brainstem.

Difference #3: Different Control Hubs

Now that we've established that the modern and ancient vagus branches plug into different parts of the brainstem, let's look at what those regions actually do, and how these vagal branches carry those functions throughout our bodies.

The Modern Vagus

First, let's look at the modern mammalian motor vagus. This branch plugs into a part of the brainstem that is anatomically known as the "ventral vagal complex" (or VVC). In addition to the vagus, the VVC also houses the source nuclei (meaning where the nerves begin) of four other cranial nerves: the trigeminal, facial, glossopharyngeal, and accessory nerves.

It is through the VVC that the vagus is closely linked to the sensory and motor functions of these four cranial nerves. To understand the implications of that, let's quickly look at what these nerves do.

The **trigeminal nerve** contributes to sensations in the face, head, and mouth. It also helps control the muscles that allow us to bite and chew. If you've ever had a dentist numb your mouth with a shot, you've experienced the impact of blocking this nerve. Not only does a portion of your face feel numb when this happens, but you probably have difficulty speaking or ingesting food without the nerve's sensory features guiding you.*

The **facial nerve** helps us control most of the muscles in our face that allow us to express emotion when talking to others.

The facial and trigeminal nerves also have branches that reach into the middle ear and regulate the absolute smallest muscles in our entire body. These tiny muscles help us dampen background sounds to better hear speech.

The **glossopharyngeal nerve** is involved with our ability to taste, salivate, and swallow. Most relevant to PVT is that this nerve contributes, along with the vagus, to regulating the motor functions of the pharynx and larynx that allow us to speak.

The **accessory nerve** is involved with our ability to control various neck and head muscles, including the muscles that allow us to

---

* Interestingly, some individuals have cardiac arrhythmias following dental procedures, which is most likely the consequence of an irritation to the sensory branch of the trigeminal communicating with the area of the brainstem controlling the cardioinhibitory fibers traveling through the vagus.

physically shrug, as well as ones that allow us to vocalize through our larynx and pharynx.

Put all these nerves together, and we see that the VVC is directly tied to many of the tiny and precise muscles that allow us to be expressive, communicative, social creatures. And the modern vagus plugs right into it.

When the modern vagus is activated and we enter the Green state of safety, our faces become more expressive. Our voices become less monotone and exhibit more prosody and nuance. We are physically better able to hear and listen to others. To go back to our Marvel metaphor, our outer Hulks melt away for our inner Bruce Banners.

Add on the vagus's ability to calm, soothe, and slow us down when activated, and it starts to make sense just how key this branch of the nerve—and the entire ventral vagal complex—is for anything related to social behavior. The modern vagus slows us down into a state conducive to socialization and also turns on the facial and vocal features that allow us to hold a conversation, be expressive, and enjoy being around others.

When we leave the Green state for the Yellow or Red, these social muscles become disengaged. When we are in a fight-or-flight state, we have flatter faces with less affect. Our voices become more monotone. We have a harder time understanding other people's voices. We even have a harder time ingesting and digesting food. (Digestive issues such as irritable bowel syndrome are very common in those who suffer from trauma. This is likely part of the reason why.) When our nervous system believes it is under an immediate threat, the bodily systems that support social behavior or our body's ability to heal and restore itself take a backseat to immediate survival.

This is also likely why so many people who live with so many seemingly unrelated conditions show these same symptoms. A flat, low-affect face and monotone voice are exceedingly common for those who have autism or deal with PTSD (or borderline personality disorder or schizophrenia or several other conditions). On paper, all of these conditions are different. But the truth is that they all likely involve the autonomic nervous system and bodies that rarely—if ever—truly feel safe. These conditions are either disruptors of our autonomic nervous system, or possibly the result of a disrupted autonomic nervous system.*

When people don't feel safe, we can literally see it on their faces and hear it in their voices.

These physical expressions of safety and danger are contagious. Simply put: We tend to mirror the autonomic state of others. When other people look and sound threatened or threatening, it signals to our bodies (via our neuroception) that maybe we should be on edge too.

We do this through the Social Engagement System.

The Social Engagement System is what I (Stephen) call the cluster of functions in our face and head that allow for sociality and connectedness. These functions come from the cranial nerves that plug into the VVC, which control the muscles in our face and head.

The Social Engagement System can be thought of as a two-way interaction system that allows us both to interpret somebody else's autonomic state and to broadcast our own state to others. This occurs through the display and interpretation of various social behaviors—largely embedded in our faces and voices—that can be activated only when our bodies feel safe.

It is through this Social Engagement System that simple social interaction can serve as a portal toward activating the vagus, making us feel safe, and improving our health and well-being. This concept is key to how an understanding of the Polyvagal Theory can allow us to live better lives.

---

* However, having common features does not imply a common external cause. For example, there is a growing public interest in the similar features of autism and PTSD that is leading to a faulty assumption that autism is rooted in trauma. It is important to note that having depressed social engagement is a powerful indicator that the autonomic nervous system has been retuned to support defense. It does not provide any insight into the causal factors leading to being locked into a state of defense. Factors such as genetics, fever, medical procedures, physical injury, loss of an effective trusted co-regulator such as a parent, and uncertainty of safety in the environment may contribute to a retuned system that adaptively becomes stuck in a state of defense.

Polyvagal Charisma

There are people who we simply like to be around because they make us feel safe. Self-help gurus like to talk about made-up statistics such as "80% of communication is body language." We're not sure where they are getting those numbers, but the premise is very true. The actual words we say to people are far less important than *how* we say them. We all intuitively understand that some people are captivating to listen to or be around—while others are unpleasant and make us feel uncomfortable. Depending on somebody's appearance or the sound and intonation of their voice, simple expressions such as "Have a nice day" or "I've always loved you" can be friendly and welcoming—or dark and menacing.

Charisma isn't some intangible mythical quality. Rather, it's the ability of certain people to make others feel safe and engaged through features like physical appearance, body language, and vocal intonation.

Let's put it this way: Facial movements and vocal prosody require the activation of the Green state. That's because the muscles that control these features have a direct line to the VVC through the modern ventral vagus, and are fully engaged only when we feel safe.

We tend to mirror the autonomic state of those we are interacting with. So if you feel and sound safe, other people around you will as well. And if you can pull that off with regularity, well, congratulations: You are a charismatic individual, and likely somebody viewed as pleasant to be around.

Once again, it is often true that *what* we say is less important than *how* we say it. Other social mammals such as prairie voles, cats, horses, and dogs chirp, growl, bark, and even sing—and successfully express their emotional state by vocalizing without relying on specific words. Dogs can't speak English, but we can tell a lot about how they are feeling by *how* they bark or growl or whimper.

We humans share these neural pathways that interpret sounds and vocalizations as threatening or soothing regardless of what words are being said. And we humans use these pathways all the time.

Anybody who has ever spoken to a dog or baby intuitively understands this. Sing the words *"Who's a good boy?"* or *"I love you"* with a high level of prosody and you're likely to be met with a wagging tail or cooing kid. But say the same words with a flat, deep, monotone voice and you're apt to make them feel scared or scolded—and to see it on their faces.

Our hardwired ability to feel safe through highly melodic and prosodic vocalizations is key to a mother's ability to transmit feelings of safety to a newborn. This is literally what loving "baby talk" and lullabies do to kids.

I (Stephen) have spent a large portion of my career focusing on this innate ability to pick up a sense of safety from prosodic vocalizations—which is largely associated with infants but doesn't go away as we grow up—and have turned it into the basis for an audio-based therapeutic treatment[6] that is currently employed by more than 4,000 practitioners around the world. (See page 121 for more information on the Safe and Sound Protocol.)

When we are in the Green state and feel safe, we simply look and sound different. And these differences are contagious as we mirror the autonomic state of others. Being around people who feel safe makes us feel safe, while being around people who feel threatened or come off as threatening makes us feel threatened and come off as threatening. And when we trigger a sense of safety in other people's neuroception—well, they like us more too.

Taken to its logical extreme, this idea is both frightening and hopeful. We live in an autonomic echo chamber. When an entire society becomes inundated with fear, it can be difficult to escape the contagion. However, those of us who succeed at making others feel safe despite it all can indeed spread these feelings and make a real difference.

MUSIC AND US

Music is a funny thing and likely universal across civilizations.

For some reason, we like experiencing specifically ordered vibrations of air waves that come within a specific frequency band. Music can make us relax or rev up. It can also elicit all sorts of emotions and is often found in social settings such as parties.

But why is it that we as humans like music? And why is it such a powerful tool for either exciting us or calming us down?

The Polyvagal Theory offers an explanation.

Our middle-ear structures are designed to pick up melodic, middle-frequency vocalizations. These sounds are instinctively interpreted by our neuroception as signs of safety and comfort via a response that is baked into us from birth. Think: a mother singing lullabies to lull a newborn to sleep, or a dog lover melodically telling a furry friend that he's a good boy.

The trigger here is the vocal prosody. Once again, that is the way the voice moves up and down in a melodic fashion. The sound of prosody triggers tiny middle-ear muscles that effectively dampen background noises so that we can better hear people talk. This effect also helps turn on our neuroception's ability to sense safety.

The act of playing an instrument, singing, or listening to music does the same thing. The melodic ordering of sound waves serves as a trigger for our Green parasympathetic nervous system—and our ability to feel safe and social.

This is why certain music might make us feel calm, collected, or social. (That social part is likely why music is basically required for a party to feel like a party.)

Just think about the music one might find playing in a spa. It is calm, melodic, and predictable. It doesn't have unexpected moments of loudness or screaming, which would shock our nervous system into a state of high alert. Whether or not there are actual vocals, the music largely sits in the middle-frequency range and probably features limited bass. These auditory features signal safety to our nervous system and allow us to relax.

But not all music is calming. Entire genres are designed to get us excited and make us scream, dance, or mosh. These songs do their job by activating our Yellow sympathetic nervous system, which puts the pep in our steps to pump our fists or slam our bodies. This is often accomplished through aggressive vocalizations, fast tempos, prominent bass lines, and a cranked-up volume knob—all of which are interpreted by our nervous systems as signs of danger, and thus as triggers for our sympathetic nervous system.[7]

Music may also bring us into the pits of sadness and grief and literally hit us in our guts. In these cases, the acoustic patterns are often characterized by lower frequency, relatively monotonic sounds that seem to trigger the dorsal vagus (more on this branch of the vagus in the following pages).

It is through these auditory properties that music allows us to manipulate our mood—and autonomic state.

———

Today, you can listen to recordings of just about anything. But long before Spotify, iPods, or even wax cylinders, music was an innately social exercise. Throughout the vast majority of human history, the only way to experience music was to play it live, and often with other people.

In this sense, music likely developed as a form of social co-regulation that would allow people to feel safe together. A sort of group expression of the same neural pathways that cause a mother's cooing to make a newborn feel safe. To play music with somebody else is to suggest safety, and allow others to suggest safety to you.

This is probably why, to this day, going to see live music tends to be a fun thing for most of us to do.

The Ancient Vagus

So the modern myelinated vagus is pretty neat, right? It lets us stay cool, calm, and collected, and hooks directly into the part of the brainstem that also lets us be expressive, social creatures.

But what about the ancient vagus?

This unmyelinated branch of the vagus is evolutionarily ancient and can be found in the majority of vertebrates stretching back eons. And, just as with the modern myelinated vagus, its functionality is closely tied to the part of the brainstem that it plugs into.

As we just discussed, the modern vagus plugs into the ventral vagal complex (or VVC), which allows the nerve to turn on a host of bodily features and functions associated with sociability and safety.

The ancient vagus, on the other hand, plugs into a section of the brainstem called the dorsal vagal complex (or DVC). While the VVC makes it possible for us to be expressive and social creatures, the DVC is deeply involved with the activation and regulation of organs that are buried in the gut and viscera. When we are not in states of severe threat, the DVC supports homeostatic functions by helping us optimize the regulation of these organs, located below the diaphragm.

This direct line from our gut and heart to the brainstem is what turns the sensory fibers in our vagus into a sort of surveillance system for our visceral organs, meaning the ones located in our chest and abdomen.

When our neuroception detects extreme danger, a feedback loop bounces the signal among our organs, senses, and brainstem—causing our entire body to transform. This transformation is deeply driven by sensory feelings that arise in our gut and heart, rather than from top-down rational thinking involving our neocortex.

This process is often talked about in terms such as "reptile brain," where a sense of severe danger or duress effectively turns off our ability to properly think and instead turns us into instinct-driven animals that might snarl, snap, or freeze without thought.

The use of the word "reptile" is apt. The Red shutdown response is a key to how many reptiles respond to threats. Rather than activating for fight-or-flight, they shut down their bodies so as to play dead and freeze to avoid detection—and to perhaps die with minimal pain.*

It is through this mechanism that the DVC and ancient vagus facilitate our capacity to freeze, dissociate, or shut down in the face of perceived threat.

This relationship between our visceral organs and our instinct-driven selves is also embedded in our language when we use terms like "operating on gut instinct" or "following our heart as opposed to our head."

When we let our gut or heart guide us, we do what we *feel* we should do, as opposed to what we *think* we should do.

---

* Dissociation may help with this.

4

The Evolution of the Polyvagal Theory

The story of the Polyvagal Theory is the story of mammalian and human evolution—and how our development as a *social* species proved crucial to our survival.

I (Stephen) first proposed the Polyvagal Theory in 1994, when I gave my presidential address to the Society of Psychophysiological Research.[1]

This idea was right there in the title of my address: "Orienting in a Defensive World: Mammalian Modifications of Our Evolutionary Heritage. A Polyvagal Theory."

But what does that mean? How is it that the long and winding path of evolution turned us into organisms where the need and ability to be social is baked right into our physiology and DNA?

To answer that question, we go back hundreds of millions of years. To the time of our ancient and asocial reptile ancestors, who roamed the earth long before us modern, social mammals.

Evolution can be thought of as a tinkerer. As species change over time, the changes that prove beneficial for survival tend to stick around and be passed along to future generations, where these adaptations continue to be used, and possibly even be repurposed for new uses.[2]

The world was (and still is) a dangerous place, and our asocial reptile ancestors needed to develop adaptations that would allow them to survive.

One such adaptation that proved especially useful was the ability to slow down their bodies. To effectively downshift the entire organism so as to conserve resources during times of scarcity, or even play dead as a way of evading predators.

This downshift effect was accomplished through the use of "cardioinhibitory" fibers that slow the heart. In ancient vertebrates, these fibers clumped together to form a strange, wandering nerve called the vagus.

What made the vagus special was that it wound its way through many different bodily systems and organs. The vagus emerged from the dorsal side of the brainstem, in a place called the dorsal vagal complex, which became the control hub for vagal pathways going to several organs in the gut and viscera, including the liver, spleen, pancreas, kidney, intestines, and colon. It is through the vagus that these organs were granted a direct line to the brain.

With the vagus connecting to so many organs and bodily systems, the ability for vagal fibers to slow things down was no longer limited to just the heart. Suddenly, these fibers were capable of slowing down the entire body at the same time by shifting the body's physiological state and reducing metabolic demands and the need for oxygen.

This gave us the first autonomic nervous systems, as early vertebrate species gained the ability to downshift their entire bodies to conserve resources or reflexively play dead as a tool for survival.

As the millennia ticked on, these asocial reptiles evolved and changed and branched off into countless different species.

Some of these species evolved to cooperate and socialize with one another as a tool for survival. This type of behavior proved particularly useful for a new category of species called mammals.

The first mammals were small. Approximately the size of a person's thumb, they were closer to a modern mouse than a walking and talking human. They were basically just reptile food.

Yet, somehow, mammals managed to survive and thrive and evolve until modern mammals came to effectively dominate planet Earth in the form of human beings.

How exactly did we pull this off?

It certainly wasn't our strength or ability to express brute force. Even after millions of years of evolution, we still aren't particularly fearsome in a bare-handed fight.

Instead, we had something else going for us. Unlike our asocial reptile ancestors, mammals could communicate, commingle, and cooperate. In ancient times, this ability allowed our ancestors to raise vulnerable offspring, team up to defend against large predators, and eventually evolve into a species that could build functioning communities and societies.

This shift toward social behavior was a monumental one, and was baked into our bodies.

If we were constantly in a state of defense or aggression (as is the case with our asocial reptile ancestors), then merely being in close proximity to members of our same species would be dangerous.

Instead, our bodies needed to find a way to downshift away from aggressive and defensive states to seek safety in others, and to project a sense of safety so that others in our species could know that we ourselves were safe to be around.

This made it possible for us to get close enough to one another to successfully cooperate and survive.

And while this ability to seek and project safety was a new one for mammals, it came from an ancient source: the same cardioinhibitory fibers that allowed our asocial reptile ancestors to downshift their physiological state to conserve resources or play dead. These structures were effectively repurposed in humans and other mammals to calm down our bodies so we could get close to others without hurting them or making them feel scared.

To accommodate this shift, the vagus's cardioinhibitory fibers morphed and moved across the brainstem.* Mammals still had (and have to this day) these fibers in the dorsal vagal complex via

---

* This journey of cardioinhibitory fibers moving from the dorsal to ventral vagal nuclei is repeated during the gestation of mammals.

the unmyelinated ancient vagus, but we now also had a new branch of the vagus that had found its way into an area of the brainstem known as the ventral vagal complex. This new branch of the vagus had a different morphology than the older one and was covered with a myelinated sheath.

What happened next can be thought of as a sort of marriage, or corporate merger. The vagus can slow down the body and shift our physiological state. The VVC is what controls the muscles that enable us to be social by listening through our ears, vocalizing through our voices, and expressing emotion through our faces.

Our vagus is what shifts our body between different physiological states. By bringing the vagus into the VVC, our social behavior became inextricably tied to our physiological state, and the same ancient neural structures that allowed reptiles to downshift their bodies in times of threat were repurposed to facilitate safe and social behavior in mammals.

With this, our voice and facial expressions became tools to broadcast our emotions and to clearly communicate to others whether we were calm and accessible or irritable and reactive.

Many of us intuitively know when it is safe to approach somebody and when they might need space, just by listening to their voice or looking at their face. This ability even extends to our interactions with other social mammals, such as dogs, cats, and horses. When we interact with these animals, we can observe the power of our voice in either calming them down or upsetting and scaring them.

These anatomical features that broadcast our emotions and physiological state form a system that I (Stephen) call the Social Engagement System.

In anatomical terms, the Social Engagement System involves the neural pathways that link the muscles in our face and head (and that control our voice) to our heart, so that the shared vagal connection that allows our heart and respiration to work in synchrony also influences our facial expressions and voice, as well as our ability to listen through our ears.

Basically: When our vagus calms down our body in times of safety, this system also opens up our face, voice, and ears to express safe social behavior to others, and receive it back from them.

Our ability to use our face and head to suck, swallow, breathe, and vocalize are expressions of these circuits. Research has shown that difficulty in coordinating these movements correlates with a profound survival risk for newborn infants and is a lead indicator of subsequent behavioral and health problems. The Polyvagal Theory emphasizes that, in addition to being a basic survival risk, such disruptions may contribute to compromised sociability and trust of others, ingestive disorders, state-regulation issues, and auditory hypersensitivities.

When the body is not calm, the entire Social Engagement System is downregulated, and our ability to express and receive signs of safety in others is diminished. Through a clinical lens, the downregulated Social Engagement System can lead to a vast pool of symptoms associated with a wide variety of diagnoses.

The Polyvagal Theory proposes that many of these symptoms (and subsequent diagnoses) are actually the result of the autonomic nervous system being in a state of defense.

This opens up the opportunity to discuss how the Social Engagement System, and features such as facial expressions and vocalization, might offer portals for clinical intervention by allowing us to retune the body toward a state of safety.

In Chapter 3, we talked about the modern obsession with directly stimulating the vagus.

The Polyvagal Theory posits that social behavior itself serves as an efficient form of vagal stimulation. And that by only focusing on the vagus as a specific nerve to be directly activated, we might miss the big picture when it comes to living a life full of healthful vagal activity— simply by being around people and places that make us feel safe.

It is likely that the ability for us to activate our vagus through these behaviors is why we as humans are drawn to activities such as singing, talking, praying, focused breathing, listening, playing instruments, and socializing.

By recruiting the muscles and neural pathways of our Social Engagement System through actions such as vocalizing and blowing air, these simple acts tap into the vagus's ability to regulate our autonomic state and consequently make us feel good, safe, and healthy.

To that, we can add another "s" to our obsession with safety and sociability: "sublime." To live a safe and social life is to live a sublime life that allows us to reach our potential as humans.

———

When I (Stephen) first proposed the Polyvagal Theory in 1994, I proposed that the search for safety was a key component of our evolution. I also suggested that the mechanisms that facilitate this search, such as the ability to express safe social behavior, are baked into our uniquely mammalian anatomy.

I suggested that these were tools, forged by evolution and repurposed from our asocial reptile ancestors, that helped us as a species survive in an unsafe world.

This is really the entire basis of the Polyvagal Theory: that mammals evolved specific mechanisms for seeking safety in an unsafe world, and that these mechanisms are closely tied to social behavior, as well as to our general health and well-being.

Believe it or not, this was a radical idea. And as is the case with any new theory, proposing it is one thing. Justifying it is something else entirely.

To that end, I turned to the field of comparative neuroanatomy.

Comparative neuroanatomy involves looking at the brains and nervous systems of different types of animals to physically infer the gradual changes of evolution.

By looking at, for example, different mammals and reptiles, we can see how parts of their brains and nervous systems may be physically the same or physically different from one another. This comparison allows us to see what parts of our neuroanatomy we share with our ancient reptilian ancestors, and what parts evolved later and thus might be unique to modern mammals.

By looking at the actual brains and nervous systems of different species of mammals and reptiles, we can also see where certain neural structures or types of cells first emerged in the brain, before perhaps expanding or migrating somewhere else in species that evolved later.

The Polyvagal Theory is concerned with how this evolutionary

journey turned modern mammals such as humans into social creatures, and how this shift resulted in an anatomy that supports
social behavior as a conduit for homeostasis, healing, and long-
term survival.

This is why you'll find so little talk about birds in this book.
While many species of birds are indeed quite social, they diverged
from reptiles millions of years after mammals, and the mechanisms that facilitate their social behavior have their own evolutionary roots. As such, the study of birds and modern reptiles is outside
the scope of the Polyvagal Theory.

It should also be noted that the Polyvagal Theory makes no
assumptions about what actually caused the evolutionary shifts that
led to mammals becoming social. Instead, it emphasizes what we
can observe from comparative neuroanatomy and the inferences that
can be extracted from an estimated phylogenetic timeline.[3] Likely,
many current assumptions regarding the timeline of our genetic history will be updated as new molecular techniques are refined.

––––––––

The specific focus of my comparative neuroanatomy research
involved tracing the evolutionary journey of cardioinhibitory structures. These are the parts of the brain and nervous system that slow
down our hearts and downshift our bodies into a parasympathetic
state. These fibers constitute a good chunk of the vagus nerve.

Both ancient reptiles and modern mammals have a vagus nerve,
which facilitates our ability to slow down our heart and enter a
parasympathetic state.

However, the Polyvagal Theory proposes that the mammalian
structures that slow us down in times of safety (and facilitate our
rest, growth, and restoration) are a *uniquely* mammalian repurpos-
ing of the ANS that was not found in ancient reptiles.

This is important. The ancient reptiles from which mammals
evolved did not have neural mechanisms that allowed them to turn
off threat responses to get close to others, co-regulate, and exhibit
maternal behavior. In addition, most reptiles do not feature synchronized heart rate and respiration.

It should be noted that, while *most* contemporary reptilian species do not exhibit maternal behavior or synchronized heart rate and respiration, some select species do. For example, alligators and crocodiles exhibit a type of maternal behavior, and monitor lizards have a respiratory-heart-rate pattern.[4]

However, an inspection of our vertebrate phylogeny informs us that, while we share a common ancestor with these reptiles (as we do with all reptiles), we did not evolve from them. This suggests that the few reptiles that do exhibit these behaviors evolved them independently from us mammals, and accomplish these behaviors through different neural mechanisms than are described by the Polyvagal Theory. Consistent with the Polyvagal Theory, there is no documentation that cardioinhibitory fibers emerging from the dorsal vagal nucleus have a respiratory rhythm in reptiles or mammals.[*]

But why does this matter? Why is it important to understand that the vagal mechanism by which we regulate and sync our breathing and heart rate is uniquely mediated via the modern ventral vagus in mammals?

The answer: By understanding this mechanism, we can also measure it. With an objective way of measuring activation of the Green parasympathetic system at our disposal, we can test various hypotheses related to the Polyvagal Theory, and literally see it in action in real time. For example, we can run experiments

---

[*] Even if the dorsal vagus had a respiratory rhythm, it would not contradict the Polyvagal Theory. That's because the PVT emphasizes the role of respiratory-heart-rate rhythms mediated by the ventral, and not dorsal, vagus.

The key point is that the observation of respiratory-heart-rate interactions in phylogenetically ancient vertebrates is irrelevant to Polyvagal Theory, since the evolutionary emergence of a respiratory rhythm from the ventral vagal complex is uniquely tied to mammalian evolution.

Interestingly, a research team (Monteiro et al., 2018) has identified cardio-respiratory interactions via a myelinated pathway originating from the dorsal nucleus of the vagus in the primitive lungfish. The authors assumed that their finding contradicted the Polyvagal Theory. However, Polyvagal Theory makes no assumptions about myelinated pathways originating from areas other than the ventral nucleus of the vagus (nucleus ambiguus) in classes of vertebrates that evolved prior to reptiles. In addition, there have been no reports of myelinated dorsal vagal fibers in amphibians or reptiles—the other classes of vertebrates that preceded mammals. This suggests that this feature evolved independently in these cases and is unrelated to our phylogenetic past.

that explore the link between our autonomic state and elements of the Social Engagement System, such as facial affect and auditory processing.

The most important metrics for measuring the calming effects of the vagus are heart-rate variability and respiratory sinus arrhythmia (or RSA).

RSA (which is extracted from, and closely tied to, heart-rate variability) is essentially a measure of how much our heart rate is syncing up with our breathing rhythms—which it turns out is a really good proxy for vagal activity (sometimes called "vagal tone") and activation of the Green state. Also crucial is that these metrics can be extracted through a simple pulse monitor, making them easily accessible using noninvasive tools.

Now that we understand how our evolution paved the way for the development of humans as social creatures,[5] we can explore just how much we truly need one another to survive and thrive—and how this need is baked into almost every fiber of our bodies.

5

Connectedness and Co-Regulation: A Biological Imperative

A not-so-"sub" subtext of this book is the importance (and dare we say: necessity) of safe social interaction to our health. To understand this, let's look back at the best-selling computer game *The Sims*.

In *The Sims*, players aren't tasked with saving princesses or blowing up bad guys. Rather, the object of the game is to simply get through the day, while tending to the needs and wants of a virtual avatar. This concept struck a chord: *The Sims*—which spawned from the brain of legendary game designer Will Wright in 2000— is, by some counts, the best-selling PC game of all time.

As you play, various status bars help you keep tabs on your character's basic "Needs," such as "Hunger," "Bladder," and "Energy" (basically sleep).

Go too long without tending to any of these Needs (we're going to capitalize it because that's what the game does), and the status bar depletes to let you know your character could really use a trip to the fridge or a quick nap. Ignore these Needs for too long, and your character becomes a complete wreck, perhaps unable to even make it across the room before collapsing on the floor or going mad.

One of the other Needs that has been in the game since its first release: a status bar labeled "Social," which can be replenished by spending time chatting with other characters. Fail to cater to this Need, and your character is apt to sit on the floor sobbing, and otherwise lack the will to go through the day.

The game is pretty spot-on in this regard. As humans, we require social interaction to be our best, smartest, healthiest, happiest, and most sublime selves. And in its absence, we're likely to end up like a character in *The Sims*.

If you've read this far, hopefully you grasp by now that the Green system is key to our ability to socialize. To make sense of all this, let's spend a minute breaking down what we mean by social interaction—and how the Green system (and ventral vagal complex) facilitates this need.

From a polyvagal perspective, social interaction is all about facilitating co-regulation. That is: our body's ability to simultaneously project and receive signs of safety with others. And, in doing so, allow us to regulate our nervous system so as to experience the states conducive to health, growth, and restoration.

Our neuroception detects the states of those around us, which triggers us to enter a similar state ourselves. So when we are around people who make us feel safe, it soothes our nervous system—which subsequently soothes theirs, and on and on the virtuous cycle goes.

The Polyvagal Theory posits that co-regulation through social behavior is a biological imperative—a need as hardwired into us as that for food or sleep. Because our survival as a species relied on the ability to identify and cooperate with trusted others, this need became baked into our DNA, and is expressed throughout our life span, beginning from the moment of birth.

Co-regulation is how our bodies maintain equilibrium in an unsafe world. It is, quite simply, a capital-N Need. In the absence of social interaction that feels safe (that part is crucial, as unsafe interactions are very different), nobody can be expected to be healthy, happy, or able to think right.

But co-regulation comes in different forms, and the moments we share with platonic friends over dinner are very different from the ones we share with partners in bed.

Let's think of it as a continuum or process, where social interaction and the subsequent autonomic co-regulation can be broken down into different phases along a flow chart. Each phase offers benefits of its own and is a necessary prerequisite for the one that follows.

We're going to put this chart here for easy reference, though it may not make much sense until you finish this section.

Co-Regulation

Safety ⟩ Proximity ⟩ Contact ⟩ Bonds

Co-Regulation Phase 1: Face-to-Face Interaction

The first step of co-regulation through social interaction involves face-to-face communication.

When we are near somebody who makes us feel safe, our Green system and VVC activate the cranial nerves that control the muscles in our face and head. This allows our Social Engagement System to display emotion in a way that is simply not possible when we're in the Yellow or Red states, which are often characterized by flat facial affect. We may not wear our hearts on our sleeves, but we definitely do on our faces. Just as dogs do with their wagging tails.

Other bodily changes occur as well, as our Green transformation funnels resources to the bodily systems that make us engaging communicators who radiate a sense of safety to others. Our middle-ear muscles shift positions to better hear the acoustic frequencies of speech, so we can pay attention to the person in front of us (instead of scanning the space for possible danger). Our voices register more prosody, moving from a monotone droll into a melodious, singsongy, welcoming legato.

And as we register these changes, the person we're talking to does so as well. Their neuroception detects us as safe, and the same bodily transformation occurs in them. This is the heart of co-regulation: We soothe each other out of an alert state of danger, and into a safe space of healing and happiness.

Now, before we go further, it's important to address the reality that not all modern social interactions actually happen this way.

Today, we can communicate without actually being in each other's presence. Humans have long since developed the ability to write, speak on the phone, and do just about everything on the internet.

But for the vast majority of human history, our species existed in a dangerous world that bore little resemblance to the one we live in today. This was a world without supermarkets, air-conditioning, or emergency services. This was a world of intense competition and danger. Of scarce resources, and abundant predators. To survive it, we needed to communicate, cooperate, and collaborate.

These social behaviors became so important to our survival that our bodies evolved a number of built-in mechanisms designed to compel us to engage in them. The impetus for this is obvious: Those who cooperated with others were more likely to survive than those who lived and operated in isolation.

We often assume that "survival of the fittest" applies to a sense of dominance and aggressiveness. But going back to the early 1960s, Theodosius Dobzhansky, a prominent Ukrainian-American geneticist and evolutionary biologist, proposed a twist on this assumption. As he put it: "The fittest may also be the gentlest, because survival often requires mutual help and cooperation."[1]

To this end, we evolved neurophysiological mechanisms for downshifting away from states of aggression and defense, and into ones of cooperation and sociability. This was a massive evolutionary shift that enabled us to feel safe around others. This adaptation may be at the core of human society and even the human domestication of other mammals such as cows, goats, dogs, and horses.

It is through this evolutionary imperative that humans evolved into social creatures, with a built-in system of biological rewards and punishments that, to this day, compel us to communicate and socialize with other people.

Fulfill this ancient need for communication and cooperation, and our bodies reward us with health and happiness by way of a downshifted nervous system that allows us to grow and heal, as well as a satisfying chemical cocktail.

Socializing is fun, parties are fun, and numerous studies have shown that people with strong social-support networks and healthy relationships tend to be happier, healthier, and longer-lived than those without.

But ignore this ancient compulsion, and our bodies punish us with illness, depression, and feelings of loneliness. Long-term social isolation is tantamount to torture. Just ask any prisoner who has been sent into solitary confinement (see Chapter 10)—or recall how all of us felt after spending weeks, months, or even years isolated during the pandemic (see Chapter 7).

Think of it as our bodies having a carrot-and-stick approach to encouraging us to work together and be social.

The carrot: Spend time safely around others, and you'll feel good and be healthier.

The stick: Stay isolated, and end up like a *Sims* character. Sad and lonely and physically unwell.

But how do our bodies know that we are fulfilling our quota for social interaction and cooperation—and thus are deserving of the carrot? Basically, how does our body know that our *Sims* "Need" bar for social interaction is being kept full?

Throughout the vast majority of human evolution, social interaction existed in one form and one form only. Before the existence of the internet, before phones, and before even the written letter, there was only one way for humans to communicate—and, by extension, cooperate—with one another: face-to-face interaction.

And so it is through face-to-face interaction, and only face-to-face interaction, that our bodies can determine whether or not we have fulfilled this quota. When we speak to another person face-to-face, our nervous systems engage an ancient, complex, and mostly subconscious dance of co-regulation that ultimately results in a rewarding rush of neurotransmitters and a feeling of satisfaction—not to mention better physical and mental health.

The *face* and *voice* became the keys, and the triggers, for telling our bodies and the bodies of others that we have fulfilled our phylogenetic contract to interact with one another in a social and safe way.

Remember those 12 cranial nerves that sprout from our brainstem, providing direct links to key parts of our bodies? Lest anybody doubt the importance of the face to the nervous system, it should be noted that a large percentage of these crucial nerves (in particular: the four that appear in the ventral vagal complex and interact with the origin point of the ventral vagus) are directly responsible for regulating the muscles involved in facial expressions, head gestures, and vocal intonations that are involved in this process.

In other words: A huge chunk of our nervous system is dedicated to the specific systems that allow us to be social with others in a face-to-face setting.

Now let's fast-forward to the modern world.

Today, most of us have easy access to the resources that are necessary for basic and superficial survival. Thanks to supermarkets and food-delivery services, it is possible—and indeed quite easy—to procure a virtually unlimited supply of food without actually having to cooperate with anybody else. Instead of teaming up to hunt, gather, or scavenge for food, a few taps of an app can result in a nutrient-rich meal (perhaps *too* nutrient rich at times) delivered directly to our door.

Even for tasks that still require cooperation, modern modes of communication make it easy for us to complete them without ever seeing another person's face. Thanks to the telephone and the internet, it is now possible—and often easier—to communicate with other people in such a way that their face is never seen. For many people, everything needed to "earn a living," so to speak, can be done solitarily through a computer.

When it comes to merely surviving, face-to-face interaction can now be considered optional for many of us. But declining this option comes at a steep price. When we fail to trigger our bodies' internal face-detection mechanism through the act of co-regulation, our nervous systems have no way of knowing that we have fulfilled our ancient need for communication and cooperation, and thus deny us the satisfaction and very real rush of happiness-inducing and health-supporting chemicals that reward us for doing so.

And don't miss the "co" in co-regulation. It can feel off-putting when a friendly attempt to engage another person is not accepted.

As an academic who has spent his career walking the halls of universities and professional conferences, I (Stephen) have frequently witnessed or experienced this firsthand. I've seen many a graduate student approach a distinguished senior faculty member with the intent to engage them in conversation—only to find the entreaty met with a cold shoulder as the faculty member walks by without acknowledgment. Such rejection might lead the student to develop a self-critical narrative, perhaps focused on their own perceived inadequacies or a belief that they are not worthy of the professor's interest or attention. Of course, the truth might be a lot more innocent. The professor could have been running late for an appointment, or perhaps didn't hear the hello in the first place. They may also simply be somebody with a low facial affect, which the student could have interpreted as being actively standoffish.

As humans, we evolved to anticipate reciprocal social interactions from others. When our nervous system believes we are about to be social, it prepares our body by downregulating our defenses and activating the features of the Social Engagement System. When the neural expectancy of friendly socialization is violated, there might be an immediate and massive shift in our nervous system toward a state of defense, which is often accompanied by a sense of emotional hurt.

I coined the term "biological rudeness" to explain our bodily reaction when we anticipate a reciprocal social engagement that does not occur. This response can be thought of as a cascade, where a lack of perceived reciprocity to a spontaneous social interaction triggers can abruptly shift an autonomic state toward one of defense. This leads to an emotional response of being offended, which may result in an aggressive reaction. We see this when minor—and perhaps unintentional—social slights spiral into actual violence. The likelihood of such a negative response is greatly increased with individuals who might be predisposed to defensive states. This could be a natural predisposition, or the result of living around violence or in a state of fear.

———

Humans need contact with other humans, just as we need food and water. This need is an ancient one that is built into our bodies like a hole in a jigsaw puzzle. Just like a missing puzzle piece, this need can be filled with subpar substitutions that bear a striking, superficial resemblance to the real thing. And in a modern world overflowing with convenience and communication technology, there is no shortage of substitutions.

As an example, video games (in particular, online multiplayer games) do an incredible job of tapping into our basic need for cooperation and human contact. These games typically require players to team up to solve puzzles and complete missions—many of which benefit from an enormous amount of planning and foresight. The games also act as massive chat rooms: virtual forums where pixelated avatars act as proxies for people, allowing them to meet and greet one another, and develop friendships and sometimes even romantic relationships. In other words, these games are almost tailor-made to fill our need for human contact.

But for all their whiz-bang graphics and programming, these games are but crude simulations. Simulations that tease our nervous systems and flirt with our need for human cooperation and interaction. Through this, they do an incredible job of priming our social nervous system into believing it is about to receive the needed dose of human interaction and cooperation. Puzzles are being solved cooperatively, words and emotions are being exchanged, conversations are being had.

But there is no face-to-face interaction. And because there is no face-to-face interaction, the body does not register the co-regulation, or provide the sense of ultimate satisfaction or biochemical reward.*

This is perhaps why the internet and video games can be so addictive: They superficially trigger the social nervous system, without ever truly giving us the specific components of social interaction that our nervous systems are searching for.

---

* Video-conferencing apps such as Zoom are a whole other story, and may provide something slightly closer to the real thing. But the unconscious dance of co-regulation involves much more than visually seeing a face, and these interactions are still nowhere near as satisfying for our nervous system as being face-to-face with a physical human.

This is also why people who are staring at screens tend to exhibit what some people jokingly call "zombie face." This is when—despite appearing to have all of their attention focused on the screen—somebody still displays a flat and unemotive face. They may be communicating with another person, but the expressive muscles and movements of the Social Engagement System that come into play for face-to-face interaction are effectively shut off.

Without the subtle facial and vocal cues that enable the face and voice keys, the nervous system is never able to give us sufficient credit for the interaction. The quota is not met, and the feeling of happiness and autonomic shift into Green that comes from communicating and cooperating with another person is not fully realized.

Before moving on, we want to quickly say that the authors of this book like video games and have smartphones. This is not intended to be some sort of antigaming or antitechnology screed. Games can be a fun and immersive hobby and are a profoundly compelling form of entertainment, storytelling, art, and learning. They also offer portals to social interaction for people who might be physically isolated, whether due to a disability or to simply being locked in during a pandemic. They help some people relax and regulate, and help others stay connected with friends.

But no form of digital technology is a true substitute for face-to-face interaction. And as we look to a future full of video calls and virtual reality and metaverses and other social simulacra, it's important to remember and cater to our ancient baked-in need to be near one another, and to find ways to spend time with one another in person.

Your nervous system—and health—will thank you.

Co-Regulation Phase 2: Intimacy

In Chapter 2, we discussed the wide variety of distinct autonomic states. There are the "pure" Green, Yellow, and Red states of sociability, fight-or-flight, and shutdown/dissociation—as well as hybrid systems such as play and intimacy.

To understand the next phase of co-regulation, let's zoom into the "intimacy" state, which comes from a combination of feeling safe (that's the Green system at work) and being physically immobilized (the Red).

We are ordering intimacy as Phase 2 of our co-regulation flowchart because it typically comes after Phase 1.

In Phase 1, our Green system allows us to be in close proximity to somebody else without acting aggressive or defensive. This proximity is necessary for the physical contact that comes with true intimacy. Think: a child lying in its mother's arms, or two partners cuddling in bed. (To be clear: While sex often—though not always—involves intimacy, we're not talking about that specifically here.)

To be intimate is to be immobilized without fear. To do this is to put forth an enormous amount of trust in another person. When this trust is violated—such as in an assault, where the proximity and contact of intimacy are turned into something violent and unwanted—it can be particularly damaging on both a physical and emotional level.

But the rewards of successful intimacy are great. It allows us to maintain a physiological state that supports health, growth, and restoration. It optimizes the ability to rest, relax, sleep, digest, and perform other bodily processes.

Successful intimacy also enables further moments of intimacy, which lead to further feelings of trust, safety, and love. It's become a common trope of television therapists to say that somebody has "intimacy issues." But intimacy really does require vulnerability, and if that vulnerability has been violated in the past, it can be enormously challenging to put it forth in the future.

The violation of the trust inherent to intimacy can be devastating and truly traumatic.

It is an increasingly well-known fact that social ties make us healthier. Countless studies confirm that those among us who have a strong social-support network do better against almost any physical or mental health malady.

But why is it? Why is it that close social bonds and healthy intimate relationships are actually restorative on a physical level?

Much of the answer comes down to the mechanisms that enable

our nervous system and our body to feel safe. We have already emphasized the role of ventral vagal pathways in mediating an autonomic state that supports feelings of safety, but the vagus does not do it alone. Rather, it shares this responsibility with other neurophysiological and neurochemical mechanisms.

Key among these: a simple and increasingly famous molecule called oxytocin—often referred to as the "love" or "cuddle" hormone.

Oxytocin: A Uniquely Mammalian Molecule

Oxytocin was first chemically mapped in the early 1950s by American biochemist Vincent du Vigneaud, who would go on to synthesize it in a lab. This would be the very first time anybody would ever synthesize a polypeptide hormone, and doing so earned du Vigneaud the 1955 Nobel Prize in Chemistry.[2]

For decades, oxytocin was believed to have a rather narrow job within our bodies. It was viewed as essential to lactation and labor but little else. Maybe it's because milk and childbirth are the biological domain of women, but oxytocin was viewed as largely inconsequential, and perhaps not even worthy of further study.

So when Sue Carter, PhD, then at the University of Maryland, discovered in the early 1990s that oxytocin (as well as the hormone vasopressin, with which it is closely linked) is deeply involved in social monogamy—that is, a mammal's ability to pair-bond (which is basically a scientist's way of saying "falling in love"), even she had a hard time believing it.[3]

Modern readers may take it for granted that "love" is a chemical process, with hormones and peptides and neurotransmitters banging around in our bodies and brains and giving us butterflies. But this idea is a relatively modern one. For centuries, the nature of love was largely viewed as the domain of poets and philosophers, with serious scientists viewing it as a learned behavior, and not something with any real chemical or neurophysiological basis.[4]

Dr. Carter's work helped prove otherwise.

Her research, which initially focused on prairie voles (basically, small field mice) but has since been expanded into humans, found that female voles who mated seemed to form social bonds more rapidly than their celibate peers who simply sat next to a potential partner. For the first time, she and her colleagues were observing that intimate behavior somehow drove these animals together, and tightened their social bonds.[5]

She began to put the pieces together. She knew that sex could release oxytocin because lactating women sometimes ejected milk during orgasm, and that oxytocin is necessary for milk ejection. She began to believe that oxytocin—which was already suspected of playing a role in a mother's ability to bond with her child—was also involved with social bonds between adults.[6]

She was right.

After a series of experiments, she and her colleagues found that oxytocin was just as crucial for the intimate bonds between adults as for the ones the molecule fused between a mother and her offspring.

Today, oxytocin is commonly associated with love, cuddles, hugs, and all the warm and fuzzy feelings they elicit. It's the name of a Billie Eilish song (sample lyric: *"Can't take it back once it's been set in motion. You know I need you for the oxytocin"*), and Dr. Carter's work with prairie voles seems to have inspired a memorable episode of the cartoon *Rick and Morty*, where mad scientist Rick creates a love potion out of vole hormones (needless to say, that's not how it actually works).

But wait, there's more!

We're now beginning to understand that even the "love" of it all is the tip of the oxytocin iceberg. Yes, the chemical is key to love and pair-bonding and all of that, but emerging research on oxytocin shows that it doesn't just make us feel warm and fuzzy, it also physically heals us and makes us more resilient in ways that scientists are still discovering.[7] New studies appear on the topic just about every day.

Which takes us back to the topic at hand and the big question of this section: Why are social behavior and intimacy physically restorative to our bodies? Why do they make us healthier and happier and longer-lived and better able to battle virtually every physical and mental health malady the world can muster?

Part of the answer is quite simple: Social behavior such as face-to-face interactions can release oxytocin. This oxytocin helps forge bonds such as what we call "love," and is also deeply involved with the body's ability to heal and the autonomic nervous system's ability to deal with the challenges of the world.

As just one example, high levels of oxytocin correlate with the speed of wound healing in humans.[8] Research is documenting the positive effects of oxytocin in treating conditions including heart disease, schizophrenia, diabetes, and certain kinds of cancer. The list goes on. Research now suggests that these all may be helped by oxytocin.

The oxytocin system (we're using the word "system" because it more accurately describes what is really a chemical cocktail with other components, such as the aforementioned vasopressin) helps protect us against the stresses and illnesses the world throws at us.[*]

When we experience stress and duress, our oxytocin levels jump to help us cope with the condition. Oxytocin, in turn, is a powerful anti-inflammatory and antioxidant, with the capacity to both calm and restore.[9] Orgasm and extreme exercise are among the various other ways to release oxytocin.[10]

The effects of oxytocin on visceral organs can be seen remarkably early in life even in single cells. If you take undifferentiated stem cells and put them in a petri dish with oxytocin, they clump together and metamorphose into tiny heart cells that beat in synchrony. Tiny, pulsing protohearts, programmed into existence by oxytocin.[11] This heart-building ability is likely central to our body's natural ability to heal heart disease and also create a functional autonomic nervous system.

In other words: The molecule that leads to love and relationships can literally heal a broken heart. You simply can't make this stuff up.

As humans, we crave safe intimacy. In its absence, we physically

---

[*] Often these positive influences co-occur or are potentiated with shifts in autonomic state that are expressed as greater vagal regulation that reflects the entire body moving into the Green state. Research in prairie voles shows that oxytocin treatments, especially in the presence of a safe companion, can promote functional coupling between sympathetic and parasympathetic systems (Yee et al., 2016).

and mentally wither and remain vulnerable to the stresses of the world. If you're reading this in the presence of a loved one, now would be a good time to put down the book and give them a hug. That fuzzy feeling of comfort may not be actual butterflies. Perhaps it's oxytocin.

Oxytocin-like molecules first appeared over 700 million years ago, long before mammals or other vertebrates roamed the earth. However, the modern oxytocin molecule evolved in parallel with mammals, roughly 150 to 200 million years ago.[12] The emergence of oxytocin laid the foundation for a biology that allowed the capacity for selective social bonds that are essential to what we humans call "love." The autonomic nervous system and oxytocin are so tightly interwoven that, according to Dr. Carter, you literally cannot have one without the other. Dr. Carter goes so far as to argue that both oxytocin and "love" are biological metaphors for safety and trust, and exist as both conduits for and expressions of this deeply ingrained biological need.[13]

Now, if you're looking for some sense of order in the universe, we'll help you: Dr. Carter is, in fact, the wife of one of this book's authors and the mother of the other. The sciences are heavily siloed, and her work as a neuroendocrinologist initially seemed far removed from my (Stephen's) work with the autonomic nervous system as a developmental psychobiologist. It was only after being married for decades that we realized we were actually studying the same processes: the social bonds that lead to trust and love, and how being in a state of perceived safety can literally heal us.

THE SECRET WORLD OF PET LOVE

If you're a dog or cat lover, get ready to nod your head in agreement: Co-regulation and intimacy don't have to be between two humans. We see it in other mammals, and it can even exist across species.

A dog lying on its belly so you can scratch it is immobilizing itself in a state of trust and safety. And who hasn't felt the unique (and soothing) joy of a friendly dog curling up next to them on a sofa? This pleasant scenario projects cues of mutual safety, trust, and co-regulation. It reflects the powerful and reciprocal influences of oxytocin and the Social Engagement System.

Studies have long shown that dog owners are happier and healthier across numerous metrics that likely include longevity, and just about everybody understands the concept of an emotional-support animal. In truth, our furry friends can offer us true love, intimacy, and co-regulation that is capable of soothing us into a state of safety, healing, and happiness.

And lest you feel selfish about turning your pet into an oxytocin machine, don't forget the "co" in co-regulation: They're likely getting as much out of the bond as you are.

This last chapter can be broken down into a pretty simple flow chart, first presented back on page 79.

Safety allows for physical proximity, which allows for intimate contact, which leads to intimate bonds. This process is facilitated by oxytocin, which both binds us together and lends its healing powers to the process.

But what happens when somebody *never* feels safe? What happens when we live in a state of constant fear or aggression and can never begin this process, much less complete it? Therein lies the counter to the healing power of love: the damaging power of trauma.

6

Trauma and Addiction

It is tempting and common for people to be dismissive of others' trauma because what they endured is viewed as perhaps "not that bad" and so they should just "get over it."

But trauma is not defined by the event. Rather, it is a function of how our nervous system responds to it. And those responses can linger with us for a very long time.

Trauma can come from a single event or a series of events. These events can be serious and short shocks to the system, or seemingly minor offenses spread out over a period of time.

To experience trauma is to experience something that our neuroception interprets as so scary or life-threatening that it triggers our ANS to enter a survival mode, and shifts the goalposts on our body's concept of how safe the world is.

In doing so, trauma reprograms our neuroception and sense of safety, so we might perceive danger in places and in situations where we didn't before.

To experience trauma is to perhaps never feel safe, and to never experience the health benefits of safety.

Trauma is not just a painful event, but a complex and (often seemingly random) web of associations that our bodies and brains tie to an event. If you present an innocent item to a rat and shock them every time they see it, they'll quickly learn to instinctively run away from that item. Likewise, when we are around things, experiences, sounds, sights, people, or just about anything else that reminds our bodies or brains of our trauma, it makes us want to run away or shut down. And while we may be conscious of this conditioning, it's also very much bodily and instinctive. We can't simply choose to turn it off.

These feelings can be viewed as our body trying to protect itself and keep us away from anything that might lead to further danger.

Unfortunately for some of us, these associations with danger and trauma can spread to almost everything around us, so the whole world triggers feelings of pain and dissociation. People or places we truly love might remind us of our trauma. As could innocuous sights, sounds, or smells that happened to be experienced alongside the worst event in our lives.

Once again: To be traumatized is to rarely or never feel truly safe. In the absence of that felt sense of safety, trauma leaves our bodies largely stuck in the hands of the aggressive Yellow and dissociative Red systems—or at least makes it a whole lot harder for us to get to Green.

We evolved to utilize these Yellow and Red systems for short bursts to evade danger. They are there to serve a real purpose and to help us survive. But it can be intensely harmful to our bodies and brains to linger in them for extended periods—or even our entire lives, as is, unfortunately, the case for many.

The Green system is crucial to our ability to heal and be happy. By cutting us off from this system, trauma also leaves us physically and emotionally vulnerable to outside stressors of all sorts and makes it more difficult to live a fulfilling life or to co-regulate with others through our Social Engagement System. That last part is particularly problematic because co-regulation is one of the chief ways our bodies heal and deal with times of stress. Meaning the traumatized people who might need the healing benefits of co-regulation the most are often the ones least able to access them.

Trauma can also make it difficult to navigate the world and creates real interpersonal problems when people and things we genuinely love—or simply can't avoid—become caught up in our body's web of traumatic associations.

We Don't Always Run

Just about everybody has the concept of trauma wrong—and that includes therapists who deal with it for a living.

There has long been a belief that the primary way we as humans respond to stress is to activate. In essence: to enter the Yellow.

The Polyvagal Theory posits that our bodies actually have multiple ways of dealing with stress and danger. Yes, we do activate to deal with threats. But we also do something else when our neuroception has picked up signals that our lives are truly and immediately threatened: We freeze, dissociate, or shut down. This is the Red response. It is a common involuntary reflex, and it has been largely ignored up until very recently.

It's also a response we see everywhere in the animal kingdom. You see it in primitive reptiles (for whom shutting down is the primary way to defend against threats), as well as in other mammals.

On YouTube, you can see videos of mice that are held in the jaws of a cat. In such a dire circumstance, the mouse will go limp and appear to be dead. This "death-feigning" behavior, as it's called, is an adaptation that might help the mouse get away from the cat. And if the mouse does indeed die on that day, this involuntary shutdown response will allow it to do so with as little pain as possible.*

This immobilization response is very much present in humans. And until we fully acknowledge it, we can't begin to properly understand what trauma does to our bodies—and how to best treat it.

---

* Curt Richter (1957) described the phenomenon of rats suddenly dying in response to life threat as the consequence of hopelessness. He proposed that this shutdown reaction was mediated by the vagus. His observations became the basis of the well-known psychological construct of "learned helplessness" (Seligman and Maier, 1967), although there appears to be no follow-up research investigating the role that the vagus contributes to the phenomenon and its generalization to humans as Richter proposed.

On Resilience

Everybody is different.

Two people can endure the same horror, and one can come out relatively unscathed while the other relives it every day of their life in every part of their body.

Outside of these long-term effects, people respond to traumatic events differently in the moment. We see this when large groups of people suffer a shared traumatic experience, be it a freeway pileup or a mass shooting. Some people activate to fight or flee, while others completely shut down. Whichever way we respond is a natural and involuntary reflex, and ultimately not up to us.

This is why a group of soldiers can endure the same horrific violence with only some of them suffering from noticeable PTSD. The human nervous system is an intervening variable for how we respond to the world around us, and the same stimuli and experiences can impact all of us very differently.

I (Seth) experienced this for myself on November 13, 2015. On that evening, I had the misfortune of being in Paris when the city erupted into a series of coordinated mass shootings and terrorist attacks. These attacks were largely clustered near the Place de la République, where I was staying. So when I stepped out of the apartment that night intending to grab a quick dinner, I saw blood on the sidewalk and a man gripping his wounded hand.

Within minutes, the sounds of sirens were everywhere, as were yells (in English) of the word "Kalashnikov."

I was locked outside my apartment while the police swept and closed the streets, and so was forced to roam the area, without any sense of whether it was safe to be outside. There had already been several attacks, and very well could be more coming. I recall specifically looking for curved streets, with the hopes that they'd make it less likely for a stray bullet to find me.

Because I was an American journalist, who happened to be in the wrong place at the wrong time, my phone also started to ring from TV news producers eager to get a sense of what was going on the ground. While on hold with these producers, I heard live audio feeds from news stations in lieu of hold music. Because I was nowhere near a TV, it was through those audio feeds that I heard just how many attacks there had been that night. And it was when CNN's Anderson Cooper mentioned to me live on the air that a nearby Cambodian restaurant had been the site of a drive-by shooting that it hit home: I had eaten at that same restaurant the night before, sitting outdoors on the terrace, exactly where and when the bullets would fly just a day later.

Safety felt elusive.

Waves of feelings began to overwhelm me, none of which were easy to pin down. There were moments where I felt like my knees might buckle, or I might cry. But the dominant feeling was one of intense activation and energy. Adrenaline seemed to numb everything else.

There was also a small sense of relief. I had never faced an instance like this in my life. And I was relieved that I had the autonomic resilience to stay lucid, and to not completely shut down. Through my knowledge of the Polyvagal Theory—and speaking to others who had suffered trauma—I knew that shutting down could just as easily have happened.

Trauma is not defined by the actual event, but by how our nervous system responds to it. One more time: Two people can endure the same horror, and one can come out relatively unscathed while the other relives it every day of their life in every part of their body.

Our individual ability to endure hardship without it traumatizing us is our capital-R Resilience, and it's different for everybody.

And just as we all have different abilities to cope with traumatic events, we also exhibit trauma differently. Clinicians have long known that different people experience PTSD with different sets of symptoms. Yes, there tend to be clusters of symptoms that pop up across patients, but no two people experience it in exactly the same way. Likewise, if you are ever diagnosed with PTSD as a patient, it does not mean you will definitely have a specific symptom.

These differences apply to treatments as well. Some treatments may prove wildly successful with one patient, while failing to move the needle at all for another.

————

Resilience is a subject I (Stephen) have been deeply immersed in since the 1970s, long before I developed the Polyvagal Theory. Indeed, my early attempts to define and quantify resilience can largely be viewed as precursors to PVT.

But before we talk about my work on the subject, let's go back in time a bit to Walter Bradford Cannon, the legendary Harvard physiologist who first coined the term "fight or flight," and popularized the term with his book *The Wisdom of the Body*.[1]

Cannon also coined another important term we've repeatedly used in this book: "homeostasis," which can be thought of as the optimal baseline for our health, growth, and restoration.[2] (In other words: To be in homeostasis is to be in the Green state.) Cannon's work in this field largely built off of the ideas of French physiologist Claude Bernard, who described this state as our *milieu intérieur*—or "internal milieu."[3]

The important thing to get about homeostasis is that our bodies desperately *want* to be in this state, but sometimes need to jump out of it to deal with immediate (and hopefully temporary) threats. In an ideal scenario, our bodies would be able to deal with a threat (or some other attention- or resource-draining scenario) and get right back to homeostasis so we can continue to heal and grow.

A lot of my work—including work that predates the Polyvagal Theory—implicitly expands upon Cannon's definition of homeostasis so that it's viewed not as a fixed point but as a range that we float within. Psychiatrist Dan Siegel calls this our "window of tolerance," which I think is a fitting term.[4]

In other words: We can handle *some* stress without leaving homeostasis, as long as we stay in our ideal range. And this range—like so much else related to trauma and stress and the nervous system—is different for everybody.

But what exactly is our window of tolerance? And assuming

every individual has their own level of resilience, is this something we can actually *measure?*

Beginning in the 1970s, I set out to do just that.

STRESS

In the mid-1980s, I (Stephen) wrote a paper on the subject of stress that attempted to unravel the ambiguity of this oft-used word.[5] This wasn't just about indulging in semantics. Rather, through my research into heart-rate variability, I was looking for ways to accurately measure this seemingly abstract concept. And if you're going to measure something, you'd better have a pretty clear definition of what it is you're measuring.

Truth is, I always found the term "stress" a bit ambiguous and confusing, since it's used to refer to whatever is causing us grief ("I'm dealing with stress"), as well as our bodily response to it ("I feel stressed"). In short, "stress" is often used to apply to both the stimulus and our body's response to it.

A polyvagal perspective shifts the discussion away from stress as some outside force and focuses on our nervous system's response to it. Just as our concept of "safety" is all about how safe our nervous systems and bodies feel (and not an impartial measure of actual threat), what matters for the polyvagal concept of "stress" is how our individual nervous systems respond to it.[6]

This new conceptualization of stress would redefine it as a measurable state during which homeostatic functions are disrupted. So if we're thrown out of our Green state of growth and restoration, we are experiencing stress.

The most important thing to understand about this is that the same stressor might cause little to no actual stress (i.e., disruption of homeostasis) in one person while massively disrupting another. Likewise, depending on our autonomic state, we might be able to brush off a specific stressor—or become paralyzed by the same event.

Everybody has a different window of tolerance for dealing with stress, and (like just about everything else in our bodies) that window of tolerance shifts based on our autonomic state and how safe we feel. So, like so many other things in this book, stress will affect us differently if we're in the Green, Yellow, or Red states.

Of course, we all intuitively know that last part, and likely experience it whenever we say or think the words "*Not now!*" in response to a stressful situation. There are simply moments when we're not capable of dealing with certain things because our body is already overwhelmed.

It all began with an attempt to understand how and why different newborns—including premature babies—seemed to handle stressors differently.

As part of this work, I (Stephen) became the first person to quantify a metric called heart-rate variability (or HRV) in this context. Obstetricians had previously been aware of HRV as a possible response to hypoxia (or insufficient oxygen) and a general life threat for the fetus and the newborn, but HRV was not carefully quantified or viewed as containing specific information related to autonomic function.

I think it's safe to assume that readers understand what heart rate is (that is: the speed at which our heart beats, typically measured as beats per minute). Heart-rate variability is obviously related, but still very different.

If you sat and measured your heart rate for a few minutes, you'd find that it doesn't stay constant at just one number. Rather, it likely flutters up and down within a fixed range. So it may be 80 one second, 75 the next, and 84 the next. This is all perfectly normal.

To be clear, I'm not talking about the obvious idea that our heart rate increases when we go for a run or otherwise engage in physical activity, but rather that some changes occur within our resting heart rate without the addition of any stressors.

The size of this range is our heart-rate variability. So if our heart rate naturally flutters across a wide range of measurements over a period of time, we have a high heart-rate variability. Likewise, if our resting heart rate is fairly static and doesn't move around much, we're said to have a low heart-rate variability.

In the late 1960s, I was the first scientist to quantify this metric. In doing so, I learned two very important things about HRV:

First, this measurement is what we scientists call an individual difference, in that it varies among us. So two different people's heart rates may naturally flutter up and down within two different ranges.

Second, while we all have a baseline HRV, our HRV does indeed go up or down as we tackle tasks that require attention, involve psychological stress, or are metabolically costly (such as running or anything else that involves physical exertion).

I also observed that having higher HRV is associated with better performance on metrics such as reaction time.

Putting it all together with my work in newborn infants, I was able to see that measuring HRV might allow us to predict which babies would survive. It soon became clear to me that HRV is actually a very accurate indication of our innate ability to handle stress and maintain homeostasis.

In other words: HRV—that is, how much our heart rate differs over a period of time—turns out to be a really good metric of our resilience and our ability to handle stressors such as traumatic incidents.

This idea has since become widely accepted by the scientific community, as well as by wearable technology manufacturers, who increasingly build the ability to measure HRV into gadgets such as cardio monitors and the Apple Watch.

But why is this? What in the world does our heart rate have to do with trauma and our ability to withstand it?

To understand this, I like to think of a simple metal spring (like a Slinky) lying on the floor. It conforms to a baseline form if left untouched, but its flexible shape also allows it to be stretched out or pushed together without breaking.

The wider the range of movement the Slinky can stretch or smush within, the better able it will be to handle a range of stressors without breaking. So a Slinky with a wide range of movement is more resilient.*

---

* Another real-world metaphor might be the "crumple zones" of a car, which are designed to smush upon impact so as to absorb the force of an accident while protecting the vehicle's passengers.

Our heartbeat effectively acts like a Slinky. Those of us with a higher HRV (meaning our heart-rate intervals have a wider range) have an autonomic nervous system that can expand and compress without breaking and leaving homeostasis.

For those individuals, their "window of tolerance" is larger, and they are likely more resilient against stress and trauma.

—————

When most people talk about resilience—and the idea that different people have differing abilities to handle stressors—they are talking in psychological terms. As if the entire process is in our heads, and begins and ends in the brain.

When I (Stephen) proposed the Polyvagal Theory in the mid-1990s, I began to view the concept of resilience as something else: an adaptive feature and physiological system that stretches throughout our entire bodies, allowing us to respond to and recover from challenges.

With the PVT, I began to view resilience as something baked into our bodies to help us recover from jolts while maintaining homeostasis and staying in the Green.

And while our resilience is innate, it is not fixed. Traumatic incidents can make us less resilient, and our Social Engagement System is metaphorically a muscle that needs to be exercised to stay in shape.

And exercise it we can! Let's go back to our previous section on play, and the PVT understanding of it as an autonomic exercise that allows us to strengthen the ability to move between the Green and Yellow systems without getting stuck in a state of danger. In this sense, the state of play (and the act of playing with others) effectively exercises our resilience as if it were a muscle, to ensure it is there for us when we need it.

In short: Safe social behavior and playing with others may make us more resilient to trauma.

However, when we leave homeostasis, we are shut out of our body's ability to heal, grow, and restore. If an event or series of events pushes us past our window of tolerance—and keeps us from getting back in—we could lose access to these abilities indefinitely.

That is effectively what trauma is, and why it is so damaging to our bodies and physical health—and not just to our brains and minds.

It forces us out of homeostasis, and may even shut the door on our ability to easily reenter this restorative state.

———————

Understanding that each of us has a different level of resilience is especially important when it comes to how we treat others who may be enduring trauma.

If we feel that somebody wasn't adequately hurt by an event, or feel confident that whatever they went through wouldn't have impacted us on a deep level, it can be tempting to be dismissive of their experiences—or to declare that they aren't really traumatized. These days, the media is rife with people telling victims that they were exaggerating the impact of an event to get attention or money.

A generous reading of such statements would be that they come from a place of ignorance. However, the effects can be quite cruel.

We can recall one prominent TV news personality telling an assault survivor live on the air that the only people who truly have trauma are soldiers who have experienced war, and that she was being disrespectful to them by claiming the term for herself.

This affront often extends to how we treat ourselves and talk about our own experiences. Millions of people who live with trauma have a difficult time acknowledging it, because to do so might imply weakness or deficiency. This was a major plot point in *The Sopranos*, in which a mob boss believed that his seeing a therapist would be viewed as such a sign of weakness, that other gangsters would kill him if they found out.

And so, instead of dealing with trauma, we bottle it up and hope it goes away.

Unfortunately, trauma doesn't simply disappear.

Instead, it just buries itself in our bodies and often comes out in bursts of unmanaged anger, aggression, and sadness—not to mention poor physical health. Left untreated, trauma hangs like a dark cloud over us and everybody close to us.

And trauma is contagious. Just as a sense of social safety can spread to others, so too can a sense of danger and trauma. We mirror the autonomic state of others. So when we are aggressive and defensive, it signals to others that they should be as well. Today, we are seeing this occur on a societal level, with many politicians and media figures using every opportunity they can to spread anger and outrage. They are, in effect, traumatizing an entire society by moving our baseline level of fear—or making such fear an omnipresent feature of our lives.

And trauma can be passed down to our children.

Transgenerational trauma is very real. We inherit the pain of our parents through exposure, and possibly even through our DNA.* Trauma is passed to those we live with and maybe even love via the harsh reality of physical or emotional abuse (where one traumatized individual spreads it by inflicting trauma on another)—or via the learned behaviors that come from living with somebody who never feels safe and acts as if everything is a threat. When we are around people who live like that, our bodies retune and adapt to live like that as well.

To be clear, we are not implying that traumatized individuals intend to harm or traumatize their families or those close to them. For many people, it's simply what they picked up from their own environments. And it's important to acknowledge that feelings of shame and guilt can make people dig in on destructive behaviors. It really is hard for anybody to admit that they've done something harmful to those around them, especially if it's something outside of their control. But the first step to breaking a vicious cycle is to acknowledge it.

---

* The emerging field of epigenetics is attempting to explain how this information is transmitted across generations. The documented transgenerational transmission of behaviors has been assumed to be dependent on the passing of DNA to offspring, although there is not currently any convincing epigenetic data to document this in humans.

Social Bonds and Trauma

In the previous chapter, we talked about the process required for us to co-regulate and intimately bond with others—and how doing so unlocks a health-and-happiness boon.

As a quick recap: A sense of safety is required for physical proximity, which is required for physical contact, which is required for the sorts of intimate bonds that release oxytocin, which heals us.[*]

Because trauma impacts our ability to feel safe, it cuts off this process at the nub. The result is that traumatized individuals often have a very difficult time forming healthy social bonds with others. This isn't just harmful in a relationship sense (where people might have a difficult time getting close to others), but it also can cause people to miss out on the beneficial and physically healthful impacts of homeostasis and the oxytocin system.

In the absence of social bonds that are born from a place of safety and trust, many people fall into the pattern of harmful relationship patterns and bonds that come from a place of fear and threat.

To be clear, fear and threat are powerful social glues—they just aren't healthy ones. And we don't mean "healthy" in a judgmental way. Rather, we mean that they literally don't heal us in the way that safe social bonds do.

When somebody never feels safe, a need for immediate survival trumps all else.

Numerous studies have shown that people who experience feelings of danger together are more likely to develop attachments with one another.[7] This feature of our physiology can be used in ways that aren't harmful (the perceived "fear" that comes from a roller-coaster or haunted house can make these attractions great dates). However, the intense correlation between fear and attachment often forces us into unhealthy bonds.

In many cases, the source of our perceived threat also acts as the salve for it. It is common for abusive partners to alternate between hot and cold. To act angry and aggressive one minute, and loving and

---

[*] See the chart on page 79.

calm the next. Through this cycle of threat and relief from threat, we might be sucked into abusive and harmful relationships that play on our nervous system's need for immediate relief from danger.

One narrative commonly used by abusive partners is that their victims are unworthy of real love, or that nobody else could ever give it to them. This is a fiction—and often a projection from somebody dealing with trauma themselves who perhaps feels deeply damaged or unworthy.

We often see our tormentors and abusers as the only people capable of stopping our torment or providing us with any sort of love.

Such feelings can be very difficult to shake. This book's authors may not know you on a personal level, dear reader, but we can tell you that no matter how much you may feel this to be true, it is not. We know it is not true for you, because it is not true for anybody.

While trauma can indeed cause intense (and even addictive) bonds, these bonds are not healing, and do not move us into the homeostatic state that our bodies seek so as to heal our mental and physical wounds. These bonds may also prevent us from finding and forming other bonds that are born from a state of safety and are thus capable of providing us with healing—while further conditioning us to believe that all love must come from a place of threat and trauma.

The Polyvagal Theory and Addiction

We live in a traumatized world.

For many of us, this manifests through feelings of pervasive stress, anxiety, chronic pain, depression, or dissociation. For many of us, our baseline physiological state is simply an unpleasant and unmanageable one. For many of us, we would do almost anything—no matter how drastic—just to *feel* different than we do.

It's no wonder, then, that we also live in an addicted world.

Study after study after study shows that a history of trauma or abuse increases the chances that somebody will misuse substances or develop an addiction. In some studies, the impact is found to be quite dramatic, with some researchers we know going so far as to suggest that addiction rarely occurs without trauma. My (Stephen) ongoing research is also documenting that the majority of individuals who suffer from chronic pain also have a trauma history.[8] Managing this pain through drugs such as opiates is, unfortunately, a common path to addiction.

In short, addiction and trauma are inextricably linked. The Polyvagal Theory offers a simple explanation as to why this is the case:

If you are stuck in a highly mobilized state of pervasive anxiety and stress (the Yellow), then "downers" such as opiates or benzodiazepines might have a numbing effect that seems to offer a temporary reprieve and regulation.

Conversely, if you are stuck in a dissociative fog (the Red), then "uppers" such as cocaine or amphetamines might mobilize you out of it.

Addiction is often treated as a crime or moral failing. The Polyvagal Theory suggests that many addictive behaviors are actually coping mechanisms driven by a body that is desperate to shift its physiological state, to regulate, and to simply feel different than it does.

Addiction is often about our need to manage our feelings.

"Feelings" are our conscious brain's interpretation of our visceral state. When our ANS is well regulated and capable of supporting homeostasis through the Green system, we experience the neurophysiological substrates upon which feelings of safety, trust, friendship, co-regulation, and love can emerge.

But if we disrupt this state, there may be a negative cascade that leaves us with feelings of threat, loneliness, pain, and despair. When we feel these negative feelings, our body's top priority becomes shifting its state so that we can feel better.

The most effective and natural way for the body to shift its state is through the calming effects of social behavior and co-regulation. When this tactic isn't available to us (or we otherwise have difficulty accessing the Green system, as is the case with many people who have experienced trauma), then the body might seek other ways to move away from these negative feelings. Often, this includes the misuse of substances.

This need to shift states is often not conscious but driven by the body on a foundational survival level. It is also compounded in people who have a trauma history, which often comes with a vulnerability to (and perhaps a deep-seated fear of) entering physiological states that might remind them of their trauma. If somebody was immobilized or physically held down during a traumatic event, then merely feeling immobilized or shut down can trigger painful associations. This can drive the use of substances to mobilize the body so as to shift away from these triggering physiological states.*

The problem with leaning on substances to regulate our feelings and autonomic state is that they offer only a temporary escape and diminishing returns.

Many people begin taking addictive substances such as opiates because they offer relief from a painful baseline state. But once the body acclimates to the substance, the substance loses its ability to make us feel better. On top of that, withdrawal can serve as a massive shock to the autonomic nervous system, putting the body into extreme defensive states. This serves only to amplify the body's need to regulate its state away from these painful feelings, including through the further misuse of substances.

People withdrawing from substances might be prone to anger or aggression. This dysregulation away from a state of calm and into defensive states such as the fight-or-flight Yellow is part of the reason why.

---

* In fact, many apparently healthful behaviors that naturally result in a calming rebound effect, such as exercise and sex, can trigger destabilization in those with a trauma history.

The possibility that consensual sex may lead to negative feelings is sometimes called postcoital dysphoria—or simply "post-sex blues." It can lead to feelings of confusion and anger from the individual who feels its effects, as well as their partners. It may also lead to the use of substances as a way of mobilizing the body so as to regulate away from this disruptive state.

This book is largely about how the body often acts in ways that our conscious self wishes it didn't. Nowhere is this disconnect between our body and our brain more evident than with addiction.

This is important. Many people who are dealing with addiction suffer from feelings of shame related to their inability to control their own behavior. These feelings can make it difficult for people to seek help or support, or to fully understand their own struggles. Shame also simply makes us feel bad, which can create an even greater need to find ways to change the way we feel.

The Polyvagal Theory suggests that we view addiction as a coping strategy. To be clear: It is often a failed and unsustainable coping strategy, but is one that nonetheless comes from the body's need to keep us safe, and to regulate its physiological state.

We've all heard of the concept of "self-medication," as individuals who might deal with mental or physical health issues lean on drugs or alcohol as a way of making themselves feel better.

This idea is consistent with the Polyvagal Theory, which suggests that individuals who are autonomically dysregulated are the most vulnerable to addiction. This dysregulation can come from a wide variety of root causes, including mental health conditions, a trauma history, or chronic pain.

This is also why being marginalized due to race, ethnic group, gender, or disability might be viewed as an addiction risk.

Marginalization frequently places individuals in a state of chronic threat and anxiety, and can limit opportunities for people to socialize and co-regulate in work, school, or community settings.

The previous chapter is about how, as humans, we evolved to rely on social behavior and co-regulation to stay sane, happy, and healthy. This is the most efficient and healthiest way for us to regulate our autonomic state. It is also not something that is always available to everybody.

When those around us present themselves as threats or treat us as outsiders, we may lose the ability to use social behavior as a calming neuromodulator. Without access to safe social behavior, the body needs to find another way to regulate its state. For many people, that ends up being addictive substances.

Those with trauma, addiction, or mental health conditions may also have difficulty getting their bodies into a state conducive to healthful social interaction. A neuroception that is biased toward detecting danger—perhaps because it has already experienced a fair share of it—is less sensitive to positive social cues and might misinterpret prosodic vocalizations, facial expressions, or bodily gestures so that friendly nods, smiles, or eye contact are seen as threats.

Like scared dogs, such nervous systems often simply don't trust the social-engagement behaviors of others as being safe. This can make it even more difficult for these people to regulate via the natural tool of social co-regulation, creating an even greater bodily need for substitutes such as substances.

And as substitutes for social co-regulation, substances are a poor one. While they may numb feelings of pain or distress, they won't lead to the physiological calmness that supports the healing processes of homeostasis. Nor will substances effectively optimize the ability of our bodies to project or detect safety in others.

———

The Polyvagal Theory doesn't just offer us an explanation as to *why* so many people lean on addictive substances. It also offers clues as to how we might treat these addictions in ways that are effective and compassionate.

To this end, the Polyvagal Institute[9] is certifying addiction-treatment centers as being "polyvagal-informed," meaning they utilize the principles of the Polyvagal Theory in how they approach and treat patients.

This approach involves framing the patient's negative feelings as the manifestation of a foundational survival mechanism that has been baked into our bodies through millions of years of evolution. The goal is to be aware of the feeling of the body moving into defensive states, without allowing these feelings to overtake the patient.

It is a common narrative that somebody—possibly the patient

themselves, possibly somebody close to them—is to blame for negative feelings. When we reframe these feelings as the natural result of an innate survival system that is triggered into a state of defense, it allows us to experience these feelings outside the prism of personal blame or shame.

This allows the patient to separate the feeling from the narrative of intention. This can be crucial to our ability to experience negative feelings in ways that don't allow them to completely overwhelm us or cause us to psychologically spiral as we search for meaning or blame in natural and common bodily feelings.

The Polyvagal Theory also suggests that a patient's physical environment can be crucial to their recovery. If the body feels threatened (as is a certainty during withdrawal), then it becomes especially important to produce an environment where aesthetic and auditory cues allow their neuroception to feel safe.

Let's put it this way: There's a reason so many drug-treatment centers are based near the breathtaking cliffs of Malibu.

The Polyvagal Perspective on Trauma

Taking what we now know about the Polyvagal Theory and autonomic nervous system, a lot of the seeming mysteries of trauma begin to make a whole lot more sense:

"Why did I freeze or dissociate when I was assaulted?
Why didn't I fight back? Does that make me complicit?"

Freezing during a traumatic incident is a natural response that is outside the realm of conscious thought or intentional behavior. When the Red system takes over, our bodies shut down and possibly even pass out. In other instances (particularly after repeated traumas), this system causes the victim to dissociate to maintain a level of physical alertness while shielding the consciousness from the harsh reality of the situation.

These responses are not choices, and do not mean a victim somehow welcomed the assault or was otherwise complicit. Simply understanding this is important when it comes to how we ascribe guilt to others and to ourselves.

"Why does everything feel, look, and sound different after my trauma?"

Our autonomic state is the filter through which we experience the world. Depending on how safe our nervous system feels, our sensory experience can completely change. This can result in things looking, feeling, smelling, sounding, and tasting different. It can also result in the feeling of a numbing or dissociative fog, where things we once loved no longer make us happy—or are now so closely associated with a traumatic incident as to trigger our nervous system's defensive Yellow or Red systems.

"Why do I hear things differently after suffering trauma?"

Let's build off of the above-mentioned sensory changes, and focus on the sense of sound.

Our middle ears feature muscles that help us pick up the sounds of human speech in a loud or crowded environment. These muscles physically change position when we leave the Green system for the Yellow to allow our ears (which are now anticipating danger) to pick up ultra low frequency sounds that might be associated with predators (think: a tiger in the bushes).

If we *never* feel safe (as is common for those suffering from trauma), then these middle-ear muscles are apt to stay in this position. The result of this is an auditory processing disorder that is very common (though often viewed as very mysterious) to those suffering from trauma, and often manifests as a hypersensitivity to background noise.

One quick aside before we move on: This book's authors have spoken to numerous people who have a hard time dealing with the creaking sounds of an empty house when they are alone. The same phenomenon is likely occurring here, as these low-frequency noises are being processed by our nervous systems as perceived threats.

"Why do certain things seem to trigger my trauma?"

Our nervous system is constantly learning and forming connections from our environment and lived experiences.

If a child eats something that tastes bitter or causes them discomfort, the experience likely keeps them from touching it again anytime soon. Likewise, almost anything that we associate with a painful or traumatic incident can trigger our neuroception into thinking danger is afoot when we encounter it in the future. This could be a smell, a color, a place, a person—almost anything. And that includes people or things we may truly love.

Not being able to handle certain mundane experiences that trauma has conditioned us into associating with danger is not a sign of weakness, nor is it something we should give others a hard time about, as it can cause them real pain.

"Why am I always so anxious?"

Trauma retunes our nervous system to pick up signs of danger where there may be none. When we are in this state, mundane stressors such as traffic, deadlines, or social media alerts may be funneled through the same neural pathways that were designed for life-threatening occurrences—and were designed only to be triggered on rare and necessary occasions.

To live our entire life in this state is to live a life where everyday occurrences feel like existential threats. This is, in a nutshell, what anxiety is.

"Why was I so shaken by the same event that somebody else was able to simply shrug off?"

We all have a different level of resilience, and instances that one person might shake off with ease could cause lifelong trauma in somebody else. Having a lower resilience to trauma and stress is not a sign of weakness, but a natural and (to some degree) measurable difference in all of us. Resilience is also something that can be exercised like a muscle through social interaction and physical play, which can help buffer us against future traumas.

"Why do I have a hard time socializing and forming bonds after trauma?"

In Chapter 5, we talked about the order of events that is needed for one to develop the sorts of safe social bonds that lead to true healing. Key to this process is the ability to feel safe around others. This can be very difficult for those suffering from trauma, which subsequently makes it difficult to socialize or form healthy relationships.

Of course, this creates yet another vicious cycle, as socializing and healthy relationships are crucial to our ability to handle trauma and stress in the first place.

"Why does trauma last for so long? And why is it so difficult to treat?"

Trauma is often mischaracterized as a purely psychological or psychiatric issue—and is usually treated as such, with talk therapy and medication viewed as the only options. And while therapy and medication can certainly help some people, these approaches still treat trauma as if it begins and ends in the brain.

Once you begin to understand the way trauma transforms us, we can approach it as a physiological issue that extends far beyond our brain and into virtually every crevice of our body.

The Polyvagal Theory also reframes trauma as a product of a nervous system that feels chronically unsafe, and posits that treatments will be most effective when they are designed with a sense of "safety" in mind—or administered in environments that make people feel safe.

Which brings us to our next section.

How the Polyvagal Theory Is Informing
New Treatments for Trauma

The truth is, I (Stephen) didn't have trauma in mind when I developed the Polyvagal Theory.

So I write with no small measure of humility that it has been astonishing to see my work adopted by the trauma world and informing how many trauma professionals now approach the subject. For this, I credit the trauma therapists who looked at PVT and saw their own work and experiences reflected in it. But once you see how PVT explains trauma—and possibly informs new treatments for it—it's impossible to unsee.

I am the founding director of the Traumatic Stress Research Consortium at the Kinsey Institute at Indiana University. As part of the consortium, we are conducting an ongoing survey of approximately 1,000 trauma therapists. This survey found that therapists ranked "polyvagal-informed information" as the single most useful and most used category of trauma treatment, with some 65% of the surveyed trauma therapists self-describing their practice as "polyvagal-informed."[*]

This translates into how therapists discuss trauma, as well as specific advances in treatment techniques.

A key tenet of the Polyvagal Theory is the paramount importance of how our bodies feel and respond to the world around us.

Every single one of us enjoys (or, as is often the case, suffers through) a wide range of bodily experiences and feelings. There are times when we feel social and lively, energized and aggressive,

---

[*] This number should be cautiously interpreted. I (Stephen) am the founding director of the consortium, and many of the surveyed therapists were somatically oriented and learned about the Polyvagal Theory during their training, suggesting that the surveyed individuals may be more likely to be familiar with PVT than the population of trauma therapists as a whole.

or perhaps paralyzed into immobilization. We feel good and we feel bad. We feel fulfilled and we feel empty. We feel a lot.

These feelings are all universal, and largely adaptive. They are not innately "bad" but, rather, exist within us to serve specific functions that evolved to help us survive and hopefully return to a state of safety.

But for those of us who suffer from trauma, specific bodily feelings can become deeply tied to our trauma. While feeling defensive or angry is never fun, healthy individuals can often move on from such feelings without too much difficulty. For those who suffer from trauma, simply *feeling* a certain feeling (whether it's defensiveness, anger, or anything else—even feelings we largely view as "positive") can act as a painful trigger that can cause massive disruption and massive pain.

This is why, with the Polyvagal Theory as a guide, Deb Dana, LCSW—clinical adviser to the Traumatic Stress Research Consortium and my coeditor on the book *Clinical Applications of the Polyvagal Theory*—reframes her therapy sessions so that she focuses not on the traumatic event but rather on the bodily feelings associated with it.

This is a major shift. The goal of talk therapy is often to create an explanation for *why* a patient feels the way they do.

The goal of polyvagal-informed therapists such as Dana is to shift that question from "why" we feel the way we do to "how."

The point is to understand our own feelings and decouple them from the trauma. In essence: Have patients get used to these universal bodily feelings so that they become less disruptive. We all feel bad feelings, just as we all feel good ones. The problem for traumatized individuals is that those bad feelings can overwhelm the ability to simply go about living.

The first step in this process is to create awareness of our bodily state, free from any narrative of it being "good" or "bad." Instead, Dana has her patients approach these states from a place of curiosity and exploration: *"This is a bodily feeling. It is not a good one or a bad one. But it is one I am feeling and this is what it feels like."*

Without this sense of awareness, we often create narratives around our negative feelings that involve blame. We blame ourselves or those close to us for making us feel bad. A loved one or the environment we're in may inadvertently trigger us, which can lead our body and brain to believe that the person or thing is the problem. This creates real interpersonal problems and no shortage of conflict. It can also cause a bias toward negativity in all our interactions, as we look for somebody to blame for our own bad feelings.

Blame is a coping strategy. But as a coping strategy, it is both easy to fall back on and highly ineffective.

A patient who is fully aware of their bodily feelings can experience these feelings outside the context of blame and, hopefully, understand what may actually be triggering them.

With awareness as a beginning, the next step is to help patients develop the ability to move in and out of these feelings and states without getting stuck in them. Life improves when patients can experience these feelings without having massive state disruptions.

Moving in and out of and controlling these states and feelings can occur through mechanisms such as breath and movement. A patient who has mastered these skills is better able to navigate through their own, often painful, bodily feelings like a ship seeking safe harbor while deftly moving past obstacles without crashing.

This sort of therapy works as a progressive exercise (or "ladder," as Dana frames it) aimed at allowing patients to become aware of their own bodily feelings, and to slowly remove these feelings from the context of pain and trauma. Patients are encouraged to "feel" feelings that they associate with trauma in short—but increasingly lengthy—bursts, and in a safe environment. If they go too far, Dana pulls them back.

Eventually, patients get used to these feelings as just *feelings*, and not as triggers for trauma. When this happens, these feelings lose their disruptive power. We can acknowledge them, honor them, feel them, appreciate them. But then also move on from them.

Shared Symptoms

Many of the symptoms that we're talking about as being related to trauma can also be found in a wide range of medical diagnoses and psychiatric conditions.

These include autism, schizophrenia, depression, borderline personality disorder, and many, many others. All of these disparate conditions feature a shared core of symptoms that include auditory hypersensitivity, difficulty extracting a human voice from background activity, flat facial affect, difficulty regulating behavioral state, a lack of prosody in the voice, and a baseline autonomic state that tends to have higher heart rates and less vagal regulation of the heart.

Many of these shared symptoms involve the physical features of the Social Engagement System and our ability to detect and express emotions.

When we talk about these conditions and "treating" them, it's important to specify that our goal is often not to "cure" somebody. There's an increasing awareness through the neurodiversity movement that many people are simply wired differently, and there's nothing wrong with that.

Sensory and autonomic hypervigilance can make sense as being sometimes beneficial from an evolutionary standpoint when one considers that such individuals may have been better tuned to pick out predators or other dangers. We've spent a lot of time talking about how resource intensive alertness and vigilance are, but social behavior also takes a lot out of us and can make it more difficult to spot potentially lethal dangers in the wild.

Rather, our goal is to make life better for people. If hypervigilance and auditory hypersensitivities make it physically painful to go through the day and cut people off from the beneficial effects of feeling safe, then that's something we need to pay attention to. Likewise, we may not be able to "cure" trauma, but we can certainly reduce its harmful impacts on people and perhaps keep it from massively disrupting their lives.

Many of these symptoms are so tightly tied to certain diagnoses that people have long viewed them as innate—and even defining—features. You see this specifically with auditory issues and autism. The two were long viewed as so tightly intertwined that the auditory issues were considered essentially untreatable as long as somebody had autism.

What we're now finding is that this is not always the case. Instead of viewing auditory issues as a key component of what makes some-body autistic, I (Stephen) think it's more accurate to view such symptoms as a side effect of a nervous system that is stuck in a state of hypervigilance and never feels properly safe. And with the Polyvagal Theory as our guide, that is something we very much can treat.

The Importance of Safety in Treatment

To be a polyvagal-informed therapist is to understand the power of our physiological state. Again: This state is the filter through which we experience the world. It is, in effect, an intervening variable that changes how we perceive and respond to everything around us. And that includes therapy.

Polyvagal-informed therapists exist within many clinical specialties, whether it's somatic experiencing (SE), eye movement desensitization and reprocessing (EMDR), cognitive behavioral therapy (CBT), internal family systems (IFS), or other therapeutic strategies. What they all have in common: the perspective that many of the issues that come from trauma can be viewed as a violation of our body's need for safety.

Polyvagal-informed therapists also understand the power of safety in the therapeutic process: If feeling safe primes our bodies to enter a state of health and restoration, then making people feel safe is likely to make almost any therapy or treatment more effective. This is true of trauma, but extends to other conditions and medical interventions as well.

With that in mind, we begin to think about new ways of treating patients—and also of designing the actual physical spaces and experiences for patients who receive treatment—so that the value of making people feel safe is viewed as paramount.

Just imagine stepping into a sterile hospital filled with buzzing fluorescent lights, sickly patients in clear view, a frantic sense of urgency, and perhaps the low-frequency sounds of ventilation machinery and aching moans filling the halls.

Now imagine a calm and serene space. A space that simply feels *safe* because it was designed with an eye toward how our neuroception and nervous system interpret sights, sounds, and smells.

The Polyvagal Theory suggests that simply being in a safer-feeling setting, and tended to by a professional with a friendly and safe-seeming bedside manner, is likely to increase the efficacy of almost any treatment by priming our nervous system to enter the Green state of homeostasis and healing.

Remember: Our body and brain physically heal faster and better when we're in the Green state. As a result, architectural, acoustic, and aesthetic features that make us feel safe may make a real difference in our body's ability to heal itself.

Beyond these general ideas, I've taken the concepts behind the PVT and used them to develop one very specific intervention that is currently (and successfully) helping reduce disruptive symptoms associated with issues that include auditory hypersensitivities, PTSD, schizophrenia, chronic pain, anxiety, depression, auditory processing disorders, long COVID, dissociation, and even Parkinson's.

The Safe and Sound Protocol

Here are a couple of simple questions:

If a newborn is upset and crying, how do you talk to them so as to calm them down?

If a beloved dog is being a good boy or girl, how do you let them know?

Hopefully, you are imagining a voice muttering "*I love you*" or "*Who's a good doggy?*"

Now imagine *how* that voice sounds. Is it monotone and stern, or singsongy and melodic?

Clearly, it's the latter.

The idea of speaking in a flat, monotone voice to a baby can be strangely upsetting to us on a visceral level. It seems to go against a hardwired nurturing instinct that urges us to coo, smile, and move our voice up and down like a musician who has mastered an instrument. We innately get that doing so will make the target of our words feel safe and loved, even if they are too young—or too much of a dog—to understand the meanings of specific words.

In these scenarios, it is not *what* we are saying that matters. It is *how* we say it.

In these scenarios, it is our prosody that is doing the work.

———

Vocal prosody is a measure of how much our pitch varies when we talk. So to speak with a high level of prosody is to speak in a sing-songy and melodic manner, where our voice moves up and down. Basically: A prosodic voice is the opposite of a monotone voice.

And while prosody may seem like an inconsequential feature of the human voice, it is, in fact, incredibly important to our nervous system. That's because prosody signals to our neuroception that somebody is safe. Such sounds act as a parasympathetic trigger and coax us into a state of calm.[*]

The process behind this shift is an unconscious reflex that is based in our anatomy itself.

As we mentioned back in Chapter 2, our ears feature tiny muscles that allow us to pick up the sounds of speech to facilitate social communication. When we feel safe and are in the Green state, we are literally better able to hear people talk to us. When we feel threatened and shift into Yellow, this feature of these muscles goes away and we become hypersensitive to ultra low frequencies that are associated with threats (think: a growling beast, or footsteps that might be following us).

This is one reason why so many people who suffer from PTSD also have auditory processing and hypersensitivity issues. If the body *never* feels safe, then these muscles are never able to shift their hearing out of this state of danger and alertness. You see this a lot with soldiers who come back from war and consequently have problems dealing with loud environments. You also see this with children who come from abusive households or dangerous upbring-

———

[*] We have documented that if the mother's voice is more prosodic, it will more effectively calm her infant following a transitory stressor (Kolacz et al., 2021).

ings. They are often unable to properly discern specific words from speech, and often accused of being poor listeners—or simply being stupid. They may even believe this themselves, not realizing what is actually happening.

Auditory hypersensitivity is also an immensely common feature in those who have autism. But while many individuals in the autism world long viewed auditory hypersensitivity as a core (and even defining) feature of the condition, I saw it as something else: a result of a body that was mobilized out of a state of safety.

This led me (Stephen) to develop the **Safe and Sound Protocol** (or SSP): a therapeutic intervention that attempts to take the core features of prosodic sounds—and their innate ability to soothe us—and use them as a tool to make the nervous system feel safe.

I wanted to deconstruct these soothing sounds into a sort of distilled essence of trust that could be used to calm us in the same way a cooing mother's singsongy voice can calm a child—or a melodic "*Who's a good boy?*" can make a dog's tail wag uncontrollably. The Polyvagal Theory suggested to me that doing this could shift the nervous system into a state of safety, and unlock the healthful benefits that come with it.

I started developing this intervention in the late 1990s, and my initial goals were narrow: to help treat auditory processing and hypersensitivity disorders in autism. I thought that using these sounds to make the nervous system feel safe could help with this, and hopefully offer real help to millions of people who have trouble hearing and listening.

In initial trials, the results were nothing short of astonishing. Almost instantly, we began to see measurable reductions in auditory hypersensitivity, improvements in auditory processing, improvements in behavioral control, and the development of spontaneous social behaviors.

Nonverbal autistic children began to spontaneously speak. Parents reported getting calls from startled teachers, who were alarmed that these formerly silent and nonresponsive kids were now attentive and engaged members of the classroom.

And it doesn't end there. A strange sort of magic occurs when you're able to take nervous systems that rarely, if ever, feel safe and give them this distilled essence of trust and safety. In addition to the auditory improvements, we also measured increased vagal regulation of the heart after test subjects went through SSP, suggesting that a wide array of under-the-hood physiological shifts were occurring as well.

A key tenet of the Polyvagal Theory is that feeling safe can transform and heal our bodies in a wide variety of ways, and these effects do not begin and end in the ears—nor are they isolated to autistic individuals.

So as this intervention—which was commercially released in 2016 by a company called Integrated Listening Systems,* which is now part of another company called Unyte Health—has spread to clinicians, therapists, and patients with different needs and goals and wants, it's been astounding (and humbling) to see it cause real and transformative change for a wide range of conditions that go way beyond my initial scope or hope. In particular, it has proved immensely powerful as a tool for adults who suffer from trauma. Beyond that, almost every day I get an email or letter from a clinician or patient who has tried SSP in a way that I never even considered and has seen an effect.

All because the nervous system feels just a little bit safer.

---

* For additional information see https://integratedlistening.com/ssp-safe-sound -protocol/

PART 2

IN THE WORLD

7

The Pandemic Paradox

Humans are a social species, and we rely on one another.

A key tenet of the Polyvagal Theory is that social interaction—particularly *face-to-face* social interaction—with safe and trusted people is a key that unlocks our body's ability to heal and buffer itself from the stresses of the world, while also allowing us to be our best and brightest selves.

Our need for being around others is nothing short of a biological imperative, crucial to our long-term survival as a species, and baked into both our DNA and nearly every aspect of our society and culture.

Isolated from others, our bodies and brains wither. Nearly every aspect of our physical and mental well-being suffers. Stressful situations that we might otherwise be able to brush off can fester into long-lasting traumas. We become unmoored and unhealthy. We suffer and become selfish.

Since early 2020, the COVID-19 pandemic has killed millions, upended the global economy, and added fuel to the fires of fear and unrest that now populate almost every corner of our world.

It also forced us to socially isolate ourselves.

COVID-19 is an infectious disease that spreads through close contact with others. In the early days of the pandemic, particularly before the widespread availability of lifesaving vaccines, we were asked to avoid close contact with others as a matter of personal survival and public health. We were told that doing so could save our lives and the lives of others.

And while the virus can be deadly, the Polyvagal Theory tells us that social isolation comes with consequences of its own.

Being around safe-seeming others is how our bodies heal and build resilience. It unlocks the Green state, which is crucial for our body's ability to funnel resources toward the systems that facilitate health, growth, and restoration: the very health, growth, and restoration that might help us survive a potentially deadly virus.

Without social interaction, our bodies are more inclined to revert to the Yellow or Red states as our baseline. This isn't just bad for our health—it's also bad for how we treat one another.

When we feel safe, we naturally express concern and altruism for others. But when we are in this Yellow state of fear (which is exacerbated by social isolation), feelings of personal survival trump all else. We act selfish, angry, and reactive—a truth that is hard to ignore as we look at the widening political and cultural schisms that have become a hallmark of recent years. There's an undeniable feeling that everybody is just a little bit *angrier* than they used to be.

To be clear, we are not saying that our need for social behavior should be prioritized above a common-sense approach to public health. To add yet another wrinkle to the situation, it's become increasingly clear that COVID-19 isn't just capable of killing us. For those who survive, it may serve as an autonomic disruptor, potentially impacting our nervous systems' ability to stay regulated and feel fully safe going forward, at least in some cases.

You can see why this chapter is called "The Pandemic Paradox."

It should be noted that, by the time you read this book, many people will have considered themselves long "done" with the pandemic. The majority of Americans have already been vaccinated, contracted the virus (perhaps multiple times), or simply decided that getting infected is an acceptable risk for a return to perceived normalcy.

The authors also acknowledge that virtually everything about the pandemic has become irreversibly politicized. How we dealt with, and continue to deal with, the pandemic has become a proxy for political and culture wars.

As such, we're not here to offer specific policy prescriptions or judgments on how people may handle the challenges of the pandemic. Instead, we're here to look at the complex and perhaps surprising ways in which the COVID-19 virus, as well as the stress and isolation that came with it, may have changed us—and why so many of us found the whole ordeal so torturous.

The Polyvagal Theory also gives us a novel lens through which to view the widening gulfs and increasing anger that have become an unavoidable part of our culture, especially since the pandemic began. Through the lens of PVT, it is possible to view these schisms as, at least in part, the product of nervous systems that have been retuned to search for threat—rather than for benevolence, compassion, and common ground. When our bodies seek and sense threats, we become a selfish, angry, and reactive species.[1]

The COVID-19 pandemic probably traumatized nearly all of us in some way and to some degree. And in doing so, it likely retuned our nervous systems en masse and on a scale that we haven't experienced as a culture in, perhaps, decades.

———

If you're reading this expecting a nice and tidy answer as to how the Polyvagal Theory tells us to deal with pandemics such as this recent one, you won't find it here. The truth—particularly before the widespread availability of lifesaving vaccines—is far more nuanced than the "Shut it all down!" or "Open it all up!" discourse that dominated the early days of the pandemic.

Social isolation was prescribed as a necessary measure to curb the spread of a deadly virus, but it was done in a way that largely failed to acknowledge the ripple effects of such measures, and how they might change people.

Epidemiologists' single-minded focus on the virus's direct threat meant that public messaging about the pandemic often failed to account for human behavior, how torturous isolation can be, and how necessary social interactions are for our health and well-being. We also failed to properly offer the mental health support that would help people endure the ordeal.

As a result, we became burned out on a massive scale.

The period of intense "lockdown" (as we all called it) proved so painful for so many people that a lot of them gave up on caring. Instead of carrying on with common-sense measures that could greatly reduce the risk of infection, many people simply decided they were done with even acknowledging the existence of the pandemic—possible infection or public health be damned.

The personal survival instincts that bubble up from a threatened nervous system also likely caused many people to be dismissive of, or perhaps unable to fully understand, how their actions might impact others. People began to look at their behavior during the pandemic as a matter of personal choice, with the idea that the only calculus that mattered was whether they themselves might get seriously ill or die.

The truth is that our actions impact others. This is true in normal times (our innate interconnectedness is a major theme of this book), but it is *especially* true during a global pandemic.

If we're young and healthy, an infection might not get us as individuals very sick, but we can easily spread the virus to a high-risk person who might end up in the hospital or dying. A tsunami of simultaneous infections can—and in many places, did—overwhelm a stretched-too-thin health-care system. Overflowing hospitals also made it difficult for anybody to schedule surgeries or seek treatment for non-COVID emergencies. Many COVID patients died in total isolation from their loved ones, unable to find comfort in a loving hand or accepting smile. Frontline health-care workers endured a prolonged period of stress and trauma that few of us can imagine.

Nobody is happy that these things happened. But when we are isolated or feel threatened, our nervous system's capacity for compassion and altruism is eclipsed by selfish survival. And widespread social isolation during the pandemic meant that, just as others needed us to step up and fully grasp the ripple effects of our actions, we as a society were the least equipped to do just that.

———

When COVID-19 first emerged in America in early 2020, we knew very little about the virus and how it spread.

This is to be expected. Science is about searching for the truth and being willing to adjust one's beliefs and actions as new evidence emerges. We were cautious in terms of how we dealt with the virus because we had to be, even if many of the suggested measures later proved unnecessary.

We disinfected our mail and wiped off food containers. We slathered anything and everything with hand sanitizer. We encouraged people to stay indoors, and even closed off hiking trails and beaches—locations for activities that we now know can be easily enjoyed safely during the pandemic.

We now know that there were (and are) safe ways for people to interact with one another and engage their Green system while minimizing the likelihood of spreading the virus. But rather than appreciating the evolving information and adjusting our behavior with the science, the airwaves became clogged with noise and voices who used any new information or changes to the prevailing wisdom as an excuse to spread misinformation and distrust.

Cynical politicians and talking heads—who either didn't understand how science works or simply pretended not to—told people that, since the latest science was now offering different advice than it had a few weeks or months prior, it meant that *all* science related to the virus was bunk and not to be trusted.

Scientists and public health officials who were tasked with offering advice based on new research and understandings became the targets of death threats. We wanted things to be cut-and-dried. We wanted easy answers. And in their absence, people were *angry*.

It seems obvious that this anger was exacerbated by the prescribed isolation. Without access to safe social interactions to offer us resilience and access to the Green state, our bodies fall into the defensive Yellow state. We become emotional and reactive, and easier to rile up. We listen to voices that tell us to hate or attack others or paint them as bogeymen who are to blame for all that is wrong in the world.

As of the time of this writing, the pandemic isn't totally behind us, but it's no longer the isolating force that it was in early 2020.

People are emerging back into the world. We are spending time with friends, socializing, and having fun together once again.

Let's just hope that, given the benefit of close contact with those who might help us co-regulate and feel safe, our cooler heads eventually prevail once again.

A Vulnerable Nervous System

Empathy is hard, and it can be difficult for people to relate to others' experiences if they differ from our own. We saw this tendency repeatedly bubble up with the pandemic when those who might have felt only mild effects from the virus or hadn't yet caught it themselves might be heard insisting that the virus should be no big deal for anybody because maybe it wasn't for them.

In reality, maladies such as COVID-19 hit everybody differently. Some suffered only minor symptoms (or none at all), and others lost their lives. Some got over the virus with ease, and others suffered long-term effects that continue to linger with them months or years later.

As is often the case, our bodies serve as intervening variables that partially determine how the virus impacts—or doesn't impact—us. Each of us has a different innate resilience to stressors such as COVID. One person's minor cold is another's life-threatening ailment.

And, as is the case with virtually every other health malady, COVID-19 tended to hit individuals with a history of adversity or trauma the hardest. This appears to be true when it came to the chances of survival, long-term health outcomes from the virus itself, and the related psychological effects that arose from dealing with everything else that came along with the pandemic.

I (Stephen) coauthored a study published in the October 2020 issue of *Frontiers in Psychiatry* that showed that noninfected individuals with a history of adversity or trauma reported higher levels of destabilized autonomic reactivity, PTSD, depression, anxiety, and worry related to COVID-19.[2]

In a second study,[3] we also reported that this was the case not only for individuals who were infected with the virus, but also for those who were simply living under the shadow of a locked-down and changed world that offered limited opportunities for safe social interaction and co-regulation. While the pandemic likely retuned nearly all of our nervous systems and impacted everybody's mental health, those with a history of adversity and trauma felt it the worst—and were far more likely to catch the virus in the first place.

A lot of the discussion around COVID-19 involved its dangers to so-called high-risk individuals who might have preexisting conditions such as asthma or diabetes, or might simply be elderly or overweight. This study suggests that we should add a trauma history to this list.

The Polyvagal Theory tells us that our unique autonomic nervous system is an intervening variable that partially determines how vulnerable or resistant we are to the stressors of the world, and that a history of trauma will make us more vulnerable to just about everything. This study suggests that this is the case for pathogens such as COVID-19.

During those early days of COVID, virtually nobody in our study with a low adversity score (meaning they did not have a history of trauma) had been infected. On the other hand, those with a high adversity score had a roughly 75% chance of having the virus. To place this into context, at the time we conducted the study, fewer than 10% of the participants had been infected.

These results were collected during the first wave of the virus, and it is likely that new variants—which have proved capable of infecting nearly everybody—might narrow or erase the gap. Still, what we found was shocking.

We also found that, while most health-care workers shared a similar likelihood with the general population when it came to being infected, those who worked in a hospital (a high-stress and traumatizing place to work, especially during a pandemic) were far more likely to catch the virus. Even those hospital workers who avoided infection were likely to express poor mental health symptoms.

The likely reason for all this is simple: Individuals who have trauma histories or deal with the effects of pervasive stress are often locked out of, or at least have a harder time accessing, the healing and buffering properties of the Green state.

The effects of trauma don't end when the incident ends. Trauma involves a physiological reaction that retunes our nervous system and impacts how our bodies respond to stress and health events long after a specific incident has passed.

We tend to think of pathogens such as COVID as all or none: If we are exposed to it, we're gonna get it.

What the pandemic has taught us is that this isn't always the case. We all have natural defenses that prevent us from becoming infected by viruses such as COVID, or from suffering severe health outcomes if we do get infected. These defenses can be buoyed through measures such as vaccines (which have been proved to dramatically improve the likelihood a COVID patient will survive or endure only a mild case, even if they do get infected) and social co-regulation. These defenses can also be weakened through factors such as having a preexisting condition, including a history of trauma.

This also likely explains why certain marginalized groups—be they persecuted minorities or individuals who live in poverty—are more likely to end up hospitalized or dead from COVID and many other health conditions.

When we talk about trauma, we often talk about it as an *event*. The Polyvagal Theory recognizes the possible severity and danger of a traumatic event but also emphasizes how our nervous system might respond to or change from it.

Trauma and marginalization have the capability of retuning our nervous system into a defensive state. As the data from our research show, this retuned nervous system is effectively a preexisting condition, capable of weakening our defenses against health concerns such as COVID—as well as almost anything else we might encounter.

Difficulties for Survivors

The effects of catching COVID-19 are often treated as a binary: Either you die from it or it's no big deal.

As with many other diseases and disorders, the reality of COVID isn't quite so simple. Just because we don't die from the disease doesn't mean we get away scot-free.

Many of us have likely heard of (or perhaps even suffered from) so-called long COVID, in which the disease leaves us with long-lasting symptoms such as fatigue, brain fog, trouble breathing, feelings of generally being "off" or "not myself," and various neurological issues—long after the initial infection has passed.

These symptoms are similar to those associated with various other conditions that result in disruption to the autonomic nervous system, and effectively tune us away from the Green and toward a state of defense. To me (Stephen), this suggested that COVID is an autonomic disruptor, and a lot of the effects of "long COVID" came from the virus's ability to do just this.

An obsession with death rates when attempting to quantify the impact of the pandemic meant that a lot of its nonfatal negative effects were ignored or dismissed. But when it comes to conditions that disrupt our autonomic nervous system—and our ability to feel safe and sound—the splash zone of these effects can seep into almost every aspect of our health and well-being.

After all, just because something doesn't kill us doesn't mean it leaves us stronger.

———

In the end, the COVID-19 pandemic presented an extraordinary challenge for all of us. Our nervous systems typically look to the presence of others as a way of co-regulating and healing. But during the pandemic, what was normally a source of healing was reframed as a potentially deadly threat. We were told to avoid socializing. Avoid hugging. Avoid sharing meals with others.

This won't be the last time humanity has to deal with a global pandemic or some other event that forces us to separate as a matter of survival. The hope is that, going forward, we will consciously look at how to maintain a sense of social connectedness, even in the face of an infectious disease. Our health and sanity may depend on it.

And while the shared trauma of enduring a global pandemic might retune our nervous systems toward a state of fear and defensiveness, it might also offer the opportunity for real empathy.

We all suffered over the past few years. By recognizing that the pain we felt (and possibly continue to feel) as individuals is shared by just about everybody else, we might be encouraged to be easier on one another, and to understand that everybody is operating on a shorter fuse as of late and that it's more important than ever to be our kindest and safest selves.

Everybody's nervous system may be newly retuned to find danger in this new world, and it's easy to respond to such signals with anger and fear of our own. But we mirror the autonomic states of those around us. And if we respond with our own anger and fear, then that's the signal that gets bounced around the autonomic echo chamber. Love and kindness are never easy, especially during these times. But by putting such feelings into this echo chamber, we're sure to feel them bounce back at us—and at the hurt and angry people out there who might need them the most.

8

The Polyvagal Theory at Work

We've all been there before. Maybe we're on vacation, relaxing by the pool. More likely, we're sitting at home. Perhaps eating dinner with our family, lounging in front of a movie, or doing whatever it is we do to wind down before bed.

Like most days, it was probably a stressful one. There was traffic, a nasty deadline or three, a pushy boss. Maybe a few coworkers were out sick, and you had to carry extra weight to make up for it. Maybe you spent nine hours on your feet—or just as much time planted in a chair, hunched over the bright light of a computer screen.

And just as you feel the stress of the day finally melting away for some semblance of peace, it happens.

Your phone vibrates.

Maybe it will be your boss asking you to burn the midnight oil with no notice. Or maybe it will be just a random piece of spam email that you can easily ignore. Either way, past experiences have conditioned you to expect the worst.

Pavlov's dog slobbered at the sound of a bell. For millions of us, our hearts race at the feeling of a vibration in our pocket.

And before you can even glance at your phone, you already feel that wave of anxiety and dread wash over you. Your body stiffens. Your breath quickens. Your stomach tightens.

And you're reminded, once again, that you can never really turn off from work.

Today, employees are often expected to be either always working or always available for work on short notice. For white-collar workers, this often takes the form of the dreaded after-hours email. For those in the retail or service industries, it can be even worse: There's often an expectation that they will be available to work any shift at any time—often without any notice.

If you don't work in that world, you might be surprised by the reality of many hourly employees. Despite only allowing employees to work *just enough* hours that they are still labeled as part-time (and thus not eligible for benefits such as health care), these employees are often still expected to block out wide swaths of hours and even days for which they may be called in with little or no notice.

When it comes to making plans over the weekend—or even for supper—well, you can just forget about it.

From a lifestyle perspective, this can be catastrophic. If you don't know when you're going to have to show up at work, you can never settle into a routine, or plan around simple necessities such as scheduling childcare or preparing meals. You also can't supplement your technically "part-time" income with another job, since you're always on call, despite not being paid for that time.

This existence is a stressful, and even traumatizing, one. Just like the email from the boss, that call to come into work can come at any time without notice. And when it does, our bodies feel it.

Even when that call doesn't come in, the prospect can hang over our heads like a cloud, preventing us from fully disconnecting or enjoying our supposed time off from work. The constant stress is real and made only worse by financial insecurity.* Put together, the result can be ruinous.

We humans—like other mammals—rely on a semblance of routine to know when we can shut down and recuperate. When we can settle into the healing state of homeostasis. In general, our nervous systems interpret predictability as safe, and the random or unpredictable as potential threats.

---

* Needless to say, the jobs that operate like this tend to be low-wage ones.

Our brains search for patterns that allow us to assess threats and safety, so that we know when to rev up as needed for survival, and when to wind down again to heal. If you want to cause a rat in an experiment to go crazy (or possibly drop dead), all you need to do is make everything random in terms of when and why things happen. When events—especially punishing or attention-sapping ones—occur at random intervals, our brains quickly learn that we *always* need to stay on high alert, and our bodies can never truly shut down or relax.

The Yellow state evolved to help us evade danger for short bursts. When stress, anxiety, and the need to be alert become an always-on way of life, bad things happen to our bodies and brains. Our health suffers. We become quick to anger and stuck in states of aggression and defense. We lose the ability to access the parts of our brain required for free and creative thinking, as well as emotional regulation. We become emotional and reactive, and stop feeling like ourselves.

For employers, the logic of such setups makes sense from a dollars-and-cents perspective: They get the always-on availability of a full-time or salaried employee, without having to pay for health care or other benefits.

But for the employees, the stress of a low-wage existence is only exacerbated by the inability to plan a routine—or to fully rest and recuperate.

Access to the Green state helps counter the intense and resource-draining effects of "being on" and activating the Yellow system. Just about everybody needs to work, but our health demands that we counter that time of activation and alertness with true relaxation. Our bodies crave homeostasis for at least a few hours every day, and require these moments to be able to handle stress and decompress from it without allowing it to fully traumatize us or burn us out.[*]

As long as our brains know that we need to be on the lookout for something—be it a saber-toothed tiger or a call from our boss—we

---

[*] We don't necessarily need to experience safety around the clock, but we do need a few hours every day with trusted co-regulators to allow our nervous system to move out of a state of threat in order to support our homeostatic functions, which are both biological and psychological.

can never truly turn off and enter the Green state for healing. We can never truly attain the feeling of homeostasis that our bodies crave, which allows us to handle bursts of stress without becoming overwhelmed or traumatized.

Of course, many of us already know how bad all this is. We know it because we've lived it, and felt it in our bodies. But as a society, we're told to work through the pain. To keep hustling. That our feelings are frivolous and don't matter.

So for many of us, the Polyvagal Theory doesn't tell us anything we don't already know here. We *get* that never being able to turn off from work is stressful and unhealthy. We *get* that we're increasingly asked to run on empty and that the side effects of this permeate almost every aspect of our well-being and ability to enjoy life.

What the Polyvagal Theory does instead is give us permission to listen to our bodies, and realize that living a life outside the shadow of pervasive stress and anxiety isn't a frivolous perk—but a true biological necessity.

The Polyvagal Theory tells us that this *matters*.

————

In many ways, the modern workplace seems almost scientifically engineered to make us feel unsafe.

The issues here can be approached from either an empathetic and humane perspective (an employee who feels safe will be happier and healthier!) or a pragmatic and cynical one (an employee who feels safe will do better work!).

The Polyvagal Theory posits that, in so many scenarios, making others feel safe benefits us as well.

This is true on a biological level, as friendly and safe behaviors bounce among people and back at us. But it's also true in ways that are easier to quantify, and perhaps more convincing for a society or industry that is largely driven by numbers and data.

If we need to be a bit cynical and focus on the bottom line to make our argument, we'll posit that a worker who feels safe is likely to be more creative, productive, and stick around longer. The modern workplace's tendency to be dismissive of this fact is shortsighted and self-defeating. It is a lose-lose for both employers and employees.

They're Watching Us

If you've called a customer service line in the past few years, the chances are pretty decent that you've been prompted to stay on the line for a quick survey.

You know the deal. A robotic voice asks you something like, "On a scale of one to five, with five being the highest, how satisfied are you with the customer service representative you just spoke to?"

For most of us, the ranking might be a mere afterthought—and something we're unlikely to engage with unless we're in a particularly good or (as is more often the case) particularly bad mood.

But to the employee on the other end of the phone, that rating may very well decide their entire professional fate. We've effectively turned frontline employees into *American Idol* contestants. The number of people who answer that question—and how they vote—often determines whether somebody gets fired or promoted.

The survey becomes a sword of Damocles hanging over the employee's head. And no matter how kind and professional an employee is (never an easy task if the worker themself is having a bad day, as we all do at times), a certain number of callers will still dial in a low rating. And even if the numbers are good today, there's no telling how they'll play out tomorrow. The threat of falling behind never truly goes away.

The modern workplace is obsessed with numbers and metrics aimed at eking every iota of productivity and compliance out of us. In the white-collar world, this often takes the form of spreadsheet-driven performance reviews. We are ranked and pitted against one another. Our bosses and coworkers might be kind, but the charts and algorithms are often cruel.

Even if you excel in this world of Excel—even if your numbers are the *best*—the pressure takes its toll. We're just as good as our latest numbers.* This feeling of pervasive insecurity funnels through the same neural pathways that were devised for quick escapes from predators. We feel stressed and anxious—even when we're not at work. Those feelings don't shut off just because we go home for the night.

And these days, we aren't just constantly measuring employees—we're also keeping tabs on their every move. Whether it's the monitoring of emails or the tracking of truck drivers with GPS, many people spend their workdays feeling like they are being watched at all times.

But this feeling of having eyes over our shoulders is an alarming one. On a primal level, it triggers our survival instincts. When we know we are being watched, we are instinctively activated into a state of alertness—and the Yellow system.

This isn't to say that employers shouldn't monitor employees' performance or keep an eye on them. But they should know that micromanaging these metrics comes with a real price. The need to be alert and on guard at all times takes its toll on us and prevents us from accessing the creative and productivity-boosting powers of the Green system.

We all need an opportunity to disengage and heal. These days, many of us are never afforded that necessity. And if you work in a profession that values creativity or problem-solving, the feeling of constantly being monitored makes it difficult to access the cranial functions that support those behaviors. On paper, these measures may seem like effective ways to get employees to work harder. But in reality, they may cause workers' performance, morale, and ability to handle the stresses of work and daily life to diminish.

Of course, employers often come to this approach from a place of fear. Fear that affording workers any sort of flexibility in their lives will cause them to quit. Fear that, if employees are free of constant monitoring and measuring, they will slack off. Fear that paying a decent wage will give employees freedom and mobility and that they won't do a job that nobody else wants to do.

---

* This reality extends to high-level corporate executives, who are judged by quarterly earnings and a fluctuating stock price.

As a result, many low-wage industries are structured around the anticipation of high turnover. It is expected that an employee will burn out or become frustrated or simply have enough and leave. But no worries if they do—there are plenty of other desperate individuals out there ready to take their place.

This model was put to a stress test during the COVID-19 pandemic and the so-called "Great Resignation." The causes for this are controversial and likely manifold, but it's probably fair to say that widespread burnout finally caught up with people, as millions realized that they could no longer continue to live with a 24-7 high-pressure existence. That almost anything—including unemployment and poverty—was preferable.

As of this writing, many businesses in all sorts of industries are, for the first time in recent memory, having a hard time finding employees.* One solution they might consider to help attract new workers and keep existing ones from leaving: put an effort into making employees feel safe, and give them ample opportunities to rest, recuperate, and reach homeostasis.

They'll be happier, healthier, and almost certain to do better work.

The Commute

Let's talk about commuting for a minute.

Commuting is often *stressful*. But when it comes to this stress, not all commutes are created equal.

Let's take two different types of commutes, each taking roughly the same amount of time.

One person spends an hour driving into a city from the suburbs, navigating gridlock traffic, listening to honking horns, inhaling heaps of exhaust fumes, and evading erratic drivers who may swerve into them at any time.

Another person spends an hour sitting on a train, listening to podcasts, reading a book, playing video games, and possibly even taking a nap.

---

* Considering how the labor market and economic cycles work, we can anticipate this sentence aging poorly for future readers.

On paper, both commutes take up the same amount of time and (for the sake of argument, let's say) cost. But for our nervous systems, these commutes are drastically different.

Sitting in traffic requires constant attention and alertness. It requires executive function and doesn't allow us to turn off for even a second, lest we end up in an accident. It almost definitionally puts us in the Yellow.

Sitting on a train allows us to tune out. It might even offer a rare moment of reprieve and relaxation. Assuming it's not too crowded and chaotic, we may reach the Green state and homeostasis.

Many people opt for long commutes to save money or to live in specific neighborhoods. Often, the calculus is limited to time, money, and real estate realities. An extra hour away from the family. An extra load of gas and some added auto maintenance. A better school district.

But a stressful commute is draining and requires our nervous system to be in a constant state of alertness.

Just as it was for our prehistoric ancestors, who may have been on the lookout for a predator hiding in the brush, sitting in traffic and staying on the lookout for swerving drivers requires us to enter the Yellow zone of alertness and engagement.

To top it off, commutes tend to come just before and just after another extended period of stress: the actual job. We all need moments to disconnect in places of safety. These moments heal us. But jumping from one stressful stretch to the other without any break in between turns what might otherwise be a potentially limited time of stress, buffered by moments of homeostatic recovery in between, into a pervasive high-pressure existence.

The pandemic forced many of us to reevaluate the costs of such commutes. Only after having months (or longer) away from the office did many of us realize just what the act of getting there did to us.

This is likely another cause of the Great Resignation (as well as the widespread desire for many to continue working from home). For many people, shown what life can be like without spending a couple of hours a day in stop-and-go traffic, the thought of returning to that life may simply be too triggering and traumatizing to handle.*

Office Spaces

When you think about a modern office, what comes to mind?

Sure, there are exceptions, but for many office workers, most days are spent planted in a chair and staring at a screen. Unless you're in the C-suite, privacy is often limited to cubicle walls that do nothing to dampen the din of typing, coworker chitchat, and the nearby copy machine. In so-called open offices, even those barriers are an unattainable luxury, as your focus on work competes for attention with every motion and murmur around you. And while not every office is lit by the bright white of long fluorescent-tube lights (which often give off an unavoidable humming sound of their own), plenty are.

Many of the design decisions that go into building such workplaces are utilitarian. Open offices are flexible, predictable, and relatively inexpensive. And why would a bottom-line-focused employer care about such frivolous features as pleasing aesthetics and acoustics?

But the Polyvagal Theory posits that these things *matter*. Our neuroception is constantly scanning the environment for bits of information that tell our nervous system how safe it is—and thus what autonomic state we need to be in. Aesthetic and acoustic features—such as a room's lighting or baseline background noise—are hugely important when it comes to this process.

The same truths here apply to other institutional environments, including schools and prisons, which we will address in later chapters. Creating environments that make us feel safe can result in real shifts to our physiology and health. And for workplaces that might want their employees to be happy, healthy, and productive, this is something that shouldn't be dismissed.

---

* Of course, there's a flipside to this: Working at home in isolation for a couple of years can make people crave the social interactions and routine predictability that may come from an actual office.

The sound of constant chatter funnels through our brains and demands our attention, forcing us out of a state of focus into the alertness of the Yellow zone.

The low-frequency background noise that often emanates from fluorescent lights, ventilation systems, and equipment such as copy machines is interpreted by our neuroception as a sign of danger.

A complete lack of visual privacy forces us into a constant state of high alert.

And spending eight or nine or 10 or more hours per day in such an environment makes it difficult to ever relax and recuperate. To ever reach homeostasis. To ever be the most productive, healthy, and focused worker that we can be. Never mind personal health and happiness.

Employers should understand the unintended consequences of the utilitarian considerations that go into designing the modern office. Making spaces that feel warmer and more welcoming won't be a cure for all the problems that workers face, but it will move the needle. And that's certainly worth something.

And if you're simply stuck in a rotten office environment, noise-canceling headphones can go a long way toward blocking the endless barrage of acoustic stimulation, and can perhaps help make your nervous system feel just a little bit safer.

Water Cooler Moments

The modern worker is often a solitary worker.

Even if we are surrounded by dozens of other workers, many of us spend our days effectively working alone, staring at computers and typing on keyboards. Even when we are brought into meetings, these get-togethers are often closer to lectures than participatory seminars.

But the human nervous system craves social interaction, to the point that it can be viewed as a biological imperative. When we are given the opportunity to be truly social, the wrappers of defense disintegrate in favor of the warm and welcoming Green state. Our brains operate with more clarity and creativity. Time flies by and things feel fun. We become more creative, better able to solve problems, and likely more productive.

Understanding this opens the door for managers to consciously integrate social interaction into the workplace. Small-group dynamics that feel collaborative should be encouraged. Meetings should feel participatory. Small talk by the water cooler or coffee machine should be viewed as a productivity booster—rather than a waste of time.

Our Green state enables social behavior, just as social behavior enables us to enter the Green state. Creating opportunities to tap into this circular, self-reinforcing system will make workers feel safer, more productive, and better buffered against the unavoidable stress of getting through the workday.

Even better if employers can also integrate elements of play into the workday through activities that are both physical and social.

Let's toss out lunchtime games of basketball as an example that I (Seth) experienced at a previous employer. Such activities don't just give people much-needed physical exercise and opportunities to work together as a team, they also help build resilience against stress by tapping into the physiological state of play.

Polyvagal Public Speaking

Years ago, the comedian Jerry Seinfeld famously poked fun at studies that purported to show that people were more terrified of public speaking than of death.

"This means to the average person, if you go to a funeral, you're better off in the casket than doing the eulogy," he joked.

All kidding aside, there's something primal and frightening about standing up in front of others and turning yourself into the center of attention. It's called stage *fright* because it fills our bodies with fear. For many, if not most, of us, the natural response is to instinctively devolve into a state of high anxiety (the Yellow state)—or even complete shutdown (the Red).

Of course, we *know* that shaking, stuttering, or shutting down is only hurting our ability to perform. But like so many other bodily responses, these reflexes are autonomic and automatic. They are completely outside the realm of our conscious control.

But that doesn't mean we're helpless to do anything about them.

I (Seth) have done a lot of TV over the past 15 years, including countless live broadcasts on news and morning shows. Back when I worked as a magazine editor, this was a big part of my job. Whenever there was a big story related to science or technology, I'd hit the airwaves and try to explain things to the public.

The first few times my magazine threw me into a television studio, beginning in roughly 2008, I felt like I was going to throw up. I was so nervous that, for days leading up to a quick two-minute TV spot, I could barely sleep. My heart went into overdrive. The back of my brain began to secretly hope that something, *anything*, would pop up that would result in cancellation. Freak hail storm. Citywide blackout. Breaking news that might bump my segment to another day.

It all felt so high stakes. The in-person audience may have been limited to a few TV hosts and camera operators, but all of the instinctive feelings and fears that come with public speaking were amplified to what felt like a cosmic degree, with the camera seeming to serve as a window to an impossible-to-quantify (but potentially infinitely large) public-speaking arena.

If things went right, perhaps a few thousand people would be tuning in. If things went wrong, my brain and body knew that a clip could go viral and make me look like a fool in front of millions.

Gulp.

And boy did it hurt. Like: physically hurt. I still feel shivers just thinking back to how uncomfortable my body felt.

Still, I somehow managed to smile and grin my way through the ordeal and did well enough that I wasn't banished as a one-and-done TV guest. And the next time I went back, it was just a little bit easier and hurt just a little bit less. The time after that, it was even easier. Until, these days, I can confidently say that talking in front of a camera is sometimes even kind of fun. Practice has smoothed out the frightening edges of a once-scary scenario until it has lost the ability to send my body into a tailspin.

We naturally fear the unknown and unfamiliar. Our nervous systems treat novel scenarios with trepidation. When we are put into unfamiliar environments—particularly ones that carry seemingly high stakes with them—it is only natural for our body's fear response to kick in, and for us to enter the anxiety of the Yellow, or the complete shutdown of the Red.

Maybe there are a few folks who are born into this world with the preternatural ability to control a crowd without fear, but for the vast majority of us, public speaking is something that needs to be practiced and perfected. Not just to get good at it, but also to put our bodies through the sort of immersion therapy that will teach us that we aren't actually in danger, and that we don't actually need to revert to our defensive physiological states.

Problem is, there are vanishingly few low-stakes opportunities to do so. For most people, the only chance to practice public speaking is to actually publicly speak. Never mind slowly dipping our toes into the water—we're expected to dive in headfirst. And if we can't cut it, we may never be given another chance—or we might do anything we can to avoid such a scenario, and all the bodily feelings it inspired, in the future.

People often ask me how I got to be comfortable with public speaking and being on TV. Yes, it took repeated opportunities to put myself out there and get better at doing the real thing, but I'm going to let you all in on a little secret: I *trained* at it in a space of safety and support. I found an environment that has all the external cues of a public-speaking affair, but where failure is viewed as an acceptable outcome with absolutely no consequence. In other words: I found the perfect place to get my nervous system used to standing up on a stage while getting over the negative bodily feelings that doing so inspired.

That training ground: karaoke bars. Best were the kind that forced me to sing on a stage in front of strangers, as opposed to being in a private room with trusted friends.

Am I a good singer? Not even remotely. But while I can't hold a tune, repeatedly jumping on karaoke stages (literally: I've been known to do quite a few jumps when I sing) made me exceedingly comfortable with performing in front of an audience. Nobody at the karaoke bar cares if we mess up. And pretty soon, neither does our brain or body. And when it came time to apply this comfort to standing on a speaking stage or in front of a camera, it translated better than I ever could have imagined.

Polyvagal Peak Performance

"Fear of public speaking makes sense," says Michael Allison, a performance coach who integrates the Polyvagal Theory into his practice. "We put a lot on the line. We want to be accepted, trusted, valued, and stay in a group. This can be a proxy for survival, as being outcast from a group might have once meant likely death."

With clients that include top athletes and executives, Allison has spent a lot of time thinking about how the Polyvagal Theory might apply to our ability to perform in high-pressure scenarios such as public speaking, and he uses it as the basis for an actionable road map for navigating these situations.

The first thing he tells clients to remember is that, beneath our conscious awareness, our physiology is constantly taking stock of the world around us via neuroception, and optimizing survival in one way or another. If we're safe and connected and grounded, our body can push resources toward our health and performance. But if we're overwhelmed, anxious, and feeling mobilized, then these feelings are going to dominate our body. These bodily feelings exist outside our conscious control, effectively relegating us to the passenger seat of our own body, and preventing us from thinking and acting in ways that we can actually control.

The first step to overcoming these feelings is to . . . well . . . *feel* them and acknowledge them. Don't ignore them or simply try to will them away. Understand them for what they are: a body responding instinctively and naturally to wherever it is and whatever is happening to it.

From there, Allison teaches his clients to employ different coping strategies that may be effective at shifting the body's state toward one more conducive to performance in high-pressure situations.

Projecting Safety

When it comes to public speaking in particular, the goal here is simple: Use what we know about neuroception to make our audience feel safe and socially engaged. We mirror the physiological state of those around us. So the best way to do this is to use our body and voice—and any other tools at our disposal—to project the feeling that we ourselves are safe, warm, and engaged. This will make an audience feel the same way.

Specific ways to accomplish this include . . .

Using The Face

Our facial expressions are controlled by an interconnected system of countless tiny muscles that allow us to express feelings and emotions with little more than a look.

This system is key to our ability to safely socialize with others and is deeply tied to the Green state. This is why people who are in the social Green are prone to smile with their mouths, crinkle their eyes, and otherwise visually emote. It's also why those who are scared into the Yellow or Red tend to have a flat facial affect.

These expressions are a key way in which we sense safety in others and then proceed to mirror it in ourselves. People who smile a lot (and with their entire face—not just their mouths) come off as safer, more charming, and more charismatic. If we're sharing a fun chat with friends, these movements are likely to occur naturally. But if we're standing on a stage and paralyzed with fear, they may require more deliberate action—and even practice.

To this end, Allison suggests his clients focus on (and practice) smiling with their entire faces: softening their eyes, gently moving their heads, and otherwise working to consciously manipulate facial muscles so that they can naturally and easily do so when it's showtime.

When others see these muscles engaged, they are likely to sense safety and warmth—and project it back at us.

Search for a Safe Face

Sure, it can be frightening to speak to a large group of strangers. But in small-group interactions, our nervous systems are quite good at locking into feelings of safety and warmth that those close to us might be projecting our way.

Let's use that.

If there's a friendly face in the crowd, Allison suggests focusing on them specifically and acting as if you are speaking only to them. Locking onto them gives us a way to focus a shifty gaze, while also registering the feelings of warmth and safety that they may be projecting our way.

Find a Routine

If you've ever watched an NBA game, you've likely seen a basketball player engage in a seemingly random pre-shot routine while standing at the free throw line.

Gilbert Arenas orbited the ball around his waist three times before every shot.

Steve Nash licked his fingers and then combed them through his hair.

Dirk Nowitzki would hum the David Hasselhoff song "Looking for Freedom" before taking his shot.

These bizarre pre-shot dances have become the stuff of sports legend, and are often pored over by fans for clues as to what the heck it all means. Are they a secret code being sent to a loved one? An uncontrollable tic? A contractual obligation to a sponsor?

The Polyvagal Theory offers a simpler explanation: Routines make us feel safe. In a high-stakes or unfamiliar situation, they give our nervous systems something recognizable and predictable to latch onto—something we've seen or experienced before, and that our bodies know how to handle. By making a novel or pressure-filled scenario just a little bit more familiar, routines help our bodies cool down.

This is why anxious people often rely on strict day-to-day routines to stay cool and collected—and also why NBA players might engage in pre-shot dances at the free-throw line.

Allison teaches his clients to take advantage of this and work out their own movement or posture routines that might dampen the innate unpredictability and pressure of stepping onto a stage or court.

Speak Socially

To humans, a prosodic voice is a safe voice. The Polyvagal Theory informs us that when our voices are melodic, we are broadcasting to others that our physiological state is calm and that we are psychologically and physically accessible to others. This is why speaking with more melodic prosody—rather than a stiff monotone—is probably the single simplest and most impactful way of getting an audience on your side.

The effect is biological and immediate.

Functionally, a prosodic voice acts like a vagal nerve stimulator for both the speaker and the audience, calming the autonomic nervous system into the Green state and tuning it to be primed for social connection. Listening to a melodic voice turns on our Social Engagement System, which activates muscles in the face and head that make it easier for audience members to actually *listen* and process what words are being spoken—while also feeling more emotionally connected to the speaker.

Beyond that, try to infuse talks with conversational and social asides. As a species, we are innately motivated to interact in a reciprocal manner, which is why our nervous systems simply act different when we are engaged on a social level as opposed to through a one-sided lecture.

Take advantage of this by speaking directly to the audience in ways that feel off-the-cuff, informal, and unscripted.

Try infusing talks with quick questions that encourage audience members to lean in, listen, and interact. I (Stephen) also like to pick up cues of connection, interest, and curiosity from the faces in the audience.*

Through these actions, we are enjoying the social nourishment of co-regulation, just as a child experiences the joy of reciprocity while playing with friends. Once there is a sense of reciprocity, large

---

* Needless to say, this made giving talks during the pandemic a grueling ordeal, since the cues of social connectedness are not easily extracted from a Zoom gallery view.

lectures will feel more personal and intimate—and we will feel safer to an unfamiliar audience, who will conversely feel safer to us.

Speak, Don't Read

The most practiced and trained speakers can still come off as stiff when they are reading from a script. Even if you need notes, speaking off-the-cuff for the bulk of a presentation makes the experience feel looser, more surprising, and more social. In the virtual world, where most of my (Stephen's) talks have been during the pandemic, I have tried to encourage conversational interview formats for my talks, which can feel like natural social interaction.

Our nervous system evolved to interpret predictability as a cue of safety. As a result, anything that veers from the predictable instantly pulls in our curiosity and attention. And while such surprises can certainly startle us and activate our defensive states (think: a sudden crash of thunder), they can also be humorous or joyful when we are feeling safe (think: a mother and her infant playing peekaboo in a safe context).

Breath Control

Back on page 49, we talked about how breathing—particularly slow exhalations—signals to the body that we are in a place of safety. Slow and deliberate exhalations effectively activate the vagal brake, slowing down our heart and bringing our entire body into the Green state.

If we're stressed, anxious, or fidgety, this is exactly what we need.

But sometimes, the opposite is called for. Sometimes, we *want* to be revved up and mobilized for action. Think: an athlete looking to squeeze every iota of energy our body has in reserve.

In such situations, the inverse type of breathing is what we need. In these cases, a long inhale followed by a short exhale will increase sympathetic activity, and tap into the Yellow.

Just be careful: This is a powerful technique that, if done improperly or excessively, may result in uncontrollable hyperventilation.

Polyvagal Posture

In 2012, social psychologist Amy Cuddy gave a TED Talk about the supposed power of specific postures when it comes to boosting our confidence and increasing our chances of success.[1]

The talk inspired much debate—and *many* clicks. As of June 2023, it has been viewed more than 68 million times.

While we don't have the real estate here to delve into her specific claims (which have proved controversial among academics, some of whom have struggled to replicate the original studies' results), the Polyvagal Theory *does* offer an explanation for how shifting our posture might impact our feelings and physiology—as well as the feelings and physiology of those around us.

"For many of the athletes I work with, I have them stand tall, open and wide, ventral side up and open, to help their body to feel comfortable, confident, and in control by deliberately bringing their posture into this 'safe' position," Allison says.

From there, he teaches his clients to also focus on their head position and eye gaze to both feel safe and project feelings of safety to others. That means keeping the head up and positioned neutrally with little muscular effort and eyes up and out, looking at the horizon while we soften the muscles around the eyes.

Allison also teaches his clients to pay attention to their own postural changes, and to view these as potential canaries in the coal mine for recognizing when our state might be shifting. A slouch could be a sign that our bodies are feeling unsafe, even if we don't yet consciously realize it.

9

Education

School is where we go to fill our brains with knowledge, skills, and the abilities needed to pick up more knowledge and more skills on our own. It is at school that numbers and letters and facts and histories and methods seep in through the open door of our senses, and implant themselves in a long-lasting way.

Of course, there's more to school than just memorizing numbers and dates. It's also an important training ground for our ability to socialize and work with others. It's where children leave the nest to make friends, resolve conflicts, team up on projects, and engage with peers, teachers, and authority figures in ways that allow for personal development, maturation, and growth.

At least, in theory.

The Polyvagal Theory posits that, for us to successfully learn, critically think, and socialize—that is, to do all the things that we go to school to do—we basically need to be in the Green state of safety. Only then are we physically capable of tapping into the higher brain functions that are required for us to grow, learn, mature, and cooperate.

With that in mind, we can boil the PVT perspective on education and schools down to a simple statement:

For a student to succeed in school, it is imperative that they feel safe. And students who feel chronically unsafe are often up against steep odds.

That's not to say that kids who feel unsafe *can't* succeed in school, just that it will be far more difficult for them to do so.

It's a simple idea, and a logical one if you've been following along. But understanding and prioritizing the concept of safety in school nonetheless forces us to rethink almost every aspect of modern education. It shifts priorities in our model of education from emphasizing the simple learning of facts, to embracing the importance of maintaining a physiology required to access the higher brain structures necessary for critical thinking, creativity, social behavior, and problem-solving.

There's a lot to unpack here, so let's break it down.

What Do We Mean by "Safety" in Schools?

The term "school safety" has been a policy buzz phrase for decades. (After all, who could possibly be against the concept of keeping students safe?)

Unfortunately, much of the effort and attention around school safety tends to focus on superficial and politically expedient measures that may purport to keep kids physically safe, but does so in ways that possibly make them *feel* very unsafe.

We are not arguing that it is not important to actually keep students safe—or litigating whether measures such as metal detectors or a constant police presence are effective at doing so. Rather, we are saying that physically keeping kids safe isn't enough. From a polyvagal perspective, it's important to also make them *feel* safe.

Unfortunately, many of these common security measures that are designed to keep us physically safe also make us *feel* unsafe, and thus come with a very real polyvagal price. They signal to our nervous systems that we need to be afraid and on guard, and not relaxed or focused on learning. They put us into a physiological state of fear and hypervigilance, and transform schools into places that prime our nervous systems to be defensive and aggressive. This can make it harder to learn, cooperate, properly behave, and socialize.

So when we talk about "safety" (in schools or anywhere else) from a polyvagal perspective, we're really talking only about how safe our bodies and nervous systems *feel*—and not how safe we actually are. According to the Polyvagal Theory, that is the key variable that our neuroception uses to shift our physiological state, which consequently transforms our health, happiness, and ability to thrive.

This is important to specify in this chapter on schools, as we can imagine people taking portions of this book (and its underlying science) out of context to push security measures that might purport to keep kids safe, while not acknowledging that being frisked, surveilled, patted down, and surrounded by weapons might also make people *feel* unsafe. The Polyvagal Theory posits that such measures might also impact students' health, happiness, and ability to succeed— while also potentially making them more aggressive or defensive.

Alternatively, focusing solely on this polyvagal definition of "feeling" safe without acknowledging that pragmatic measures sometimes do need to be taken to keep people physically safe is similarly inadequate.

So yes, schools should keep kids safe. That goes without saying. But in an ideal world, they would do this in a way that doesn't also make people *feel* unsafe.

Why Is It So Important for Students to Feel Safe?

Students who don't feel safe at school—or at home, for that matter—enter the classroom with a nervous system locked into the Yellow or Red state of defense.

The Polyvagal Theory suggests that these defensive states interfere with our ability to tap into the higher brain functions required to learn and socialize. As a result, children who deal with feelings of threat are at an immense disadvantage when it comes to succeeding in school.

Often, these students are cited for behavioral issues. After all, if our nervous system is in the Yellow fight-or-flight state—which evolved to help us outrun or outfight an immediate threat—we're almost definitionally locked into a state of adrenaline, alertness, and activation. In which case, good luck sitting still and listening to a teacher.

When our bodies are tuned for defense, our very physiology shifts so that our anatomy—including how our senses, brain, and nervous system function—is optimized for immediate survival. Not only does this state interfere with our ability to properly learn and socialize, it also changes the way we physically hear speech, as our middle-ear structures shift away from the sounds of the human voice to better pick up the ultralow frequencies that our nervous systems associate with predators.[1]

The result is that students who feel unsafe often have a hard time hearing or processing what a teacher is telling them, and are often treated as either stupid or deliberately insubordinate because they aren't picking things up as quickly as the "good" students in the class.

If you were to dig deep into which students end up in remedial classes, it's a safe bet that a large share of them deal with bullying at school, abuse at home, or simply live in unsafe homes or neighborhoods. They may also deal with pervasive environmental or sensory factors that make the nervous system feel unsafe. This could include lead poisoning or severe air pollution. It could also include the constant sound of traffic or sirens interrupting the ability to sleep or to sufficiently reach a state of homeostasis or calm at home.

Teachers and administrators routinely reprimand and punish these students for being unable to sit still and listen, as if it were a conscious decision. But the nervous system and our autonomic state are not dictated by our will, and our bodily state is not compliant with our intentions. And for kids who are locked into a fight-or-flight state of mobilization and defense, it can be nearly impossible to fulfill the role of a focused and well-behaved model student.

These students are not necessarily intellectually challenged or stupid or trying to cause problems. Rather, they may feel perpetually threatened, and are often responding reflexively to this reality in the same way that any of us would, given the circumstances. Understanding this can go a long way toward finding opportunities to break through common educational challenges while treating these students with dignity and compassion.

Bullying

In the previous section, we briefly mentioned bullying, and it should be obvious why.

For students who are forced to spend hours on end in close proximity to somebody who is physically or psychologically tormenting them, it can be difficult to ever truly feel safe. Even low-level bullying can, when applied for extended periods, prove deeply traumatic to children (or adults, for that matter).

When this book's authors came of age, schoolyard bullying usually ended at the schoolyard. But with students now largely living their lives online, cyberbullying can easily become an unending menace, with bullies possessing the nearly nonstop ability to harass or embarrass their victims via social media at any hour of any day.

To live our lives under the shadow of a bully is to live our life feeling threatened. Not only does this harm both our health and our ability to succeed in school, it also, in turn, makes us even more threatening to others and more likely to misbehave.

Our nervous systems are very good at responding to the people and cues around us. So if we are threatened by somebody, we're likely to reflexively respond to their aggressive state by either mirroring this aggression or reacting with hurt and vulnerability. But while the Polyvagal Theory helps explain the real harm that bullying can cause, it also recognizes that this behavior often comes from a place of real pain or trauma.

It perhaps goes without saying that many bullies themselves deal with torment, abuse, or neglect at home and bring these feelings and coping strategies with them to school, where these defensive behaviors and states can spread like a virus.

It is through this that bullying and abuse beget more bullies and abuse, and limit students' ability to succeed in school on both an academic and a social level.

The same thing can happen to students who are subjected to draconian discipline. Many academic traditions emphasize that a student's job is to sit down and shut up. And while corporal punishment in schools may not be as common as it once was, we still see it pop up in the news regularly.

According to the Polyvagal Theory, beating students into submission through harsh discipline is likely to be counterproductive. A scared or threatened student will lose access to the Green state, harming their ability to learn and behave; this results in a cycle as increasingly bad behavior begets ever more discipline—and ever more bad behavior.

Let's Talk About Lunch and Hunger

There are a lot of factors that can cause a student to feel unsafe at school. It can come from an abusive household or bullying at school. It can also come from malnourishment and hunger, which actively spark our body's survival instincts.

In case it isn't obvious, a lot of these triggers are disproportionately tied to being poor. It's often assumed that well-off students do better in school because of the things money can buy: better-funded schools, pricey tutors, well-educated parents who have the time to help with schoolwork.

But perhaps just as important is the fact that malnourishment and economic insecurity simply make people feel unsafe. If a student can't afford breakfast and lunch—or is unsure whether their family will have a roof over their head—one can see why they may be primed to enter and live in a state of survival.

Think about how much more aggressive a dog is when it's been starved. The same thing happens to us humans.

Unfortunately, compassion is hard. As humans, it's not easy for all of us to fully understand what somebody else might be going through. If we've never been truly hungry, it can be almost impossible to understand what this means for our day-to-day existence, and how truly traumatic and exhausting it can be.

So while free breakfast and lunch programs at schools are an effective treatment for malnourishment, there's an unfortunate tendency for states, schools, school districts, and administrators to either cut back on these programs or deliberately and publicly shame kids who take advantage of them.

In 2016, a Birmingham, Alabama, school district began literally stamping "I Need Lunch Money" on the hands of kids who couldn't afford to buy meals.[2] In 2019, Warwick, Rhode Island, made a rule that any student with unpaid lunch debt could be served only a simple sunflower-butter-and-jelly sandwich, as opposed to a hot lunch.[3] Other school districts bar kids who can't pay for lunch from participating in extracurricular activities. In 2019, administrators at a Pennsylvania school district sent out letters threatening to put kids who couldn't afford lunch into foster care.[4]

You don't need to read *The Scarlet Letter* to understand how such public branding can result in shame, bullying, and ostracizing. Shame is a powerful motivator for feelings of threat and defensiveness, and can cause immense and possibly irreparable trauma and harm to innocent kids who are already fighting economic insecurity and hunger. It also further conditions kids to view school as a place of fear and pain, pushing them further and further away from the physiological states that will set them up to succeed and be happy—while also encouraging them to drop out or play hooky to avoid a setting that they might associate with these negative feelings.

School Design

In Chapter 2, we discussed how our nervous systems take cues from the environment around us and process them as signals of either safety or threat. With these cues as a guide, our neuroception then shifts our autonomic state among the Green, Yellow, and Red systems.

It is through our neuroception that the physical environment of a school can radically shift our physiology—and thus our ability to learn.

Many schools are designed to feel like prisons, with few windows and little natural light. Sounds often crash around walls in ways that feel startling and frightening.

I (Stephen) have spent a lot of time in recent years attempting to deconstruct how we can use the principles of the Polyvagal Theory to design spaces that are more conducive to learning. I have even gone so far as to help design a school in Chicago for autistic students who may be particularly sensitive to this sensory experience.[5]

In simple terms, this can be accomplished by paying attention to acoustic properties so as to minimize upsetting background noise, such as the hum that might come from fluorescent-tube lights or the vibrations from elevators and ventilation systems. Rooms should be designed so that they offer real sunlight and feelings of warmth, while limiting visual distractions. In the school for autistic children, the windows were raised to present a view of trees and the sky, but not of traffic and people walking by.

How Can Teachers Help?

The role of education in Western culture has long been focused on rote memorization.

The polyvagal perspective on learning offers another pathway, which emphasizes the behaviors that are innately tied to—and consequently engage and activate—the Green system. That means encouraging socialization, conversation, and group problem-solving.

Treating school like a shared journey of discovery makes it more likely that kids will actually *learn*. After all, when we are actively social and in the Green state, our physiology is primed to absorb and process new information. This approach also recognizes that school is an important training ground for our ability to socialize and work with others.

As kids grow up, they are likely to forget almost every fact and figure they were taught in school. What they won't forget (and what is perhaps the single most useful skill for many future careers): how to work with others to cooperate and solve problems. Not to mention the confidence boost that comes from successfully doing so.

To this end, schools and educators should find ways to mix socialization with learning. And while group seminars and conversational-style classes are ideal for this, we recognize that these formats can be challenging from a purely logistical perspective when one considers shrinking budgets and ballooning classroom sizes.

But if we're going to treat grade school classes like university lectures, it's important to balance such settings with smaller breakout rooms and conversations (which have long been a staple of large-scale college lectures for this very reason). These conversations should be held in spaces that feel warm and inviting, are not overwhelming from a sensory perspective, and do not trigger the nervous system to enter a state of threat or self-protection.

School as an Autonomic Exercise

Proponents of art and music education frequently tout the idea that students who take these classes are likely to do better in other subjects, such as math.[6]

But why is this? How can drawing pictures or playing music possibly impact our ability to succeed at algebra?

The Polyvagal Theory offers an explanation.

Performing or listening to music in a group setting is a potent vagal exercise. Singing or blowing into an instrument activates the vagus nerve, and primes us to enter the Green state. The same can be said for art, which might act as a neural exercise that forces us to engage the processes associated with the Green state.

Once in the Green state, almost any type of learning should come easier for us. Students are also likely to be more cooperative and better behaved.

Recess

Speaking of seemingly frivolous activities, the past few decades have seen schools increasingly cut recess or play periods. But just like music and art, recess plays an important role when it comes to students' ability to learn and succeed.

In Chapter 2, we talked about the concept of "play" as a vagal exercise that tunes and tones our ability to seamlessly shift between the Green and Yellow states. This is immensely important for building resilience and allowing us to get through hard times without getting stuck in defensive states.

The Polyvagal Theory further defines play as a social activity.

So while solitary activities certainly have their place, team sports and group games are a far more effective vagal exercise.

Schools should be supportive of these activities, as should parents who might fail to see the value in team sports. Your kid may not be likely to make it to the NBA, but their well-tuned nervous system could make it easier for them to listen and learn in class, and also offer increased autonomic resilience for their future.

10

Incarceration

We live in an incarcerated society. According to the Bureau of Prison Statistics, as of the end of 2020, more than 5.5 million people were in prison or jail, or on probation or parole.*

Our chances of incarceration are greatly increased if we are a racial minority. Black men are roughly six times more likely than white men to be incarcerated, and Latino men roughly 2.5 times more likely.[1] Roughly one in every 12 Black men in their 30s is in prison or jail on any given day.[2]

For millions and millions of Americans (not to mention their friends and family), life in prison is a harsh and unavoidable reality.

And harsh it is. Those who call prison home must adapt to a pervasive threat of violence, an almost total lack of privacy, limited contact with loved ones who might help them co-regulate, and a physical environment filled with unwanted and alarming stimulation, alerts, lights, and sound. And that's not even addressing the torturous effects of solitary confinement.

This is not a subject I (Stephen) come to abstractly. I have seen it firsthand. During the summer of 1967, in between my first and second years as a graduate student, I worked as a prison guard.

While there, I witnessed the aftermath of prisoners who had endured sexual assault. I watched as a revolving door as inmates

---

* That number is actually an 11% drop from the previous year, partially due to the COVID-19 pandemic leading some prisons and jails to reduce their populations.

would be released, then show back up again weeks or months later, often returning to welcoming cheers. I saw the life and hope squeezed out of people, and saw peaceful prisoners take on aggressive and sometimes violent postures as a matter of survival.

We're not here to argue the many, many debates about criminal justice in the modern era. However, the Polyvagal Theory makes it clear that our current approach to incarceration isn't just harmful to prisoners' health in ways that may not be obvious; it's also likely counterproductive when it comes to dissuading crime and violence.

It should also be stated that our goals in this section here are not political but, rather, informative. Incarceration is a fact of life and an inescapable part of the fabric of our society. But if we're going to subject millions of people to it, it behooves us to understand the inconvenient truths and consequences when it comes to prisoners' health, trauma, and ability to possibly reenter society as productive and nonviolent citizens.

Often, we *want* prisons to have a positive effect on those incarcerated and society at large. The Polyvagal Theory forces us to look at what it actually does to them and to us.

From a biological perspective, incarcerated individuals are people. That might sound like a silly thing to say, but when the airwaves are filled with rhetoric describing criminals as monsters, it's an important distinction to be made. They share the same autonomic nervous system and neuroception system as the rest of us. The same things that make us feel safe or afraid also make them feel safe or afraid. And when they feel safe or afraid, their bodies and brains respond and transform in ways that are familiar to all of us.

With the Polyvagal Theory as our guide, we can thus understand just how the prison experience might transform or traumatize somebody, impacting their ability to downshift away from a state of aggression and to hopefully someday reenter the world as a peaceful member of society.

Prison is an unsafe place. This is true in a literal sense, with violence a potentially commonplace occurrence, depending on where somebody is incarcerated. But it's also true in a polyvagal sense. For our nervous systems, the prison environment simply *feels* unsafe.

Looking back at my experiences, I'm reminded of the communal sleeping and showering arrangements that deprived prisoners of the smallest modicum of privacy or personal time—and thus the ability for the nervous system to rest and recuperate and reach homeostasis for even a minute.*

I think about how anything and everything could be turned into a weapon and used without warning. A sock filled with a bar of soap was a particularly popular way to beat somebody without leaving many marks.

Prisoners spend their days—and often years—surrounded by signs and signals that are, often rationally, interpreted by their neuroception and nervous system as cues of danger. Life is full of similar signals, and many of us are lucky enough to experience them for only brief bursts before returning to a place of perceived safety. But when one spends years living in a state of prolonged fear and pervasive danger, as is almost definitional for inmates, the defensive Yellow and Red physiological states become the baseline. We become quick to anger and impulse, minor social infractions are treated as triggers for violence, and we effectively lose access to the critical brain structures and anatomical features required to handle problems socially and diplomatically.

If you wanted to engineer an environment that made people more aggressive and violent, you'd be hard-pressed to find a more suitable space than a modern prison: a place of constant fear and threat, without any opportunity for the nervous system to recover back to a state of homeostasis in a place of safety and privacy. To live like this is to effectively be locked into the defensive Yellow and Red states, and cut off from the ability to access the Green.

If you want to take an emphatic view of that scenario, it means that prisoners (who are people, no matter what crime they were convicted of) will see their mental and physical health suffer in astonishing ways. If you want to take a selfish or societal view, it

---

* The sleeping arrangements at my location were not typical cells, but wide-open dormitory-style rooms filled with beds.

means that these prisoners will inevitably become more aggressive and violent and probably more likely to commit more crimes—an outcome that no rational person could want.

To view the modern prison system through the lens of the Polyvagal Theory is to see a deeply broken institution that, at best, is ineffective at dissuading crime and, at worst, perpetuates and serves as a factory for the antisocial and violent behaviors it is purportedly designed to deter.

Once again, we're going to break this chapter down into bite-sized sections so we can address some of the issues at play here. What follows might come off as a bleeding-heart screed that fails to understand the harsh realities of dealing with dangerous criminals. That couldn't be further from the truth.

Again: I (Stephen) worked at a prison. I saw this firsthand. The Polyvagal Theory acknowledges the inconvenient (and perhaps not politically expedient) truth that all humans—including felons—respond to and are transformed by their environments.

To put it simply: When we are in chronically unsafe spaces, we respond with aggression and potentially violence. Likewise, when we feel safe, we are better able to socialize, handle problems peacefully, and access the higher brain functions that are required for rational and thought-through behavior.

A lot of "tough on crime" rhetoric treats prisoners as inhuman, as if extending them the smallest bit of well-being, kindness, or safety will somehow encourage them to commit more crimes. This is a mistake not only from a moral perspective but also from a practical one. If we don't acknowledge that prisoners respond to their environments in the same way all humans do, we are apt to make fatal errors in how we treat them that will likely turn them into even greater threats.

Once again, let's go back to dogs as an example. Hitting a dog as a form of punishment might make it momentarily meek, but will certainly make it far more likely to bite back in the long term. The same can be said about the way we treat criminals.

The modern punitive approach to criminal justice largely stems from the idea that the prison experience should be so unbearably harsh that potential criminals will think twice about committing crimes. This viewpoint is a myopic one and fails to understand that many aggressive and criminal behaviors are driven not by rational thinking but by a nervous system locked into a state of defense and fear. The prison population is also disproportionately filled with graduates of the foster care system or individuals who have suffered childhood abuse.

Perhaps some criminal acts are fully thought through by people who are capable of rationally evaluating the potential risk and reward, but many more likely come from an instinct-driven nervous system that is locked into a defensive or aggressive state. They may also be driven by drugs or mental illness that further conspire to make the nervous system feel threatened, while limiting access to the higher brain functions required to fully think through our actions.* Many other prisoners are also likely incarcerated despite not actually having committed crimes, or because they could not afford the robust legal defense that often keeps well-heeled convicts from doing hard time.

It should be a shared aim of everybody—criminals, their families, and a society that craves peace and order—to get violent criminals out of a biobehavioral state that supports aggression. Our current approach to prison often serves only to calcify it.

As a society, our goals with the modern prison system are largely punitive. We have mostly given up on the idea that prison can rehabilitate somebody, and that there might be a pathway toward real reintegration into society. Instead, we've done almost everything we can to close those doors—even after people leave prison. The Scarlet F of being a felon can make it incredibly difficult to get a job or find a place to live. This financial or housing insecurity can further feed a nervous system stuck in a defensive place of fear.

This is not to suggest that crime be forgiven or tolerated. But, with the Polyvagal Theory as our guide, there are real paths toward

---

* If we had to guess, the criminals that are more likely to have come to their crimes through a rational approach are white-collar or financial criminals, who also tend to have shorter and easier times in prison than the prison population as a whole.

treating prisoners in a way that might offer them the chance to reha-bilitate and reenter society—rather than reoffend and recidivate.

An Autonomic Echo Chamber

As humans, we mirror the autonomic state of those around us. When we are around people that feel and project safety, our neu-roception clocks into this sense of safety, and likewise allows us to feel and project safety to others.

This creates a sort of pinball effect, where a contagious sense of warmth and safety bounces among people who are in close prox-imity to one another.

But the opposite is true as well. Feelings of fear and danger—and the consequent reorientation of our bodies into a state of defense—are just as contagious.

Prisons are full of people who have a history of committing vio-lent or transgressive acts, and who are then placed into a closed-off environment populated with others who may have the same.

And that environment? It simply feels unsafe—even without the presence of countless prisoners radiating their own threatened autonomic states.

Tight quarters, unwelcoming architectural and aesthetic fea-tures, and constant sounds of alert and alarm are interpreted by our neuroception as signals of danger. In the case of people who live in prisons, those signals can be a 24-7 presence. There might simply be no relief, and no ability to ever enter the healing state of homeostasis that our body craves.

These factors conspire to turn prison into an autonomic echo chamber, where a feeling of pervasive danger bounces among inmates[*] and reorients nervous systems into a state of defensiveness and further violence. These feelings are then funneled back into the environment in an endless feedback loop, further exacerbating the problem.

---

[*] And guards.

THE POLYVAGAL THEORY AND CONSENT

In March of 2022, *The New York Times* published an op-ed[3] criticiz-ing a proposed change to the Model Penal Code (a standard criminal code that states use to create their own specific laws) when it comes to determining what constitutes rape.

The proposed change, which was written by the American Law Institute, basically says that inaction can be interpreted as consent. So if somebody doesn't actively fight back, they are not actually being assaulted—legally speaking.

This definition ignores the science and the realities of human behavior.

In 2015 I (Stephen) was an author on a paper in the journal *Biofeed-back* entitled "When Not Saying NO Does Not Mean Yes: Psychophys-iological Factors Involved in Date Rape." In this paper we described how the nervous system may immobilize in response to a threat, and that a lack of response is not the equivalent of giving consent.[4]

Once again: Just because somebody didn't fight back doesn't mean they weren't assaulted. When our nervous systems sense pro-found danger, we often respond by freezing, shutting down, and dissociating. This response is not voluntary, but autonomic (again: meaning automatic).

Simply understanding this will allow us to write laws that reflect how we as humans actually respond to traumatic scenarios, rather than how we imagine we would respond if we were in the victims' shoes. It will also allow us to respond to certain crimes in ways that don't unnecessarily retraumatize victims—or force them to question their own experiences.

Co-Regulation and Conjugal Visits

As humans, we rely on the physical presence—and physical contact—of loved ones to co-regulate and downshift our autonomic state to the Green. Prisoners are deprived of this, and instead are forced to share tight quarters with others who may make them feel very unsafe.

Prisons often have very strict rules governing visitors and contact with the outside world. Phone calls are often limited to short conversations, and visitation often occurs in chaotic and loud rooms shared with countless other prisoners and visitors. So while prisoners may receive rare glimpses of loved ones, they are seldom given the chance to truly co-regulate with them—or to socialize with anybody who is not going through a similarly stressful living experience.

And then there's the question of conjugal visits. Despite movies perhaps convincing us otherwise, conjugal visits are increasingly rare. As recently as the early 1990s, 17 states allowed for them. As of 2022, that number had dwindled to just four (California, Connecticut, New York, and Washington). They are also banned in federal prisons.

The reason for the disappearance of conjugal visits is largely a political one: Allowing intimacy with a loved one might seem like a reward, when prison is designed to be a punishment.

But the Polyvagal Theory suggests that co-regulation with loved ones—including intimate co-regulation—is a biological imperative. It is not a frivolous reward, but a crucial part of our ability to handle stress and downshift our nervous system away from a state of defense and aggression.

To be blunt about it: Sexual activity, on a biological level, calms a defensive nervous system. To go back to dogs, you don't want to mess with one who is in heat.

We are sympathetic to the political reality that something like conjugal visits might seem like a reward for dangerous criminals, and that nobody in power wants to come off as soft on crime. But this approach ignores the way our nervous system works on a neurophysiological level, and is likely to make dangerous criminals only more dangerous—just as it would to anybody else.

The Polyvagal Theory suggests that allowing more contact with the outside world, as well as more (and more intimate) contact with loved ones, will make prisoners better able to survive the stresses of prison without them resorting to or being stuck in a state of defensiveness and aggression.

The Green system can be viewed as a use-it-or-lose-it muscle that needs to be exercised. To help with this, visits should occur in warm and welcoming environments that are free of excess noise and crowds. Prisoners should be given the opportunity to be physically present with people they love. And even if visits are not conjugal, they should feel private and intimate.

This isn't about rewarding criminals—it's about giving them the basic ability to regulate their own physiology and behavior.

Lastly, we acknowledge that, while visits from loved ones may help prisoners co-regulate, they aren't always an option or a common occurrence. This is why it's important for prison employees and authorities to understand how they can make prisoners feel safe, and perhaps allow them some semblance of co-regulation.

This can be done by emphasizing one-on-one, or at least small-group, interactions with prisoners. Talking to prisoners in ways that feel empathetic and like the employee is listening will calm the prisoners' autonomic nervous systems away from a state of defense. It's also important to give prisoners opportunities to separate from larger-group dynamics. This isn't just about privacy but about stepping away from a culture that might require one to be aggressive or defensive to survive or fit in.

Another way to allow prisoners to co-regulate might involve animals. A 2019 study published in the *Prison Journal* showed that a Washington State pilot program that brought dog training to prisons helped with prisoner empathy, self-efficacy, and anxiety.[5] Anybody who has ever leaned on a furry friend for comfort will understand why.

Solitary Confinement

Back in Chapter 5, we talked about how humans are wired for social interaction. It is a biological imperative, and something (like food and water) that we *need* to survive and stay healthy and sane.

This brings us to the topic of solitary confinement: a harsh measure that is often used in prisons and jails.

A 2015 study commissioned by the Bureau of Justice Statistics found that roughly 20% of federal inmates had spent time in "restrictive housing," including solitary confinement. And while some prisoners endure it for only a few days, others are kept in solitary for months, years, or even decades. The same study found that roughly 10% of prison inmates spent 30 days or longer in such conditions over a one-year period.[6]

Solitary confinement isn't just about putting a misbehaving prisoner in time-out. From a polyvagal perspective, solitary confinement is an almost immeasurably cruel experience. If one wanted to empirically prove that humans need contact with other humans to survive, and that co-regulation is a true biological imperative, they need only look at what happens to prisoners in solitary. Cut off from other people, prisoners who endure it regularly report hallucinations, mental breakdowns, uncontrollable rages, dissociation, an increased chance of attempting suicide, and severe PTSD.

In a study with prairie voles that I (Stephen) coauthored, we found that social isolation had a profound impact on vagal regulation, resulting in exaggerated heart-rate reactions to other prairie voles and behavioral features of severe anxiety and poor behavioral regulation.[7] Interestingly, the administration of oxytocin, which normally is released through intimate relationships, protected against the negative behavioral and autonomic consequences of isolation.[8]

As humans, we too rely on the presence of others to co-regulate. Our very biology and social structure are based around interacting and mingling with others.

Cut off from others for even brief periods, our brains and bodies wither and flail. Our ability to think rationally or to peacefully handle conflicts disappears.

But let's say you simply don't care about the health and well-being of a prisoner. Perhaps you view them as a murderer or monster that does not deserve our sympathy.

Even if you subscribe to such a crass worldview, our shared goal should be to make people—particularly prisoners—less violent and less monstrous.

According to the Polyvagal Theory, solitary confinement will have the opposite effect. As with many counterproductive measures in modern prisons, the increased use of solitary confinement often stems from a political desire to come off as tough on crime.

In truth, it likely only makes the problems worse. As a punitive measure against misbehaving prisoners, it is almost guaranteed to make them misbehave even more.

> *"Well, maybe they'll think more about the*
> *consequences before they commit a crime."*

Once again: They simply can't. Solitary confinement shuts people out of the Green state of sociability, and keeps them from accessing the neural pathways required for such rational analysis. Solitary confinement turns us into instinct-driven animals who are simply incapable of evaluating the risks and rewards of our actions.

Perhaps there are situations in which isolating a prisoner is necessary for their safety or the safety of other prisoners or guards. However, the increasingly common use of solitary confinement as a form of punishment is cruel, counterproductive, and, from a polyvagal perspective, incredibly difficult to justify.

Art and Theater in Prison

Back in 2002, the radio show *This American Life* produced an episode about a group of prisoners in Missouri who staged a production of *Hamlet.*[*]

The episode largely focused on the emotional and performance layers that come from having actual killers play literary ones. But from a polyvagal perspective, it's difficult to not think about what engaging with the arts does to a prisoner's nervous system.

In the prior chapter on schools, we discussed how art classes might help make students better at math. The likely reason: Engaging in the arts effectively exercises the Green system (which, again, can be thought of as a use-it-or-lose-it muscle), and makes it easier for students to tap into its higher brain processes. This is likely to make them better at critical thinking, and better able to absorb information in almost any other subject.

---

* "Act V" (Episode no. 218) aired August 9, 2002. https://www.thisamericanlife .org/218/act-v

And while the Green system primes us to think and learn, it also makes it possible for us to socialize and handle problems peacefully and diplomatically. When we are in the Green, we are better able to handle stress without losing control or acting violently. And just as arts programs in school might help students learn, it is likely they can help prisoners act peacefully.

For prisons and prisoners alike, that seems like a win.

And while almost any form of art might be effective in this regard, theater may be a particularly powerful pathway. That's because theater is social and, in many ways, a real form of play (the final product is even called a play). The act of play allows us to exercise our ability to slide between the Green and Yellow systems without getting stuck in either. This is perhaps why many forms of therapy involve acting and role-playing: Play serves as an autonomic exercise and helps us build resilience.

Theater also involves the deliberate and strategic modulation of both our voice and facial muscles. To act is to manipulate one's facial expressions and control the tenor and prosody of the voice. The cranial nerves and muscle systems required to control these features are reliant on accessing the Green system. To act is, quite literally, to practice the use of the Social Engagement System, which might make it easier to access when we really need it.

The Polyvagal-Informed Prison

Understanding what's *wrong* with modern prisons, the next logical question is: How can we possibly design them to be better?

What would a polyvagal-informed prison look like?

In many ways, the same principles that can be used to inform the designs of spaces such as schools, clinics, and hospitals also apply here. The goal should be to design environments that facilitate the nervous system's ability to feel safe and access the Green state.

That means paying attention to the sensory environment. The architecture of institutional environments such as prisons tends to be utilitarian and focus on surveillance and cleanliness. In a polyvagal-informed space, the architecture also focuses on how the setting makes us feel. And the goal should be to make people—even felons—feel safe.

A lot of this can be accomplished through acoustics. Institutional environments that amplify low-frequency rumbling, ambient sounds from heavy machinery such as ventilation systems, or high-pitched screams make our neuroception and nervous systems feel unsafe. Finding ways to dampen these sounds might give inmates' nervous systems the ability to cool off, rather than forcing them into a constant state of alert. Such fixes are not going to solve every problem with prisons, but they are relatively low-hanging fruit that might help to a surprising degree.

And then there's the issue of prison privacy. We understand that there are real practical and safety reasons why prisoners are afforded little privacy. However, it's important to acknowledge that this comes at a real price. On a biological level, we require safe and private places to eat, digest, and sleep—bodily functions that are tied to the Green system on an anatomical level.

Without feelings of safety and privacy, our bodies never truly turn off their defensive states. Instead, our nervous system and bodily systems need to always be "on" and scanning their environment for signs of threats. This is exhausting, unhealthy, and makes us more likely to act aggressively and without thinking.

The primary role of the autonomic nervous system is to funnel resources to the proper bodily systems. When we feel safe, our body turns on anatomical systems that allow it to be social and physically heal. When we feel threatened, we activate into a defensive or aggressive mode. Our bodies are physically incapable of doing both at the same time.

Understanding this as a binary neural decision where somebody who feels safe is likely to act socially and calmly, while somebody who feels threatened is likely to act impulsively and aggressively, forces us to reevaluate just about every aspect of how we treat prisoners.

All this is a long-winded way of saying that if our goal is to curb violence and crime, it's likely that making prisoners feel safe might actually help the rest of us stay safe as well.

Epilogue: The Polyvagal Life

Few days pass when I (Stephen) don't receive at least a few messages from people looking to share their own polyvagal stories.

These messages come from clinicians and trauma survivors. From architects and recovering addicts. From elementary school teachers and yoga teachers. From prisoners and pastors.

Needless to say, it has been a surprising and humbling experience to see my ideas adopted by a wide range of people, across a wide range of disciplines.

It has also been an illuminating one.

It is one thing to propose an idea. It is something else altogether to see how people might apply it to their own lives and experiences. Through this dialogue, I continue to grow my own understanding of the Polyvagal Theory and how it might offer explanation, acknowledgment, and hope to the realities of living in this challenging and often unpredictable world.

To that end, the last few chapters of this book have offered a polyvagal perspective on real-world scenarios and institutions such as schools and the workplace. While we hope you find these chapters helpful, we're going to be honest here: The real goal of them has nothing to do with those specific use cases.

Instead, we hope that outlining the polyvagal perspective on a few specific scenarios might trigger the pattern-recognition part of the human brain so that readers might draw their own connections and conclusions about how these principles might apply to their own experiences and lives.

Despite the neuroanatomy and evolutionary history involved with fully explaining the Polyvagal Theory (thank you for bearing with all that, by the way), its core idea is a simple one that we summed up in a single sentence on the very first page of this book:

> *"How safe we feel is crucial to our physical*
> *and mental health and happiness."*

This is a text about the transformative power of feeling safe. With that understanding comes a very simple call to action:

> *"What can we do to make ourselves,*
> *and other people, feel safe?"*

Answering that question is at the heart of what it means to live a polyvagal-informed life.

To that end, we'll finish this book with a short list of principles that we see as embedded in the Polyvagal Theory, and that might offer us all a blueprint for living a happier, healthier, more sublime life—no matter our personal circumstances or experiences.

We explore all of these ideas elsewhere in this book in greater detail, so view this as your end-of-text cheat sheet. A CliffsNotes guide that you can turn back to anytime you need a polyvagal refresher course.

- When we feel safe, our bodies transform in a way that optimizes us for social connectedness, health, growth, and restoration. This is the healing state of homeostasis.

- When we feel unsafe, threatened, or dysregulated, our bodies respond by activating defensive systems that optimize us for immediate survival—at the cost of our ability to heal, grow, and restore.

- When we feel unsafe, threatened, or dysregulated, our bodies will instinctively do whatever it takes to end these feelings.

- When we are deprived of opportunities to feel safe, our mental and physical health suffers, as do many aspects of the human experience.

- In the modern world, many people are almost entirely deprived of opportunities to feel safe. This manifests as anxiety, trauma, stress, unchecked emotions, and poor health.

- Whether we feel safe or unsafe, our bodies telegraph these feelings to those around us—including our children.

- We often mirror the feelings and states of those around us. Likewise, those around us mirror whatever feelings and states we project into this "autonomic echo chamber."

- Our autonomic state and how we feel are intervening variables that bias and change our behavior, sensory experiences, and ability to be happy and healthy.

- Through our neuroception, the sensory environment we are in—including acoustics and aesthetics—can be a powerful tool for shifting our autonomic state, how we feel, and how our body operates.

- Neuroception is an automatic process driven by external cues of threat and safety, and is outside our conscious control. However, we can be informed by our reactions to it, and use our knowledge about what makes us feel safe or unsafe to navigate the world around us.

- Trauma is not just psychological. It is also physiological and can cause real changes in the body.

- All of us have different innate levels of resilience. The same event may prove deeply traumatic for one person, while barely impacting another.

- Many mental and physical health diagnoses can be characterized by a nervous system that is biased toward feeling unsafe.

- Many people assume that we always respond to threats by running or fighting. In truth, when our bodies feel threatened, we sometimes respond by freezing, dissociating, or shutting down. This response is autonomic (meaning automatic), and outside our conscious control.

- Feeling safe is necessary for living a good life and bonding with others.

- Feeling safe can support therapeutic interventions in both mental and physical health by putting the body into a state that is primed for healing.

- Feeling safe can support our ability to learn, relax, rehabilitate, and be productive. This can inform how we design institutions such as schools, hospitals, clinics, drug-treatment centers, work environments, and prisons.

- When we feel threatened, we have a difficult time transmitting feelings of safety to others.

- When other people come off as threatening to us, it is often because they themselves do not feel safe.

- We often respond to threatening others in ways that only make them feel more threatened and more likely to lash out at us in return.

- In order to feel safe, and express safety to others, our bodies need to downregulate our defensive systems.

- Our bodies downregulate these defensive systems to enter a state of safety by using the vagus nerve, which acts as a neural brake.

- The vagus plugs into the part of the brainstem that controls social behaviors such as vocalizations, facial expressions, and our ability to listen to speech. As a result, we can only fully access some social behaviors when we feel safe.

- Safe social behavior effectively acts as a trigger for our vagus, calming us down and downregulating our defensive systems.

- Our bodies use co-regulation through social behavior and bonding with others to downregulate our defensive systems to allow the body to feel safe and heal.

- This need for social behavior is baked into our evolutionary history and DNA, and helps us understand virtually every aspect of our society and culture.

- In the absence of healthy relationships or opportunities to co-regulate, we seek other ways to downregulate our defensive systems. This often takes the form of addictive substances and behaviors.

- When people don't feel safe, they can't access the higher brain functions required for critical thinking. This offers an explanation for why politicians and media figures often try to make people feel unsafe.

- The act of "play" can be viewed as a neural exercise that allows us to recruit our mobilizing defense systems, without becoming aggressive or getting stuck in them.

- By mixing social behaviors and play into activities such as work and school, we can better access the higher brain functions that allow us to be creative, productive, and happy.

In short: Let's all try to be safe to each other—and to ourselves.

Acknowledgments

Stephen Porges:

Almost 30 years ago, the Polyvagal Theory (PVT) emerged from my research. The theory was initially presented during my presidential address to the Society for Psychophysiological Research on October 8, 1994, in Atlanta, Georgia. At that time, I was unaware that the theory would be embraced by clinicians and applied in areas outside of academic science, including education, business, and medicine. I had conceptualized the theory as a structure for testable hypotheses within the research community. Consistent with my initial expectations, the theory has had a transdisciplinary impact in science and has been cited in thousands of peer-reviewed publications representing several disciplines. However, the main impact of the theory has been to provide plausible neurophysiological explanations for personal bodily experiences, especially those described by individuals who have experienced trauma. For these individuals, the theory provided an understanding of how their bodies have involuntarily and adaptively been retuned in response to life threat, often losing the resilience to return to a state of safety.

The theory has led me on a personal journey of exploration of the core human need to connect and trust. I have learned that sociality literally nourishes our nervous system and serves as, perhaps, the most potent and relevant "neuromodulator" to calm our nervous systems so as to optimize and support the homeostatic functions of health, growth, and restoration. This journey has shifted from a path of discovery through experimentation to a journey of witnessing the voices of others, especially those whose nervous systems have been retuned through adverse experiences. Thus, the implications of Polyvagal Theory in mental health, education, and society would not have emerged without witnessing those who have shared their experiences with me. They have shared how Polyvagal Theory provided them with a manageable framework to understand, without judgment, the heroic reactions of their nervous systems in their quest for safety and survival. I gratefully acknowledge those individuals and especially the power of their personal narratives of recovery. They have taught me that, although behavior and physiological state can be driven by foundational brainstem mechanisms, understanding PVT has enabled their conscious and intentional higher brain circuits to make meaning of their experiences.

My experiences with survivors of adversity have emphasized the important role of communicating features of Polyvagal Theory. Their feedback to me suggests that, for many, knowledge of Polyvagal Theory has been a pivotal transformative moment leading to self-understanding. Perhaps Polyvagal Theory may provide the psychoeducational elements for humanity to become more accessible to the two domains of co-regulation: 1) bidirectional brain–body communication; and 2) bidirectional biobehavioral co-regulation. These two domains form the basis of both health and sociality. This leads us to communication, the primary focus and justification for this book.

As a scientist, my communication skills have been tailored over decades to write in the objective and frequently dense language of science. This works well when the target audience is limited to scientists within one's own discipline. It becomes more difficult when the research is transdisciplinary and traverses discipline boundaries, which characterizes Polyvagal Theory. I have tried to translate the scientific lexicon associated with Polyvagal Theory to the clinical and applied world. It is a difficult task and highlights contradictory goals of building a strong scientific basis and translating the science into a language that can be easily understood and applied by others (e.g., mental health providers, medical health providers, educators, business managers, etc.) who are not scientists. This book is our response to that task, and acknowledges my son Seth's gifts in communication through the written and spoken word. Seth is a remarkably talented writer and thinker. As he has demonstrated in this book, Seth has the rare ability to extract the essence of complex concepts in an easily accessible language. Working with Seth has provided me with an opportunity to witness my son's brilliance in translating Polyvagal Theory into an accessible language. As Seth's proud father, I am in awe by his understanding of Polyvagal Theory and am curious about how he became so fluent in the theory.

Polyvagal Theory did not evolve or expand without the help and commitment of several people who have played important roles in helping me translate my ideas into a coherent theory. Unlike many of my colleagues, who treat and study trauma, trauma was not a focus of my research or part of my theoretical agenda. Without traumatologists being interested in Polyvagal Theory, there would not have been an entrée for the theory to contribute to the treatment of trauma. This entrée was due to three pioneers in traumatology: Peter Levine, Bessel van der Kolk, and Pat Ogden. I graciously acknowledge their influence on my work and their generosity in welcoming me on their journey to understand and rehabilitate the disruptive effects of trauma. It was through their passion to help their clients, their commitment to learn, and their curiosity to understand the processes involved in experiencing and recovering from trauma that they embraced insights from Polyvagal Theory into their treatment models.

Foremost, I want to acknowledge my wife and Seth's, mother, Sue Carter. For decades she has listened to, witnessed, and shared ideas that were to become the Polyvagal Theory. Sue's landmark work, discovering the role of oxytocin in social bonds, and her general interest in the neurobiology of social behavior served to focus my thinking on the role the autonomic nervous system and physiological state played in not only health, but also in social behavior. Without Sue's enduring support, love, and intellectual curiosity, Polyvagal Theory would not have evolved. Moreover, Sue's loving, maternal support in nurturing Seth contributed to his personal brilliance, while allowing me to be a "good enough" father.

I am sincerely grateful to Sue's contribution. This book is truly a product of this support and love.

As the reader can surmise, the Porges home has been an intellectual incubator for the neuroscience of sociality, especially focusing on the autonomic nervous system and the neuropeptides of oxytocin and vasopressin. Within this culture there is another Porges: Eric. Eric is Seth's brother. Eric elected to follow within the "family business" and is a neuroscientist at the University of Florida. Not surprisingly, he conducts research on vagal stimulation with a focus on how it may reduce PTSD symptoms. In fact, Eric and his colleagues have developed (and patented) an innovative noninvasive vagal nerve stimulator that targets vagal afferents in the ear and uses the body's own shifts in vagal regulation of the heart to control stimulation. Thus, we would like to acknowledge the welcoming and accessible intellectual culture of exploration and curiosity that has enabled our entire family to find meaning in our paths of inquiry.

A special thanks to Deborah Malmud, our editor at Norton. Deborah enthusiastically welcomed the idea of *Our Polyvagal World*. She worked with us to transform our manuscript into a vehicle for the Polyvagal Theory. We are pleased to add our book to the expanding polyvagal bookshelf at Norton.

Seth Porges:

Early in this book, we write that—once you strip away the neuroanatomy and complex terminology—the Polyvagal Theory is, at its core, a worldview. It is a lens through which we can explain our own lived experiences, and understand the experiences of others.

As a way of seeing the world, it is a perspective marked by a sense of optimism and hope. One that presents love and social behavior and simply taking care of ourselves and those around us as a pathway out of a tortured and divided world. One that gives us permission to have fun and play with friends and pets. One that recognizes that we are all connected, and that we ignore this innate truth about ourselves at our own peril. One that values the sense of safety and co-regulation that comes from the folks who we love and who love us and make us feel safe.

All this is my way of saying that, whatever sense of catharsis and pride must accompany the publication of any author's book, the fact that I was able to do this with my father immediately multiples that by a million.

So, first and foremost, I want to thank Dr. Porges. He gifted me with not just life, but with a good life. I cannot imagine I ever will be as proud of anything in my professional life as I am of this collaboration.

This may be a unique, collaborative text in that it wasn't born from set interviews or interactions between the authors, but rather from years of dinner conversation osmosis. Dr. Porges—or "Dad," as I call him—is the type of person who we are all playing catch-up with. My honest hope is that this book stands as a monument to a loving father and a brilliant thinker.

Further thanks must also go to the rest of my immediate family (Sue, Elsa, Eric, Jenny, Minna), and also my extended family of friends, colleagues, collaborators, and co-conspirators. If this book only reflected the lived experiences of its authors, it would be both boring and useless. To the many individuals who have been willing to share their own pasts, pains, and joys, I just want to say: It is your lived experiences that have served as the puzzle pieces that made this book possible.

Thank you.

Glossary

Note: This glossary is designed for readers who may want more technical or scientific information about the topics at hand. As such, it might use more technical language than is found elsewhere in the book.

Appeasement. Based on survivor experiences and Polyvagal Theory, appeasement is offered as a replacement for the term "Stockholm syndrome." Stockholm syndrome has been frequently used to describe the appearance of trauma survivors' developing emotional attachments to their abusers. In contrast, appeasement, when operationally defined through the Polyvagal Theory, explains how survivors may appear to be emotionally connected with their perpetrators to effectively adapt to life-threatening situations by calming the perpetrator. Use of the term "appeasement" demystifies the reported survivor experiences and provides a science-based explanation for narratives of survival that may initially appear to be contradictory. By understanding the potent reflexive neurobiological survival mechanisms embedded in appeasement, individuals and families can approach their survival from a perspective that supports resilience and a healthy long-term recovery that normalizes their coping responses as survival techniques (see Bailey et al., 2023).

Attachment. Attachment is a psychological construct reflecting a strong emotional bond between two individuals, such as the relationship between a mother and her child. Polyvagal Theory focuses on the features of safety manifested in the Social Engagement System that facilitate co-regulation and enable attachment to occur. Prosodic voices, positive facial expressions, and welcoming gestures trigger, through neuroception, feelings of safety and trust that spontaneously emerge when the Social Engagement System is activated. Functionally, feeling safe via the Social Engagement System is a prerequisite for attachment.

Autonomic afferent nerves. Autonomic afferent nerves are neural pathways that send information from the visceral organs to the central nervous system (i.e., brain and spinal cord). They are also called sensory fibers, because they send signals from organs informing brainstem regulatory structures of the status of the organs. The afferent nerves in the autonomic nervous system, many of which travel through the afferent branch of the vagus, function as a surveillance system in which the brain is continuously monitoring the status of visceral organs.

Autonomic balance. Autonomic balance is a construct that represents the balance between the sympathetic and parasympathetic branches of the autonomic nervous system. Although several organs receive innervation from both branches of the autonomic nervous system, autonomic balance assumes a linear additive model in which both branches have similar magnitudes of influence. For example, since the sympathetic nervous system increases heart rate and the parasympathetic nervous system decreases heart rate through the vagus (the major neural component of the parasympathetic nervous system), a high heart rate would be interpreted as a manifestation of an autonomic balance biased toward sympathetic excitation. In contrast, a slow heart rate would be interpreted as a bias toward parasympathetic excitation.

Although "autonomic balance" is a frequently used term, it is often used to indicate dysfunction in the autonomic nervous system (e.g., atypical autonomic balance). From a polyvagal perspective, a focus on autonomic balance obfuscates the importance of the phylogenetically ordered response hierarchy of how the autonomic nervous system reacts to challenges. According to Polyvagal Theory, when the Social Engagement System with the myelinated ventral vagal pathways is engaged, a unique autonomic state emerges that supports an optimal autonomic balance in the regulation of subdiaphragmatic organs. This optimal autonomic balance to subdiaphragmatic organs, via sympathetic and unmyelinated dorsal vagal pathways, is the emergent product of the activation of the ventral vagal pathways.

Autonomic efferent nerves. Autonomic efferent nerves are neural pathways that send information from the central nervous system (i.e., brain and spinal cord) to visceral organs. They are also called motor fibers, because they send signals to organs instructing them to respond. The efferent nerves in the autonomic nervous system travel primarily through the vagus and the spinal sympathetic nervous system and function to adjust (calm or activate) specific visceral organs.

Autonomic nervous system. The autonomic nervous system is a component of the peripheral nervous system that regulates involuntary physiological processes, including heart rate, blood pressure, respiration, digestion, and sexual arousal. It contains three anatomically distinct divisions: sympathetic, parasympathetic, and enteric.

Autonomic state. Within Polyvagal Theory, autonomic state and physiological state are interchangeable constructs. Polyvagal Theory describes three primary circuits that provide neural regulation of autonomic state. These are ventral vagal, dorsal vagal, and sympathetic pathways. Autonomic state reflects activation of these pathways. In general, there is a focus on each circuit providing the primary neural regulation for a specific state. This would result in the ventral vagal circuit supporting social-engagement behaviors, the sympathetic nervous system supporting mobilized defensive (fight/flight) behaviors, and the dorsal vagal circuit supporting immobilized defensive behaviors. However, autonomic state can support mobilization and immobilization behaviors that are not defensive when coupled with activation of the ventral vagal circuit and the Social Engagement System (see *Autonomic balance*, above). Thus, by coupling the Social Engagement System with the sympathetic nervous system there is an opportunity to mobilize without moving into defense. This is observed in play, in which the aggressive effects of movements are contained by social-engagement behaviors. Similarly, when the Social Engagement System is coupled with the dorsal vagal circuit, cues of safety (e.g., prosodic voice, facial expression) enable immobilization to occur without recruiting defense (e.g., shutdown, behavioral collapse, dissociation). This is observed during intimacy and in trusting relationships. Thus, through the coupling of social engagement with mobilization and immobilization, the three autonomic circuits support five states associated with different classes of behavior: social engagement, fight/flight, play, shutdown, and intimacy. Additional hybrid states that simultaneously mix autonomic states have been used to describe freeze, fawn, and appease.

Biological imperative. Biological imperatives are the needs of living organisms required to perpetuate their existence. This list frequently includes survival, territorialism, fitness, and reproduction. Polyvagal Theory emphasizes that the need to connect with others is a primary biological imperative for humans. The theory emphasizes that, through connectedness, physiology is co-regulated to optimize mental and physical health. The theory focuses on the role that the Social Engagement System plays in initiating and maintaining connectedness and co-regulation.

Connectedness. Polyvagal Theory refers to social connectedness and trusting relationships as a biological imperative. Humans can also feel connected to their pets, which are usually other mammals with reciprocal Social Engagement Systems.

Co-regulation. Within Polyvagal Theory, co-regulation involves the mutual regulation of physiological state among individuals. For example, within the mother–infant dyad, not only is the mother calming her infant, but the infant's response of relaxing and calming to the mother's vocalizations, facial expressions, and gestures has the reciprocal effect of calming the mother. If the mother is unsuccessful in calming her infant, the mother's physiological state also becomes dysregulated. Co-regulation can also extend to groups, such as families. For example, following the death of a family member, the presence of others may support the biobehavioral state of the grieving person.

Cranial nerves. Cranial nerves emerge directly from the brain, in contrast to spinal nerves, which emerge from segments of the spinal cord. Cranial nerves are functionally conduits that, in general, contain both motor and sensory pathways. Humans have 12 pairs of cranial nerves (I–XII). They are the olfactory nerve (I), optic nerve (II), oculomotor nerve (III), trochlear nerve (IV), trigeminal nerve (V), abducens nerve (VI), facial nerve (VII), vestibulocochlear nerve (VIII), glossopharyngeal nerve (IX), vagus nerve (X), accessory nerve (XI), and hypoglossal nerve (XII). Other than the vagus, which provides pathways for both sensory and motor communication with several visceral organs, cranial nerves primarily relay information to and from regions of the head and neck.

Death feigning/shutdown. In mammals under certain conditions, the nervous system reverts to a primitive defense response characterized by appearing to be inanimate. This defense pattern is frequently observed in vertebrates, such as reptiles and amphibians, that evolved prior to the phylogenetic emergence of mammals. However, mammals are great consumers of oxygen and the immobilization required in feigning death is associated with a decrease in the capacity to oxygenate the blood and an inability to deliver sufficient oxygenated blood to the brain to support consciousness. This massive depression of autonomic function is due to activation of the dorsal vagal circuit, which depresses respiration (apnea) and slows heart rate (bradycardia). Polyvagal Theory proposes that death feigning is an adaptive response to life threat when options for fight/flight behaviors are minimized, such as during restraint or when there is an inability to escape. During conditions of life threat, the nervous system through neuroception may revert to the ancient immobilization defense system. Polyvagal Theory emphasizes aspects of this life-threat response in understanding trauma reactions. The theory functionally operationalizes a trauma response as the body's physiological response to life threat that would include features of death feigning such as fainting (vasovagal syncope), defecation, and dissociation.

Dissociation. Dissociation is a process of losing a sense of presence resulting in experiencing a disconnection and a lack of continuity between thoughts, memories, surroundings, and actions. For many people, dissociation is within the range of normal psychological experiences and is manifested as daydreaming. For some people, dissociation is sufficiently disruptive that it results in a loss of personal identity and creates severe difficulties in relationships and in functioning in everyday life. Trauma history is frequently associated with the severe disruptive effects of dissociation and may result in a psychiatric diagnosis. Polyvagal Theory interprets dissociation in response to life threat as a component of an immobilization or death-feigning defense response. Polyvagal Theory interprets dissociation as an adaptive reaction to life-threat challenges that, unlike the effects of a prolonged death-feigning response, would not compromise the neurobiological needs for oxygen and blood flow. Based on Polyvagal Theory, one could speculate that there may be gradations in reactions to life threat, from total shutdown and collapse, mimicking the death-feigning responses of small mammals, to an immobilization of the body during which muscles lose tension and the mind dissociates from the physical event.

Dissolution. Dissolution is a construct introduced by the philosopher Herbert Spencer (1820–1903) to describe evolution in reverse. It was adapted by John Hughlings Jackson (1835–1911) to describe how brain damage and brain disease function similarly to a process of "de-evolution," in which evolutionarily older circuits become disinhibited. Polyvagal Theory adapts dissolution to explain the phylogenetically ordered hierarchy in which the autonomic nervous system responds to threats with progressively evolutionarily older circuits.

Dorsal vagal complex. The dorsal vagal complex is located in the brainstem and consists primarily of two nuclei: the dorsal motor nucleus of the vagus and the nucleus of the solitary tract. This area integrates and coordinates sensory information from visceral organs via sensory pathways in the vagus that terminate in the nucleus of the solitary tract with the motor outflow originating in the dorsal motor nucleus of the vagus that terminate on visceral organs. Both the nucleus of the solitary tract and the dorsal motor nucleus of the vagus have a viscerotropic organization in which specific areas of each nucleus are associated with specific visceral organs. The motor pathways from this nucleus provide the unmyelinated vagal pathways that travel through the vagus and primarily terminate in subdiaphragmatic organs. Note that a few of the unmyelinated vagal pathways may also terminate on supradiaphragmatic organs such as the heart and bronchi. This is the likely mechanism for bradycardia in preterm infants and is potentially related to asthma. The vagal pathways originating in the dorsal motor nucleus of the vagus have been referred to in various publications as the dorsal vagus, the subdiaphragmatic vagus, the unmyelinated vagus, and the vegetative vagus.

Efferent nerves. Efferent nerves are the neural pathways that send information from the central nervous system (i.e., brain and spinal cord) to a target organ. They are also called motor fibers, because they send signals to organs that influence how the organs function.

Enteric nervous system. The enteric nervous system consists of a mesh-like system of neurons that governs the function of the gastro-intestinal system. The enteric nervous system is embedded in the lining of the gastrointestinal system, beginning in the esophagus and extending down to the anus. The enteric nervous system is capable of autonomous functions, although it receives considerable innervation from the autonomic nervous system. Polyvagal Theory assumes that optimal functioning of the enteric nervous system is dependent on the dorsal vagal circuit not being recruited in defense. That occurs when the ventral vagal circuit is activated.

Fight/flight defense system. Fight and flight behaviors are the predominant mobilized defense behaviors of mammals. Activation of the sympathetic nervous system is necessary to support the metabolic demands required to flee or fight. Withdrawal of the ventral vagal circuit and a dampening of the integrated Social Engagement System facilitate efficient and effective activation of the sympathetic nervous system in supporting the metabolic demands for fight and flight behaviors.

Heart-rate variability. Heart-rate variability (HRV) reflects the variation in the time between heartbeats. A healthy heart does not beat with a constant rate. Only a heart without neural innervation would beat at a relatively constant rate. Much of the variability in heart rate is determined by vagal influences, especially through the myelinated ventral vagus, which is manifested in respiratory sinus arrhythmia (RSA). Other contributions to HRV may come through the dorsal vagus. Blocking vagal influences to the heart with the drug atropine will remove virtually all HRV.

Homeostasis. Homeostasis reflects the neural and neurochemical processes through which our body regulates visceral organs to optimize health, growth, and restoration. Although the word is derived from the Greek word meaning "same" or "steady," homeostasis is better understood as the product of a negative-feedback system that oscillates around a "set" point. In some physiological systems, the greater amplitude of the oscillations (i.e., rhythmic deviations from the set point) is a positive indicator of health (e.g., respiratory sinus arrhythmia). In other situations, it is a negative indicator of health (e.g., blood pressure variability). Oscillations in physiological systems are primarily a reflection of neural and neurochemical feedback mechanisms.

Interoception. Interoception is the process that describes both conscious feelings and unconscious monitoring of bodily processes by the nervous system. Interoception, similarly to other sensory systems, has four components: (1) sensors located in internal organs to evaluate internal conditions, (2) sensory pathways conveying information from the organs to the brain, (3) brain structures to interpret sensory information and regulate the organs' response to the changing internal conditions, and (4) motor pathways that communicate information from the brain to the organs and consequently change the state of the organs. In Polyvagal Theory, interoception is the process that provides the signal to the brain of changes in physiological state (see Porges, 1993). In contexts in which there are cues of risk or safety, interoception would follow the process of neuroception. Interoception may result in a conscious awareness of a bodily response. In contrast, neuroception occurs outside conscious awareness.

Intervening variable. Polyvagal Theory positions autonomic state as an intervening variable mediating stimulus–response relationship.

Thus, the nervous system's interpretation of contextual cues shapes our reactions. Within this conceptualization, depending on the individual's autonomic state, the same contextual cues and challenges may result in different behavioral, cognitive, and physiological reactions. By placing autonomic state as the intervening variable in an S–R or cause-and-effect world, pragmatic survival behaviors of fight and flight or shutdown, as well as complex problem-solving strategies that would lead to escape, are consequential and dependent on the facilitatory function of the ANS in optimizing these strategies. Similarly, turning off threat reactions and calming autonomic state, via the ventral cardioinhibitory vagal pathway, will promote interpersonal accessibility, while simultaneously supporting the co-regulation of autonomic state.

Middle-ear muscles. The two smallest striated muscles in the body, the tensor tympani and the stapedius, are located in the middle ear. The middle ear is the portion of the auditory system between the eardrum and the cochlea (inner ear). Middle-ear structures include the ossicles and the muscles regulating the stiffness of the ossicle chain. When these muscles are tense, they stiffen the ossicle chain and increase the tension of the eardrum. This process changes the characteristics of sound that reaches the inner ear. The inner ear transduces sound into a neural code that is transmitted to the brain. The tensing of the middle-ear muscles reduces the influence of low-frequency sounds and functionally improves the ability to process the human voice.

Middle-ear transfer function. As middle-ear muscle tone changes, there is a change in the transfer of acoustic energy through the middle-ear structures to the inner ear. Borg and Counter (1989) described a role of the middle-ear muscles in facilitating the extraction of human speech by dampening the transmission of low-frequency noise from the external environment to the inner ear. The Borg and Counter model explains why auditory hypersensitivity is a symptom of Bell's palsy, a condition characterized by a lateralized paralysis of the facial nerve including the pathway regulating the stapedius muscle in the middle ear. Borg and Counter (1989) provide a scientific basis to investigate whether improvements in auditory processing would occur if neural regulation of the middle-ear muscles were rehabilitated through the exercises embedded in the Safe and Sound Protocol. The extrapolation from normalizing the middle-ear transfer function to improved vagal regulation of the heart is based on the theoretical model elaborated in Porges and Lewis (2010) and linked to the Social Engagement System described in the Polyvagal Theory (Kolacz et al., 2018; Porges, 2011).

Neural exercise. Polyvagal Theory focuses on specific neural exercises that provide opportunities to exercise the regulation of physiological state. According to the theory, neural exercises consisting of transitory disruptions and repairs of physiological state through social interactions would promote greater resilience. Play such as peekaboo is an example of a neural exercise that parents frequently employ with their children.

Neural expectancy. Within Polyvagal Theory, neural expectancy refers to the predisposition wired into our nervous system that anticipates a reciprocal response to a spontaneous social-engagement behavior. Neural expectancies promote social interactions, bonding, and trust. When neural expectancies are met, calm states are supported. Violations of these expectancies may trigger physiological states of defense.

Neuroception. Neuroception is the process through which the nervous system evaluates risk without requiring awareness. This automatic process involves brain areas that evaluate cues of safety, danger, and life threat. Once these are detected via neuroception, physiological state automatically shifts to optimize survival. Although we are usually not aware of the cues that trigger neuroception, we tend to be aware of the physiological shift (i.e., interoception). Sometimes we experience this shift as feelings in our gut or heart or as an intuition that the context is dangerous. Alternatively, this system also triggers physiological states that support trust, social-engagement behaviors, and the building of strong relationships. Neuroception is not always accurate. Faulty neuroception might detect risk when there is no risk or identify cues of safety when there is actually a risk.

Nucleus ambiguus. The nucleus ambiguus is the source nucleus of the motor fibers of the ventral vagus. It is located in the brainstem ventral to the dorsal motor nucleus of the vagus. Cells in the nucleus ambiguus contain motor neurons associated with three cranial nerves (glossopharyngeal, vagus, and accessory), which control striated muscles of pharynx, larynx, upper portion of the esophagus, and neck through somatomotor pathways and the bronchi and heart through myelinated ventral vagal pathways.

Nucleus of the solitary tract. The nucleus of the solitary tract is located in the brainstem and serves as the primary sensory nucleus of the vagus.

Ontogeny. Ontogeny is the study of the origination and development of an organism throughout the entire life span.

Parasympathetic nervous system. The parasympathetic nervous system is one of the two main divisions of the autonomic nervous system. The primary neural pathways of this system are vagal and support health, growth, and restoration. However, Polyvagal Theory emphasizes that, under certain life-threatening conditions, specific vagal pathways that would normally support homeostasis and health can respond defensively and inhibit health-related functions.

Phylogenetically ordered hierarchy. Polyvagal Theory proposes that the components of the autonomic nervous system react to challenges following a hierarchy in which the phylogenetically newer circuits react first. This pattern of evolution in reverse is consistent with the Jacksonian principle of dissolution (see above). Functionally, the order of reactivity proceeds through the following sequence: myelinated ventral vagus, sympathetic nervous system, unmyelinated dorsal vagus.

Phylogeny. Phylogeny is the science that describes the evolutionary history of a species. As a science, it provides evolution-based methods for taxonomic grouping of organisms. Within Polyvagal Theory, there is an interest in the phylogenetic transitions in autonomic function among vertebrates, with a focus on the transition from primitive extinct reptiles to mammals.

Physiological state. See *Autonomic state.*

Prosody. Prosody is the intonation in voice that conveys emotion. Polyvagal Theory emphasizes that prosody is mediated by vagal mechanisms and, similar to heart-rate variability (i.e., respiratory sinus arrhythmia), it conveys information about physiological state.

Respiratory sinus arrhythmia. Respiratory sinus arrhythmia (RSA) is characterized by rhythmic increases and decreases in heart rate occurring at the frequency of spontaneous breathing. The amplitude of this periodic heart-rate process is a valid index of the influence of the ventral vagus on the heart.

Safety. Polyvagal Theory proposes a neurophysiological model of safety and trust. The model emphasizes that safety is defined by feeling safe and not by the removal of threat. Functionally, feeling safe is determined by the visceral organs projecting information to the brain that it is supporting homeostatic functions. Feeling safe is dependent on three conditions: (1) the autonomic nervous system cannot be in a state that supports defense; (2) the Social Engagement System needs to be activated to downregulate sympathetic activation and functionally contain the sympathetic nervous system and the dorsal vagal circuit within an optimal range (homeostasis) that would support health, growth, and restoration; and (3) to detect cues of safety (e.g., prosodic vocalizations, positive facial expressions and gestures) via neuroception. In everyday situations, the cues of safety may initiate the sequence by triggering the Social Engagement System via the process of neuroception, which will contain autonomic state within a homeostatic range and restrict the ANS from reacting in defense (Porges, 2022). This constrained range of autonomic state has been referred to as the "window of tolerance" (see Ogden et al., 2006; Siegel, 1999) and can be expanded through neural exercises embedded in therapy. A recent scale evaluating the neuroception of psychological safety has been developed that psychometrically measures safety along three dimensions: social engagement, compassion, and body sensations (Morton et al., 2022).

Safety in therapeutic settings. From a polyvagal perspective, feeling safe is an important mediator influencing the effectiveness of most therapeutic manipulations, including medical procedures, psychotherapy, and psychoeducation. The theory assumes that physiological (autonomic) state functions as an intervening variable influencing the effectiveness of treatment. More specifically, the theory assumes that for a treatment to be effective and efficient it is necessary to keep the autonomic nervous system out of states of defense. Engagement of the Social Engagement System with its ventral vagal pathways ensures that the autonomic nervous system supports health, growth, and restoration and is not easily recruited in defense. Note that this principle of "feeling safe" as the precursor of treatment is not currently well integrated into educational, medical, and mental health treatment models. In addition, the physical environments in which therapy is delivered are seldom vetted for cues (e.g., low-frequency background sounds, street noises, ventilation-system sounds, vibrations from elevators and escalators) that would trigger, via neuroception, defensive states of the autonomic nervous system, which would interfere with the effectiveness of the treatment.

Self-regulation. "Self-regulation" is a term frequently used to describe an individual's ability to regulate their own behavior without the aid of another person. Self-regulation is often a defining feature of a child's ability to deal in the classroom or in a novel situation. Polyvagal Theory does not treat self-regulation as a learned skill but interprets self-regulation skills as a product of the nervous system that can maintain feelings of safety in the absence of receiving cues of safety from another person. The theory emphasizes that, through the processes of co-regulation, an individual develops a capacity to self-regulate. The theory emphasizes that the mutual, synchronous, and reciprocal interactions among individuals that define co-regulation function as a neural exercise enhancing the ability to self-regulate in the absence of opportunities to co-regulate.

Social Engagement System. The Social Engagement System is the two-way system by which the muscles and movements of our face and head allow us to express and receive signals of safety during social interactions. It consists of a somatomotor component and a visceromotor component. The somatomotor component involves special visceral efferent pathways that regulate the striated muscles of the face and head. The visceromotor component involves the myelinated supradiaphragmatic vagus that regulates the heart and bronchi. Functionally, the Social Engagement System emerges from a heart–face connection that coordinates the heart with the muscles of the face and head. The initial function of the system is to coordinate sucking, swallowing, breathing, and vocalizing. Atypical coordination of this system early in life is an indicator of subsequent difficulties in social behavior and emotional regulation.

Somatomotor. Somatomotor pathways are motor pathways regulating striated muscle. The pathways regulating the striated muscles of the face and head travel through cranial nerves, and those regulating the muscles of the limbs and trunk travel through spinal nerves.

Special visceral efferent pathways. Special visceral efferent fibers originate from motor nuclei in the brainstem (ambiguus, facial, and trigeminal) that develop from the branchiomotor column (i.e., ancient gill arches) of the embryo and innervate striated muscle fibers (muscles of mastication involved in ingestion, facial musculature involved in emotional expression, muscles of the pharynx and larynx involved in vocalizations, and muscles of the middle ear involved in listening) associated with the pharyngeal arches. Special visceral efferent pathways compose the somatomotor component of the Social Engagement System.

Stimulus–response versus stimulus–organism–response models. Research is generally conducted within the framework of a mechanistic stimulus–response (S–R) model. This model is basically used to test historic cause-and-effect hypotheses. In the S–R model, response variance is assumed to be determined by stimulus variance. If the stimulus produces variations in response, the traditional experimental design treats the variations as experimental "error." In contrast, Polyvagal Theory emphasizes the mediating (i.e., intervening variable) influence of the state of the autonomic nervous system at the time of experimental manipulation on the qualities of the response. Polyvagal-informed research assumes that responses are not solely the product of the stimulus but also in terms of the state or condition (e.g., autonomic state) of the organism prior to the stimulus. The research would be formulated within the framework of a stimulus–organism–response (S–O–R) model. Thus, the changing characteristics of the organism might index the reliability of the stimulus producing a response or predict the response features.

Subdiaphragmatic vagus. The subdiaphragmatic vagus is the branch of the vagus that connects brainstem areas with organs located below the diaphragm. The motor fibers in this branch of the vagus originate primarily in the dorsal nucleus of the vagus. These motor fibers are predominantly unmyelinated.

Supradiaphragmatic vagus. The supradiaphragmatic vagus is the branch of the vagus that connects brainstem areas with organs located above the diaphragm. The motor fibers in this branch of the vagus originate primarily in the nucleus ambiguus, which is the source nucleus in the brainstem for the ventral vagus. These motor fibers are predominantly myelinated.

Sympathetic nervous system. The sympathetic nervous system is one of the two main divisions of the autonomic nervous system. The sympathetic nervous system functions to increase blood flow throughout the body to support movement. Polyvagal Theory focuses on the role of the sympathetic nervous system in increasing cardiac output to support movement and fight/flight behaviors.

Vagal afferents. Approximately 80% of the neural fibers in the vagus are afferent (sensory). Most vagal sensory fibers travel from the internal organs to an area of the brainstem known as the nucleus of the solitary tract. Of note, medical training provides a very limited understanding of vagal afferents. Thus, medical treatments seldom acknowledge possible influences due to feedback from the treated organ to the brain.

Changing sensory feedback has the potential to influence mental and physical health (e.g., vagal nerve stimulation).

Vagal brake. The vagal brake reflects the inhibitory influence of vagal pathways on the heart, which slow the intrinsic rate of the heart's pacemaker. If the vagus no longer influences the heart, heart rate spontaneously increases without any change in sympathetic excitation. The intrinsic heart rate of young healthy adults is about 90 beats per minute. However, baseline heart rate is noticeably slower due to the influence of the vagus functioning as a "vagal brake." The vagal brake represents the actions of engaging and disengaging the vagal influences on the heart's pacemaker. It has been assumed that the vagal brake is mediated through the myelinated vagal fibers originating in the ventral vagus. Although the unmyelinated vagal fibers appear to mediate clinical bradycardia in preterm neonates, this process has not been conceptualized in the vagal brake construct. Thus, discussing clinical bradycardia as a product of a vagal brake should be clarified by emphasizing that it is through a vagal mechanism different from the protective ventral vagal influence.

Vagal paradox. Vagal influences to visceral organs have been assumed to be protective. However, vagal influences can be lethal by stopping the heart or disruptive by triggering fainting or defecation. These responses, often linked to fear, are mediated by the vagus. The vagal paradox was initially observed in research with preterm infants in which respiratory sinus arrhythmia was protective and bradycardia was potentially lethal. This created a paradox, since both respiratory sinus arrhythmia and bradycardia were mediated by vagal mechanisms. The contradiction was solved by the introduction of the Polyvagal Theory, which linked these responses to different vagal pathways.

Vagal tone. The construct of vagal tone is usually associated with the more tonic influence of the myelinated ventral vagal pathways on the heart and is frequently indexed by the amplitude of respiratory sinus arrhythmia.

Vagus. The vagus is the 10th cranial nerve (CN X). The vagus is the primary nerve in the parasympathetic division of the autonomic nervous system. The vagus functions as a conduit containing motor pathways originating in the nucleus ambiguus and the dorsal motor nucleus of the vagus and sensory fibers terminating in the nucleus of the solitary tract. The vagus connects brainstem areas with structures throughout the body, including the neck, thorax, and abdomen. Polyvagal Theory emphasizes the phylogenetic changes in the autonomic nervous system in vertebrates and focuses on the unique change in the vagal motor pathways that occurred with the emergence of mammals.

Vegetative vagus. See *Dorsal vagal complex*.

Ventral vagal complex. The ventral vagal complex is an area of the brainstem involved in the regulation of the heart, the bronchi, and the striated muscles of the face and head. Specifically, this complex consists of the nucleus ambiguus and the nuclei of the trigeminal and facial nerves regulating the heart and bronchi through visceromotor pathways and the muscles of mastication, middle ear, face, larynx, pharynx, and neck through special visceral efferent pathways.

Visceromotor. Visceromotor nerves are motor nerves within the autonomic nervous system that originate in the brainstem and regulate smooth and cardiac muscles and glands.

Psychiatric Diagnoses Through the Lens of the Polyvagal Theory: Examples

Anxiety disorders. Anxiety is frequently defined from a psychological (emotional feelings of fear or uneasiness) or psychiatric (e.g., anxiety disorders) perspective. Polyvagal Theory emphasizes the autonomic state that underlies the psychological feelings that define anxiety. Polyvagal Theory assumes that anxiety is dependent on an autonomic state characterized by concurrent activation of the sympathetic nervous system with a downregulation of the "ventral" vagal circuit and the Social Engagement System. Basically, anxiety is our brain's interpretation of our autonomic nervous system being in a state of threat, and anxiety disorders occur when our autonomic nervous system is locked in a state of threat. These points are elaborated in an accessible article that I (Stephen) authored, published in *Psychology Today*.[1]

Autism. Autism spectrum disorder (ASD) is a complex psychiatric diagnosis that includes communication problems and difficulties relating to people. Polyvagal Theory focuses on the observation that a diagnosis of ASD involves features that reflect a depressed Social Engagement System. Thus, many individuals with ASD have voices without prosody, have auditory hypersensitivities, have auditory processing difficulties, do not make good eye contact, have flat facial expressivity especially in the upper part of their faces, and have severe behavioral-state-regulation difficulties that are frequently manifested in tantrums. Polyvagal Theory is not focused on the antecedent cause of these problems, but takes an optimistic perspective and assumes that many of the features of the depressed Social Engagement System observed in ASD are state-dependent and may be reversed through an understanding of how the nervous system, via neuroception, responds to cues of safety. Intervention strategies based on the Polyvagal Theory emphasize reengagement of the Social Engagement System. Polyvagal Theory does not make any assumptions regarding features in ASD other than a depressed Social Engagement System.

Borderline personality disorder. Borderline personality disorder (BPD) is a psychiatric diagnosis including features of mood instability and difficulties in regulating emotion. From a polyvagal perspective, the regulation of mood and emotion involves the neural regulation of the autonomic nervous system. Thus, the theory would lead to hypotheses that BPD would be associated with a challenged Social Engagement System and especially the efficiency of ventral vagal pathways in downregulating sympathetic activation. This hypothesis has been tested and supported (Austin et al., 2007).

Depression. Depression is a common and serious mood disorder that influences feelings, thoughts, and behavior. Polyvagal Theory assumes that clinical states of depression have a physiological profile that would be explained by the Polyvagal Theory as "depressed" sympathetic activity and enhanced dorsal vagal activation in the absence of sufficient ventral vagal activation. Hypothetically, the profile would include a downregulation of the Social Engagement System and atypical coordination between sympathetic and dorsal vagal pathways. The latter point may lead to behavior oscillating between high levels of motor activity coincident with sympathetic activation and lethargy coincident with depressed sympathetic activity and increased dorsal vagal activity.

Post-traumatic stress disorder (PTSD). PTSD is a psychiatric diagnosis reflecting the consequences of experiencing a traumatic event such as sexual assault, severe injury, war, earthquake, hurricane, or bad accident. Polyvagal Theory focuses on the response to the event and not the qualities of the event. This focus on the response is consistent with the observation that there are great variations in individual reactions to a common "traumatic" event. A common "traumatic" event may be devastating to an individual and disrupt their life, while having less of an effect on others who may be more resilient. Because of the range of reactivity and recovery trajectories, Polyvagal Theory focuses on the profile of the reaction to infer shifts in neural regulation of autonomic state and emphasizes the dorsal vagal life-threat response. Based on Polyvagal Theory, many of the problems associated with PTSD are emergent features following a life-threat response that are manifested as a dysfunctional Social Engagement System and a low threshold for either the sympathetic nervous system or the dorsal vagal circuit to respond in defense.

References

Anderson, M. J., & Tuerkheimer, D. (2022, May 16). "The thinking about consent has evolved drastically. This code may turn the clock back." https://www.nytimes.com/2022/05/16/opinion/metoo-sexual-assault-consent.html

Bailey, R., Dugard, J., Smith, S.F., & Porges, S. W. (2023). Appeasement: Replacing Stockholm syndrome as a definition of a survival strategy. European Journal of Psychotraumatology.

Bernard, C. (1865). *Introduction à l'étude de la médecine expérimentale* (No. 2). JB Baillière.

Borg, E., & Counter, S. A. (1989). The middle-ear muscles. *Scientific American, 261*(2), 74–80. https://doi.org/10.1038/scientificamerican0889-74

Bowen, D., & Kisida, B. (2019). Investigating Causal Effects of Arts Education Experiences: Experimental Evidence from Houston's Arts Access Initiative. Research Report for the Houston Independent School District (ED598203). ERIC. https://eric.ed.gov/?id=ED598203

Cannon, W. B. (1929). Organization for physiological homeostasis. *Physiological Reviews, 9*(3), 399–431. https://doi.org/10.1152/physrev.1929.9.3.399

Cannon, W. B. (1939). *The wisdom of the body.* W. W. Norton.

Carter, C. S. (1992). Oxytocin and sexual behavior. *Neuroscience & Biobehavioral Reviews, 16*(2), 131–144. https://doi.org/10.1016/s0149-7634(05)80176-9

Carter, C. S. (1998). Neuroendocrine perspectives on social attachment and love. *Psychoneuroendocrinology, 23*(8), 779–818. https://doi.org/10.1016/s0306-4530(98)00055-9

Carter, C. S. (2017). The oxytocin–vasopressin pathway in the context of love and fear. *Frontiers in Endocrinology, 8.* https://doi.org/10.3389/fendo.2017.00356

Carter, C. S. (2022). Oxytocin and love: Myths, metaphors and mysteries. *Comprehensive Psychoneuroendocrinology, 9,* 100107. https://doi.org/10.1016/j.cpnec.2021.100107

Carter, C. S., Ahnert, L., Grossmann, K. E., Hrdy, S. B., Lamb M. E., Porges, S. W., & Sachser, N. (2005). *Attachment and bonding: A new synthesis.* MIT Press.

Carter, C. S., Kenkel, W. M., MacLean, E. L., Wilson, S. R., Perkeybile, A. M., Yee, J. R., Ferris, C. F., Nazarloo, H. P., Porges, S. W., Davis, J. M., Connelly,

J. J., & Kingsbury, M. A. (2020). Is oxytocin "nature's medicine"? *Pharmacological Reviews, 72*(4), 829–861. https://doi.org/10.1124/pr.120.019398

Cuddy, A. (2012, June). Your body language may shape who you are [Video]. TED Conferences. https://www.ted.com/talks/amy_cuddy_your_body_lang uage_may_shape_who_you_are

Dale, L. P., Cuffe, S. P., Kolacz, J., Leon, K. G., Bossemeyer Biernacki, N., Bhullar, A., Nix, E. J., & Porges, S. W. (2022). Increased autonomic reactivity and mental health difficulties in COVID-19 survivors: Implications for medical providers. *Frontiers in Psychiatry, 13.* https://doi.org/10.3389/fpsyt .2022.830926

Dobzhansky, T. (1962). *Mankind evolving.* Yale University Press.

du Vigneaud, V., Ressler, C., & Trippett, S. (1953). The sequence of amino acids in oxytocin, with a proposal for the structure of oxytocin. *Journal of Biological Chemistry, 205*(2), 949–957. https://doi.org/10.1016/s0021-9258 (18)49238-1

Gorner, P., & Tribune Science Reporter. (2006, April 27). Easter Seals announces pioneering autism effort. *Chicago Tribune.* https://www.chicagotribune.com/ news/ct-xpm-2006-04-28-0604280141-story.html

Gouin, J. P., Carter, C. S., Pournajafi-Nazarloo, H., Glaser, R., Malarkey, W. B., Loving, T. J., Stowell, J., & Kiecolt-Glaser, J. K. (2010). Marital behavior, oxytocin, vasopressin, and wound healing. *Psychoneuroendocrinology, 35*(7), 1082–1090. https://doi.org/10.1016/j.psyneuen.2010.01.009

Grippo, A. J., Lamb, D. G., Carter, C. S., & Porges, S. W. (2007). Social isolation disrupts autonomic regulation of the heart and influences negative affective behaviors. *Biological Psychiatry, 62*(10), 1162–1170. https://doi.org/10.1016/j. biopsych.2007.04.011

Grippo, A. J., Trahanas, D. M., Zimmerman, R. R., Porges, S. W., & Carter, C. S. (2009). Oxytocin protects against negative behavioral and autonomic consequences of long-term social isolation. *Psychoneuroendocrinology, 34*(10), 1542–1553. https://doi.org/10.1016/j.psyneuen.2009.05.017

Gutkowska, J., & Jankowski, M. (2012). Oxytocin revisited: Its role in cardiovascular regulation. *Journal of Neuroendocrinology, 24*(4), 599–608. https://doi. org/10.1111/j.1365-2826.2011.02235.x

Hering, H. E. (1910). A functional test of heart vagi in man. *Menschen Munchen Medizinische Wochenschrift, 57*, 1931–1933.

Hrynkiw, I. (2016, June 13). 'I need lunch money,' Alabama school stamps on child's arm. *Advance Local.* https://www.al.com/news/birmingham/2016/06/ gardendale _elementary_student.html

Jackson, J. H. (1884). The Croonian lectures on evolution and dissolution of the nervous system. *British Medical Journal, 1*, 703. https://doi.org/10.1136/bmj .1.1215.703

Jacob, F. (1977). Evolution and tinkering. *Science, 196*(4295), 1161–1166. https:// doi.org/10.1126/science.860134

Jong, T. R. D., Menon, R., Bludau, A., Grund, T., Biermeier, V., Klampfl, S. M.,

Jurek, B., Bosch, O. J., Hellhammer, J., & Neumann, I. D. (2015). Salivary oxytocin concentrations in response to running, sexual self-stimulation, breastfeeding and the TSST: The Regensburg Oxytocin Challenge (ROC) study. *Psychoneuroendocrinology, 62*, 381–388. https://doi.org/10.1016/j.psyneuen.2015.08.027

Kolacz, J., Dale, L. P., Nix, E. J., Roath, O. K., Lewis, G. F., & Porges, S. W. (2020). Adversity history predicts self-reported autonomic reactivity and mental health in US residents during the COVID-19 pandemic. *Frontiers in Psychiatry, 11*. https://doi.org/10.3389/fpsyt.2020.577728

Kolacz, J., daSilva, E. B., Lewis, G. F., Bertenthal, B. I., & Porges, S. W. (2021). Associations between acoustic features of maternal speech and infants' emotion regulation following a social stressor. *Infancy, 27*(1), 135–158. https://doi.org/10.1111/infa.12440

Kolacz, J., Lewis, G. F., & Porges, S. W. (2018). The integration of vocal communication and biobehavioral state regulation in mammals: A polyvagal hypothesis. *Handbook of Behavioral Neuroscience, 25*, 23–34.

Kovacic, K., Kolacz, J., Lewis, G. F., & Porges, S. W. (2020). Impaired vagal efficiency predicts auricular neurostimulation response in adolescent functional abdominal pain disorders. *American Journal of Gastroenterology, 115*(9), 1534–1538. https://doi.org/10.14309/ajg.0000000000000753

Monteiro, D. A., Taylor, E. W., Sartori, M. R., Cruz, A. L., Rantin, F. T., & Leite, C. A. C. (2018). Cardiorespiratory interactions previously identified as mammalian are present in the primitive lungfish. *Science Advances, 4*(2). https://doi.org/10.1126/sciadv.aaq0800

Morton, L., Cogan, N., Kolacz, J., Calderwood, C., Nikolic, M., Bacon, T., Pathe, E., Williams, D., & Porges, S. W. (2022). A new measure of feeling safe: Developing psychometric properties of the neuroception of psychological safety scale (NPSS). *Psychological Trauma: Theory, Research, Practice, and Policy.* Advance online publication. https://doi.org/10.1037/tra0001313

Porges, S. W. (1985). Spontaneous oscillations in heart rate: Potential index of stress. In G. P. Moberg (Ed.), *Animal stress* (pp. 97–111). Springer. https://doi.org/10.1007/978-1-4614-7544-6_7

Porges, S. W. (1992). Vagal tone: A physiologic marker of stress vulnerability. *Pediatrics, 90*(3), 498–504. https://doi.org/10.1542/peds.90.3.498

Porges, S. W. (1993). The infant's sixth sense: Awareness and regulation of bodily processes. *Zero to Three, 14*(2), 12–16.

Porges, S. W. (1995). Orienting in a defensive world: Mammalian modifications of our evolutionary heritage. A Polyvagal Theory. *Psychophysiology, 32*(4), 301–318. https://doi.org/10.1111/j.1469-8986.1995.tb01213.x

Porges, S. W. (2003). Social engagement and attachment. *Annals of the New York Academy of Sciences, 1008*(1), 31–47. https://doi.org/10.1196/annals.1301.004

Porges, S. W. (2004). Neuroception: A subconscious system for detecting threats and safety. *Zero to Three (J), 24*(5), 19–24.

Porges, S. W. (2007). The polyvagal perspective. *Biological Psychology, 74*(2), 116–

143. https://doi.org/10.1016/j.biopsycho.2006.06.009

Porges, S. W. (2011). *The Polyvagal Theory: Neurophysiological foundations of emotions, attachment, communication, and self-regulation.* W. W. Norton.

Porges, S. W. (2020). The COVID-19 pandemic is a paradoxical challenge to our nervous system: A polyvagal perspective. *Clinical Neuropsychiatry, 17*(2), 135.

Porges, S. W. (2021). Polyvagal Theory: A biobehavioral journey to sociality. *Comprehensive Psychoneuroendocrinology, 7,* 100069. https://doi.org/10.1016/j.cpnec.2021.100069

Porges, S. W. (2022). Polyvagal Theory: A science of safety. *Frontiers in Integrative Neuroscience, 16.* https://doi.org/10.3389/fnint.2022.871227

Porges, S. W., Bazhenova, O. V., Bal, E., Carlson, N., Sorokin, Y., Heilman, K. J., Cook, E. H., & Lewis, G. F. (2014). Reducing auditory hypersensitivities in autistic spectrum disorder: Preliminary findings evaluating the listening project protocol. *Frontiers in Pediatrics, 2.* https://doi.org/10.3389/fped.2014.00080

Porges, S. W., & Lewis, G. F. (2010). The polyvagal hypothesis: Common mechanisms mediating autonomic regulation, vocalizations and listening. *Handbook of Behavioral Neuroscience, 19,* 255–264.

Porges, S. W., Macellaio, M., Stanfill, S. D., McCue, K., Lewis, G. F., Harden, E. R., Handelman, M., Denver, J., Bazhenova, O. V., & Heilman, K. J. (2013). Respiratory sinus arrhythmia and auditory processing in autism: Modifiable deficits of an integrated social engagement system? *International Journal of Psychophysiology, 88*(3), 261–270. https://doi.org/10.1016/j.ijpsycho.2012.11.009

Porges, S. W., & Peper, E. (2015). When not saying no does not mean yes: Psychophysiological factors involved in date rape. *Biofeedback, 43*(1), 45–48. https://doi.org/10.5298/1081-5937-43.1.01

Prison Policy Initiative. (2003). Lifetime chance of being sent to prison at current U.S. incarceration rates. https://www.prisonpolicy.org/graphs/lifetimechance.html

Rajabalee, N., Kozlowska, K., Lee, S. Y., Savage, B., Hawkes, C., Siciliano, D., Porges, S. W., Pick, S., & Torbey, S. (2022). Neuromodulation using computer-altered music to treat a ten-year-old child unresponsive to standard interventions for functional neurological disorder. *Harvard Review of Psychiatry.* Advance online publication. https://doi.org/10.1097/hrp.0000000000000341

Richter, C. P. (1957). On the phenomenon of sudden death in animals and man. *Psychosomatic Medicine, 19*(3), 191–198.

Richter, D. W., & Spyer, K. M. (1990). Cardiorespiratory control. In A. D. Loewy & K. M. Spyer (Eds.), *Central regulation of autonomic function* (pp. 189–207). Oxford University Press.

Romo, V. (2019, May 10). After backlash, Rhode Island school district rolls back 'lunch shaming' policy. *NPR.* https://www.npr.org/2019/05/10/722259141/after-backlash-rhode-island-school-district-rolls-back-lunch-shaming-policy

Sageman, M. (2004). *Understanding terror networks.* University of Pennsylvania Press.

Seligman, M. E., & Maier, S. F. (1967). Failure to escape traumatic shock. *Journal of Experimental Psychology*, *74*(1), 1–9. https://doi.org/10.1037/h0024514

The Sentencing Project. (n.d.). Growth in mass incarceration. https://www.sentencingproject.org/criminal-justice-facts/

Siebold, G. L. (2007). The essence of military group cohesion. *Armed Forces & Society*, *33*(2), 286–295.

Siegel, D. J. (1999). *The developing mind: Toward a neurobiology of interpersonal experience*. The Guilford Press.

van der Kolk, B. (2014). *The body keeps the score: Brain, mind, and body in the healing of trauma*. Penguin.

Vera, A. (2019, July 21). Pennsylvania school district tells parents to pay their lunch debt, or their kids will go into foster care. *CNN*. https://www.cnn.com/2019/07/20/us/pennsylvania-school-lunch-debt-trnd/index.html

Williams, J. R., Insel, T. R., Harbaugh, C. R., & Carter, C. S. (1994). Oxytocin administered centrally facilitates formation of a partner preference in female prairie voles (*Microtus ochrogaster*). *Journal of Neuroendocrinology*, *6*(3), 247–250. https://doi.org/10.1111/j.1365-2826.1994.tb00579.x

Winhall, J., & Porges, S. W. (2022). Revolutionizing addiction treatment with the felt sense polyvagal model. *International Body Psychotherapy Journal*, *21*(1), 13–31.

Woodworth, R. S. (1929). *Psychology* (2nd ed.). H. Holt.

Yee, J. R., Kenkel, W. M., Frijling, J. L., Dodhia, S., Onishi, K. G., Tovar, S., Saber, M. J., Lewis, G. F., Liu, W., Porges, S. W., & Carter, C. S. (2016). Oxytocin promotes functional coupling between paraventricular nucleus and both sympathetic and parasympathetic cardioregulatory nuclei. *Hormones and Behavior*, *80*, 82–91. https://doi.org/10.1016/j.yhbeh.2016.01.010

Other Resources

Books

Porges, S. W. (2011). *The Polyvagal Theory: Neurophysiological foundations of emotions, attachment, communication, and self-regulation*. W. W. Norton.

Porges, S. W. (2017). *The pocket guide to the Polyvagal Theory: The transformative power of feeling safe*. W. W. Norton.

Porges, S. W. (2017). *Die Polyvagal-Theorie und die Suche nach Sicherheit: Traumabehandlung, soziales Engagement und Bindung*. Probst Verlag.

Porges, S. W. (2021). *Polyvagal safety: Attachment, communication, self-regulation*. W. W. Norton.

Porges, S. W., & Dana, D. (2018). *Clinical applications of the Polyvagal Theory: The emergence of polyvagal-informed therapies*. W. W. Norton.

Additional Papers

Austin, M. A., Riniolo, T. C., & Porges, S. W. (2007). Borderline personality disorder and emotion regulation: Insights from the Polyvagal Theory. *Brain and Cognition, 65*(1), 69–76.

Dale, L. P., Kolacz, J., Mazmanyan, J., Leon, K. G., Johonnot, K., Bossemeyer Biernacki, N., & Porges, S. W. (2022). Childhood maltreatment influences autonomic regulation and mental health in college students. *Frontiers Psychiatry.*

Flores, P. J., & Porges, S. W. (2017). Group psychotherapy as a neural exercise: Bridging Polyvagal Theory and attachment theory. *International Journal of Group Psychotherapy, 67*(2), 202–222.

Gray, A., & Porges, S. W. (2017). Polyvagal informed dance/movement therapy with children who shut down: Restoring core rhythmicity. In C. A. Malchiodi & D. A. Crenshaw (Eds.), *What to do when children clam up in psychotherapy: Interventions to facilitate communication* (pp. 102–136). Guilford Press.

Guccione, C., Heilman, K., Porges, S. W., Gentile, S., Caretti, V., & Halaris, A. (2022). Autonomic measures in differentiating depressive disorders: A potential aid. *Clinical Neuropsychiatry, 19*(1), 29.

Kolacz, J., Kovacic, K. K., & Porges, S. W. (2019). Traumatic stress and the autonomic brain-gut connection in development: Polyvagal Theory as an integrative framework for psychosocial and gastrointestinal pathology. *Developmental Psychobiology, 61*(5), 796–809.

Kolacz, J., & Porges, S. W. (2018). Chronic diffuse pain and functional gastrointestinal disorders after traumatic stress: Pathophysiology through a polyvagal perspective. *Frontiers in Medicine, 5,* 145.

Lucas, A. R., Klepin, H. D., Porges, S. W., & Rejeski, W. J. (2018). Mindfulness-based movement: A polyvagal perspective. *Integrative Cancer Therapies, 17*(1), 5–15.

Porges, S. W. (2001). The Polyvagal Theory: Phylogenetic substrates of a social nervous system. *International Journal of Psychophysiology, 42*(2), 123–146.

Porges, S. W. (2003). The Polyvagal Theory: Phylogenetic contributions to social behavior. *Physiology & Behavior, 79*(3), 503–513.

Porges, S. W. (2009). The Polyvagal Theory: New insights into adaptive reactions of the autonomic nervous system. *Cleveland Clinic Journal of Medicine, 76*(Suppl. 2), S86.

Porges, S. W. (2016). Trauma and the Polyvagal Theory: A commentary. *International Journal of Multidisciplinary Trauma Studies.*

Porges, S. W. (2021). Polyvagal Theory: A biobehavioral journey to sociality. *Comprehensive Psychoneuroendocrinology,* 100069.

Porges, S. W., & Carter, C. S. (2017). Polyvagal Theory and the social engagement system. In P. L. Gerbarg, P. R. Muskin, & R. P. Brown (Eds.), *Complementary and Integrative Treatments in Psychiatric Practice* (pp. 221–241). American Psychiatric Association Publishing.

Porges, S. W., & Furman, S. A. (2011). The early development of the autonomic nervous system provides a neural platform for social behaviour: A polyvagal perspective. *Infant and Child Development, 20*(1), 106–118.

Porges, S. W., & Kolacz, J. (2018). Neurocardiología a través de la óptica de la teoría polivagal. In R. J. Gelpi & B. Buchholz, B. (Eds), *Neurocardiología: Aspectos fisiopatológicos e implicaciones clínicas* (pp. 343–352). Barcelona, España Elsevier.

Reed, S. F., Ohel, G., David, R., & Porges, S. W. (1999). A neural explanation of fetal heart rate patterns: A test of the Polyvagal Theory. *Developmental Psychobiology: The Journal of the International Society for Developmental Psychobiology, 35*(2), 108–118.

Reed, S. F., Porges, S. W., & Newlin, D. B. (1999). Effect of alcohol on vagal regulation of cardiovascular function: Contributions of the Polyvagal Theory to the psychophysiology of alcohol. *Experimental and Clinical Psychopharmacology, 7*(4), 484.

Sullivan, M. B., Erb, M., Schmalzl, L., Moonaz, S., Noggle Taylor, J., & Porges, S. W. (2018). Yoga therapy and Polyvagal Theory: The convergence of traditional wisdom and contemporary neuroscience for self-regulation and resilience. *Frontiers in Human Neuroscience, 12*, 67.

Notes

Chapter 2
1 (Carter et al., 2005)
2 (Jackson, 1884)
3 (Bailey et al., 2023)

Chapter 3
1 (Porges, 2021)
2 (Kovacic et al., 2020)
3 (Richter & Spyer, 1990)
4 (Hering, 1910)
5 (Porges, 1992)
6 (Porges et al., 2013, 2014; Rajabalee et al., 2022)
7 (Kolacz et al., 2018, 2021; Porges & Lewis, 2010)

Chapter 4
1 (Porges, 1995)
2 (Jacob, 1977)
3 (Porges, 2021)
4 (Porges, 2003)
5 (Porges, 2021)

Chapter 5
1 (Dobzhansky, 1962, pp. 150–152)
2 (du Vigneaud et al., 1953)
3 (Carter, 2022)
4 (Carter, 1998)

5 (Williams et al., 1994)
6 (Carter, 1998)
7 (Carter et al., 2020)
8 (Gouin et al., 2010)
9 (Carter et al., 2020)
10 (Carter, 1992; Jong et al., 2015)
11 (Gutkowska & Jankowski, 2012)
12 (Carter et al., 2020, 2022)
13 (Carter et al., 2020)

Chapter 6
1 (Cannon, 1939)
2 (Cannon, 1929)
3 (Bernard, 1865)
4 (Siegel, 1999)
5 (Porges, 1985)
6 (Porges, 2022)
7 (Sageman, 2004; Siebold, 2007)
8 (Winhall & Porges, 2022)
9 https://www.polyvagalinstitute.org

Chapter 7
1 (Porges, 2020)
2 (Kolacz et al., 2020)
3 (Dale et al., 2022)

Chapter 8
1 (Cuddy, 2012)

Chapter 9
1 (Kolacz et al., 2018, 2021; Porges & Lewis, 2010)
2 (Hrynkiw, 2016)
3 (Romo, 2019)
4 (Vera, 2019)
5 (Gorner, P., & Tribune Science Reporter, 2006)
6 (Bowen & Kisida, 2019)

Chapter 10

1 (Prison Policy Initiative, 2003)

2 (The Sentencing Project, n.d.)

3 (Anderson & Tuerkheimer, 2022)

4 (Porges & Peper, 2015)

5 (Flynn et al., 2019)

6 (Beck, 2015)

7 (Grippo et al., 2007)

8 (Grippo et al., 2009)

Glossary

1 "A Sigh of Relief," September 2021, https://www.psychologyto-day.com/us/articles/202109/sigh-relief

Index

abusive environments, 25, 42–43, 103–5, 183; *See also* childhood abuse
academic success, 154–55, 162, 175
accessory nerve, 60–61
acoustics
  classroom, 160, 161
  neuroception and, 20, 179
  office, 143–44
  in prisons, 176
  in treatment settings, 119
addiction, 105–10
adrenaline, 7, 96, 156
adversity history, 12n*, 130–31
aesthetics
  neuroception and, 20, 110, 179
  office, 143–44
  in prisons, 169
  in treatment settings, 119
aggression
  autopilot program promoting, 7
  in educational settings, 155, 156, 158, 159
  fawning to reduce, 42, 43
  neuroception and orientation toward, 20, 26, 27
  in prison settings, 165–68, 176
  rejection and, 83
  for reptiles, 70
  and survival of the fittest, 80
  trauma and, 102–3, 105
  withdrawal and, 107
  in work settings, 137
  in Yellow state, 37, 93
Allison, Michael, 148–50, 153
altruism, 126, 128
alveoli, 53
American Law Institute, 170
ancient branch of vagus nerve, 58–59, 66–67, 70–71
anger
  autopilot program promoting, 7

in COVID-19 pandemic, 126, 127, 129, 134
  and hunger, 14
  narratives that engineer, 29–30
  neuroception and orientation toward, 27
  trauma and, 102–3, 105, 115
  withdrawal and, 107
  in work settings, 137
ANS, *See* autonomic nervous system
antisocial behavior, 167
anxiety
  about public speaking, 145–48
  about work performance, 137, 138, 140
  addiction and, 105, 106, 108
  breathing to reduce, 50, 55, 152
  in COVID-19 pandemic, 130
  inmates with, 172
  narratives designed to induce, 29–30, 48
  Safe and Sound Protocol for treating, 119
  trauma and, 105, 112
anxiety disorders, 199–200
apnea, 57, 58, 187
appeasement, 16, 42–44, 183
Apple Watch, 100
Arenas, Gilbert, 150
art, 162, 174–75
ASD, *See* autism spectrum disorder
attachment, 104–5, 183–84
attention, 6, 7
auditory hypersensitivity
  with autism, 121, 200
  with Bell's palsy, 191
  neuroception and, 22, 23
  for trauma survivors, 22, 111
  treatment for people with, 117, 119–21
auditory processing disorders, 22, 23, 111, 117–20

autism spectrum disorder (ASD)
　auditory processing disorders and,
　　117–18
　classrooms designed for students
　　with, 161
　facial expression and prosody
　　with, 61, 62n★
　Polyvagal Theory as lens for, 200
　Safe and Sound treatment for
　　people with, 121–22
autonomic afferent nerves (sensory
　fibers), 51, 184, 197–98
autonomic balance, 11–12, 184–85
autonomic echo chamber, 64, 169,
　179
autonomic efferent nerves (motor
　fibers), 185
autonomic nervous system (ANS),
　5–17
　as autopilot system, 5–7
　COVID-19 pandemic and,
　　130–34
　defined, 5, 185
　in educational settings, 162
　effect of breathing on, 49
　first, 69
　freeze effect and, 14–17
　Hulk metaphor for, 10–12, 21, 61
　intervening variables and, 13–14
　as lens for sensory experience,
　　7–12
　oxytocin and, 90
　phylogenetically ordered hierarchy
　　in, 36, 193
　of prison inmates, 169, 176
　and safety, 194
　subsystems of, 7–12
　traditional model of, 14–15,
　　35–38, 56–57
autonomic state (physiological
　state), 179; *See also* traffic-light
　model of states
　defined, 8, 185–86
　feelings of safety and, 9–11
　as intervening variable, 14, 191
　mirroring of, 64
　neuroception and, 20, 26, 44
　posture as indicator of, 153
　and resilience, 99
　sensory experience and, 8–9, 32,
　　111
　substance misuse to shift, 106–7
autopilot system of body, 5–7, 9, 32

baseline heart-rate variability, 100
behavioral issues
　prison inmates with, 173–74
　students with, 156–57, 159
　for trauma survivors, 117

Bell's palsy, 191
Bernard, Claude, 97
biological imperatives
　co-regulation, 78–79, 173
　defined, 186
　feelings of safety, 31–32
biological rudeness, 83
birds, 24n★, 74
Birmingham, A.L., 160
Black men, incarceration rates for,
　164
blame, 110, 115–16
blood oxygenation, 53
bodily experience, 114–16
body
　autopilot system of, 5–7, 9, 32
　disconnection of brain and, 108
　vagal pathways to/from, 47–48
bonding, 87–90, 104–5, 113
borderline personality disorder
　(BPD), 61, 117, 200
Borg and Counter model, 191–92
bradycardia, 57, 58, 187, 189, 198
brain
　disconnection of body and, 108
　pattern recognition by, 137
　resources for, 31
　vagal nerve stimulation by, 51
　vagal pathways to/from, 47–48
brainstem
　breathing and, 52–54
　middle-ear muscles and nerves
　　in, 21
　origin of vagus nerve in, xv–xvi,
　　45–47, 50, 59, 180; *See also
　　specific structures*
breathing
　ANS control of, 6, 49
　controlled, 6, 46, 48–50, 152
　heart rate, calm, and, 52–55
　vagal stimulation through, 52
bronchi, 53
bronchioles, 53
bullying, 157–60
Bureau of Justice Statistics, 172–73
Bureau of Prison Statistics, 164
burnout, 128, 137, 138, 141

calm, 107n★
　activating vagus nerve for, 46
　autopilot program promoting, 7
　breathing and, 49–50, 52–55
　heart rate and, 52–55
　music and, 65–66
　PNS and, 8
　for prisoners, 171, 172
cancer, 89
Cannon, Walter Bradford, 97
cardiac arrhythmia, 60n★

cardioinhibitory fibers, 53–54, 69–71, 75
Carter, Sue, 87–88, 90
cats, 90–91
CBT (cognitive behavioral therapy), 118
charisma, 63–64
Chicago, I.L., 161
childhood abuse, 120, 157–59, 168
chronic pain, 105, 106, 119
Clinical Applications of the Polyvagal Theory (Dana and Porges), 115
cognitive behavioral therapy (CBT), 118
common cardiorespiratory oscillator, 52
communication
 in classroom, 161–62
 co-regulation and, 79–82, 84
 in traffic-light model of states, 44
commuting, 141–43
compassion, 128, 157, 159
conjugal visits, 170–71
connectedness, 186
consciousness, loss of, *See* freeze (shutdown) response
consent, 17, 170
controlled breathing, 6, 46, 48–50, 152
Cooper, Anderson, 96
cooperation, 80, 82, 84, 161, 162
co-regulation, 77–91, 180–81
 addiction as substitute for, 107–9
 with audience, 151–52
 as biological imperative, 78–79, 173
 in COVID-19 pandemic, 130, 133
 defined, 186–87
 dissolution and, 36–37
 face-to-face interaction phase of, 79–85
 and fawning, 43
 and importance of social interaction, 77–97
 intimacy phase of, 85–87
 oxytocin's role in, 87–90
 with pets, 90–91
 in prison settings, 164, 170–73
 self-regulation and, 195
 trauma and, 93, 104
corporal punishment, 158–59, 167
COVID-19 pandemic, 125–34
 effects of, on survivors, 132–33
 evolving scientific response to, 129–30
 Great Resignation and, 141–43
 incarceration rates in, 164n⋆
 nervous system response to, 130–34

social isolation during, 81, 125–28
vulnerability in, 12n⋆
cranial nerves
 in co-regulation, 79, 81–82
 defined, 187
 functions of, 60–61
 and nucleus ambiguus, 193
 vagal interactions with, 45, 62
 vagus vs. other, xv–xvi
criminal behavior, drivers of, 167–68
criminal justice, 165, 167–68, 173–74
critical thinking, 174–75
crumple zones metaphor for resilience, 100n⋆
Cuddy, Amy, 153
customer service surveys, 139
cyberbullying, 158

Dana, Deb, 115, 116
dancing, 41, 44
danger signals
 mirroring of, 103
 priming of neuroception with, 20–21
 in prison settings, 166, 169
 for trauma survivors, 93, 111, 112
 vagal transmission of, 46–47
 and Yellow state, 34–35
date rape, 170
death, fear of, 145
death feigning, 94, 187, 188; *See also* freeze (shutdown) response
death rates, in COVID-19 pandemic, 133
defensive states
 during COVID-19 pandemic, 129, 132, 133
 and criminal behavior, 168
 in educational settings, 156–57
 neuroception and orientation toward, 20
 and polyvagal-informed treatment, 109
 in prison settings, 166
 for reptiles, 70
 for trauma survivors, 115
 in work settings, 137
 in Yellow state, 37
depression
 in COVID-19 pandemic, 130
 Polyvagal Theory as lens for, 200–201
 Safe and Sound Protocol for treating, 119
 shared symptoms of trauma and, 117
 trauma and, 105

depression (*continued*)
  vagal stimulation to treat, 50
Descartes, René, xi, 48
diabetes, 50, 89
digestive system, SNS activation
    and, 10
dignity, 157
discipline, at school, 157–59
discovery, 161
dismissiveness, 92, 102, 128
dissociation
  addiction and, 105, 106
  defined, 188
  and Red system, 35, 37–38
  Safe and Sound Protocol for
    treating, 119
  in traffic-light model of states, 44
  as trauma response, 15, 16, 25–
    26, 93, 94, 105
  as unconscious reflex, 38
dissolution, 36–38, 188, 193
Dobzhansky, Theodosius, 80
dogs
  aggression in, 159, 167
  co-regulation with, 90–91, 172
  emotional displays by, 79
  fearful, 109
  play by, 40
  sexual activity and calm for, 171
  vocalizations by, 63
  vocal prosody with, 119–20
dorsal vagal complex (DVC)
  autonomic state and activation
    of, 185
  cardio–respiratory interactions
    and, 75n*
  death feigning and, 187
  defined, 188–89
  heart rate variability and, 190
  origin of ancient vagus in, 67,
    69–71
  psychiatric disorders and, 201
  Social Engagement System and,
    186
du Vigneaud, Vincent, 87
DVC, *See* dorsal vagal complex

economic insecurity, 159–60
educational settings, 154–63
  autonomic nervous system in, 162
  bullying in, 158–59
  impact of teacher behaviors,
    161–62
  malnourishment and hunger in,
    159–60
  meaning of safety in, 155–56
  recess in, 162–63
  school design, 160–61
  socialization and learning in, 156–57

efferent nerves (motor fibers), 185,
    189, 196, 197
Eilish, Billie, 88
EMDR (eye movement
    desensitization), 118
emotions, 14, 48, 64–66; *See also*
    feelings
empathy, xix, xxii
  during COVID-19 pandemic,
    130, 133–34
  personal hardship and, 17
  in prison settings, 172
  in work settings, 138–39
enteric nervous system, 189
epigenetics, 103n*
epilepsy, 50
exhalation, 49, 53–55, 152
eye movement desensitization
    (EMDR), 118

Facebook, 29
face-to-face interactions, 79–85, 125
facial expressions
  co-regulation and, 79, 82, 85
  during public speaking, 149
  SNS vs PNS activation and, 10
  in theater, 175
  of trauma survivors, 117
facial nerve, 60
fawning, 16, 42–44
fear
  and attachment, 104–5
  in COVID-19 pandemic, 126,
    133, 134
  and criminal behavior, 168
  living in a state of, xx–xxii, 83
  narratives designed to induce, 30
  neuroception and orientation
    toward, 20
  performance monitoring based
    on, 140
  in prison settings, 169
  of public speaking, 145–48
feelings
  acknowledging, 148
  addiction to manage, 106–7
  avoiding school and, 160
  negative, 106–7, 109–10, 160
  in polyvagal-informed treatment,
    109–10, 114–16
feelings of safety, xv, 178–80; *See
    also* Safe and Sound Protocol
    (SSP)
  autonomic state activated by,
    9–11
  and bidirectionality of vagus
    nerve, 47–48
  as biological imperative, 31–32
  bonding and, 104, 105, 113

charisma and, 63
co-regulation and, 79, 91
dissolution and, 37
in educational settings, 154–56
and Green system, 33–34
importance of, 27
increasing, 24–25
priming neuroception with, 20–22
prison design to evoke, 175–76
projecting, 148–50, 153
transformative effects of, xxi–xxii
treatments that evoke, 118–19
vagal signals related to, 46, 48
work-related benefits of, 138–39
fight-or-flight response, 189
danger signals activating, 10
facial and vocal features in, 61–62
sympathetic nervous system and, 8
in traditional model of ANS, 15
in traffic-light model of states,
34–35
foster care system, 168
freeze (shutdown) response; *See also*
Red state
and ANS, 14–17
neuroception and, 35
in traffic-light model of states,
42–44
to trauma, 92–94, 96, 110–11
friendly faces, in audience, 149–50
Frontiers of Psychiatry, 130

glossopharyngeal nerve, 60
Great Resignation, 141–43
Green state
accessing, at work, 140, 144, 145
accessing, during COVID-19
pandemic, 129, 131
addiction and access to, 106–7
appeasement to induce, 43
behavior associated with, 33–34,
44
during commute, 142
controlled breathing and, 48, 55,
152
co-regulation and, 78, 79, 85
dissolution process and, 37
engagement in arts and, 174–75
facial expression and prosody in,
63–64, 149, 151
harsh discipline and, 159
homeostasis in, 97, 98, 119
intimacy and, 41–42, 86
learning in, 154, 160–62
long COVID and, 133
measuring activation of, 75, 76
middle-ear muscles in, 111, 120
modern vagal branch and
activation of, 59, 61

music as trigger for, 65
need for, 93
for newborns, 57–58
oxytocin release and, 89n*
play and, 38–41
prison inmates' access to, 166,
171, 172, 174–76
resilience as ability to remain in,
101
social isolation and, 126
turning off work to enter, 137–38
vagal brake and, 46–47, 56, 58
vagal nerve stimulation to induce,
51
guilt, 103
gut instincts, 36–37, 67

Hamlet (Shakespeare), 174
healing, 93, 104, 119, 122
hearing
neuroception and, 21–23
by students in Yellow state, 157
for trauma survivors, 111, 117,
120–21
heart disease, 89
heart rate, 117
breathing and, 52–55, 74–75
calmness and, 52–55
and SNS vs. PNS activation, 10
heart-rate variability (HRV), 76,
98–101, 190
Hering, Heinrich, 54
homeostasis, 11–12, 67, 190
bonding for, 104, 105
and healing, 119
and office space, 144
for prisoners, 166
in prison settings, 169
resilience and, 97–98, 101–2
routine for, 136–37
hopelessness, 94n*
hospitals, 118, 131
hourly employees, 136–38
HRV, *See* heart-rate variability
Hulk metaphor for ANS, 10–12,
21, 61
human evolution, 30–32, 68–76
humanity, of incarcerated
individuals, 165
hunger, 14, 159–60
hyperventilation, 49, 55, 152
hypervigilance, 117–18, 155
hypoxia, 99

IFS (internal family systems), 118
immobilization behaviors
and consent laws, 170
defined, 186
as trauma response, 14–17, 94

incarceration, 164–65; *See also*
    prison settings
Indiana University, 114
individual differences, defined, 100
infants, 88, 120n*, 186; *See also*
    newborns
inhalation, 49, 54–55
insecurity, 140
Integrated Listening Systems, 122
internal family systems (IFS), 118
internal milieu, 97
interoception, 190, 192
intervening variable(s)
    autonomic state as, 14, 118, 179,
        195
    defined, 191
    mood as, 13
    in resilience, 95
    in S-O-R models, 13–14, 197
    in viral infection, 130, 131
intimacy
    co-regulation and, 85–87, 90–91,
        171
    as hybrid state, 41–42, 44
    in prison settings, 171
intrinsically photosensitive retinal
    ganglion cells, 19n*
irritability, 14
irritable bowel syndrome, 52, 61
isolation, *See* social isolation

Jackson, John Hughlings, 36, 188, 193

karaoke, 147
kindness, 134
Kinsey Institute, 114

Latino men, incarceration rates for,
    164
learned helplessness, 94n*
learning
    art/music education and, 162
    in Green state, 47
    physical spaces to promote, 160–61
    Polyvagal Theory on, 154
    and socialization, 156–57
Lewis, G. F., 192
life threats, 35, 92, 187
lighting, 19–20, 160–61, 164
linear additive model, 184
loneliness, 81
long COVID, 50, 119, 132–33
love, 86–91, 105, 134
loved ones
    prison inmates' contact with,
        170–72
    transmitting trauma to, 103
lunch debt, 160

malnourishment, 159–60
mammals; *See also specific types*
    domestication of, 80
    evolution of, 30–32, 68–76
    freeze response for, 94
    modern motor branch of vagus
        nerve in, 58–66
    oxytocin in, 87–90
    routines for, 136
    social behavior by, 72–73
    vocalizations by, 63
marginalization, 108, 132
maternal behavior, 74–75, 88,
    120n*, 186
medical conditions, 116–18, 197–
    98; *See also specific conditions*
meetings, 144, 145
mental health
    Polyvagal Theory as lens for,
        199–201
    of prison inmates, 166–68
    trauma and, 116–18
metal detectors, 28, 155
middle-ear muscles
    co-regulation and, 79
    defined, 191
    music and, 65
    in neuroception system, 21–22
    and SNS vs. PNS activation, 10
    trauma and, 111
middle-ear transfer function, 191–92
mirroring, 64, 103, 149, 169
mobilization behaviors, 185–86
Model Penal Code, 170
modern motor branch of vagus
    nerve, 58–66
monogamy, social, 87–88
Monteiro, D. A., 75n*
mood, as intervening variable, 13
motor fibers, 185
movement-based routines, 150
music, 46–47, 64–66, 162
myelination, 59, 66

Nash, Steve, 150
National Basketball Association
    (NBA), 150
natural light, 160–61
negative feelings, 106–7, 109–10,
    160
neural exercise, 40, 162, 181, 192
neural expectancy, 83, 192
neuroception, 18–44, 179
    addiction and, 109
    autism spectrum disorder and, 200
    in autonomic echo chamber, 64,
        169
    and autonomic states, 44

in co-regulation, 79
and definition of safety, 27–30
described, 18–23, 32, 192
effect of trauma on, 23–25
fawning and appeasement
        responses, 42–43
fight-or-flight response, 34–35
freeze response, 35
individual differences in, 25–27
interoception vs., 190
during intimacy, 41–42
and physical environment, 143
during play, 38–41
of prosody, 120
of psychological safety, 194–95
search for safety as driver of
        human evolution, 30–32
self-reinforcement in, 20–21
and signals from vagus nerve, 46
Social Engagement System and,
        33–34
Spider-Sense metaphor for, 19
and traditional model of ANS,
        35–38
traffic-light metaphor for
        autonomic states, 32–33
neurodiversity, 117
neurophysiological model of safety
        and trust, 194
newborns
heart-rate variability in, 99–100
neuroception by, 31
prosody use with, 63–64, 119–20
Social Engagement System of, 72
vagal activation in, 57–58
The New York Times, 50
Nowitzki, Dirk, 150
nucleus ambiguus, 193
nucleus of the solitary tract, 193

office space, 143–44
ontogeny, 193
open offices, 143
optic nerve, xv
orgasm, 88, 89
"Orienting in a Defensive World"
        (Porges), 68
ossicles, 191
outrage, 29
oxytocin, 87–91, 104, 173

pain
chronic, 105, 106, 119
response to, 19
tolerance for, 10
parasympathetic nervous system
        (PNS); *See also* Green state
activation of, 8–12, 21, 33–34

balance between sympathetic and,
        11–12, 184–85
defined, 193
in traditional model of ANS, 38,
        39, 56–57
Paris terrorist attacks (2015), 95–96
Parkinson's disease, 119
past experience, neuroception and,
        25–26
peak performance, at work, 148–52
Pediatrics, 57
performance monitoring, 139–41
performing arts, 174–75
pets, co-regulation with, 90–91
phylogenetically ordered hierarchy,
        36, 193
phylogeny, 193–94
physical assault, xx, 15–16
physical contact
and intimacy, 86
need for, 83–84
in prison settings, 170–72
physical environment
and neuroception, 20
for polyvagal-informed treatment,
        110, 118–19
in prisons, 164, 167
in schools, 160–61
trauma triggers in, 112, 116
at work, 143–44
physical exertion, 39, 100
physical health
and feelings of safety, 24
intimacy and, 86–88
of prison inmates, 166–67
of trauma survivors, xx–xxi
physiological state, *See* autonomic
        state
play
building resilience with, 175
as hybrid state, 38–41, 44
as neural exercise, 40, 181
during recess, 162–63
and resilience, 101–2
at work, 145
PNS, *See* parasympathetic nervous
        system
politics
during COVID-19 pandemic,
        126, 129
narratives that make us feel unsafe
        in, 28, 30
and punitive approach to criminal
        justice, 167–68, 171, 173
school safety in, 155
polyvagal-informed design
for addiction treatment centers,
        109–10

politics (*continued*)
  for offices, 143–44
  for prisons, 175–76
  and Safe-and-Sound Protocol,
    119–22
  for trauma treatment, 114–16,
    118–19
  and universality of safety, 27
Polyvagal Institute, 109–10
Polyvagal Theory (PVT)
  on addiction, 105–6, 108
  bodily experience in, 114–15
  concept of stress in, 98–99
  on dissociation, 25–26
  explaining behavior with, xix–xx
  on fawning and appeasement, 42
  feelings of safety in, 27
  on harsh discipline, 159
  on human/mammalian evolution,
    30–32, 68–76
  hypothesis testing related to, 54,
    75–76
  improving performance with,
    148–52
  on incarceration, 165, 167–69, 173
  on learning, 154
  on posture, 153
  principles embedded in, 178–81
  proposal of, 68
  on psychiatric diagnoses, 199–201
  on resilience, 101
  on routines, 150
  on social behavior in mammals,
    72–73
  and Social Engagement System, 72
  on social isolation, 127
  summary of, xv, xix, 178
  traditional model of ANS vs.
      model in, 14–15, 35–36, 38
  on trauma, xviii, 110–13, 114, 132
  on work-related stress, 138
Porges, Eric, 50–51
Porges, Stephen, 68, 115, 192
postcoital dysphoria, 107n*
post-traumatic stress disorder
    (PTSD)
  in COVID-19 pandemic, 130
  Polyvagal Theory as lens for, 201
  resilience and development of, 95
  Safe and Sound Protocol for
    treating, 119
  symptoms of, 61, 62n*, 96–97,
    120
  vagal stimulation to treat, 50, 52
posture, 150, 153
prairie voles, 87–88, 89n*, 173
predictability, 152
priming neuroception, 20–22

prison settings, 164–76
  activation of ANS in, 169
  art and theater in, 174–75
  as chronically unsafe spaces,
    165–67
  and consent laws, 170
  co-regulation in, 170–72
  effects of punitive approach to
    criminal justice, 167–68
  and incarceration as fact of life,
    164–65
  polyvagal-informed design for,
    175–76
  solitary confinement in, 172–74
privacy
  in office spaces, 143, 144
  in prison settings, 164, 166, 172,
    176
prosody
  and charisma, 63–64
  for co-regulation, 79
  defined, 194
  and effect of music on state, 65
  PNS activation and, 10
  in public speaking, 151–52
  in Safe and Sound Protocol,
    119–21
  in theater, 175
  for trauma survivors, 117
PTSD, *See* post-traumatic stress
    disorder
public speaking
  fear of, 145–48
  improving, 148–52
  posture during, 153
punishment, in schools, 157–59
punitive approach to criminal
    justice, 167–68, 173–74
PVT, *See* Polyvagal Theory

rape, 170
rational analysis, 174
rats, 92, 94n*
reactivity, 127, 129, 130
reading, during presentations, 152
recess, 162–63
Red state; *See also* freeze (shutdown)
    response
  adaptive function of, 39, 40
  appeasement and, 43
  behavior associated with, 33, 35, 44
  controlled breathing to shift out
    of, 48
  in COVID-19 pandemic, 126
  dissolution process and, 36–38
  facial expression and voice in, 61,
    149
  fawning and, 43

intimacy and, 41–42, 85, 86
for prison inmates, 166
during public speaking, 145, 147
for reptiles, 67
sensory experience in, 111
Social Engagement System and, 79
students in, 156
substance misuse to shift out of, 106
trauma and, 93, 94, 110
vagal brake in, 56, 58
reintegration, after incarceration, 168–69
rejection, 82–83
relaxation, 135, 137
remedial classes, 157
reptiles
ancient vagal branch of, 58
comparative neuroanatomy for mammals and, 73–74
freeze response for, 94
and mammalian evolution, 67–70
Red state for, 36n★, 38
safety as driver for mammals vs., 30–31
social behavior by mammals vs., 24
resilience, 179
in COVID-19 pandemic, 129, 130
crumple zones metaphor for, 100n★
HRV as measure of, 98–101
individual differences in, 38, 112–13
of inmates, 175
oxytocin and, 88–90
play and, 162–63
play to build, 41
Slinky metaphor for, 100–101
social behavior, play, and, 101–2
social isolation and, 126
as trauma response, 95–103
respiration, heart rate and, 52–53
respiratory sinus arrhythmia (RSA), 54, 76, 190, 194
rest-and-relax response, 8, 10
restrictive housing, 172–73
rewards, visits with loved ones as, 171–72
Richter, Curt, 94n★
Rick and Morty (TV show), 88
routine, 136–37, 150
RSA, *See* respiratory sinus arrhythmia

sadness, 102–3
Safe and Sound Protocol (SSP), 119–22

safety; *See also* feelings of safety; threats to safety
meaning of, 27–30, 155–56
neurophysiological model of trust and, 194–95
search for, 30–32, 73
in therapeutic settings, 118–19, 118–22, 195
universality of, 26–27
vagal transmission of signals of, 46–47
schizophrenia, 61, 89, 117, 119
school design, 160–61
school safety, 155–56
SE (somatic experiencing), 118
security measures, 27–28, 155–56
Seinfeld, Jerry, 145
selfishness, 126, 127
self-medication, 108
self-regulation, 195
sensory branch of vagus nerve, 58n†
sensory experience
autonomic nervous system and, 7–12
autonomic state as lens for, 7–12, 32
conscious and unconscious components of, 19
neuroception and, 21–23
in prison, 175–76
trauma and, xxi, 12, 111
vagal pathways from body to brain, 47–48
sensory fibers, *See* autonomic afferent nerves
sexual activity, 88, 89, 107n★, 171
sexual assault, xvii, 86, 164, 170
shame, 103, 108, 110, 159–60
shutdown response, *See* freeze response
Siegel, Dan, 97
Sims, The (game), 77–78, 81
Slinky metaphor for resilience, 100–101
smiling, 149
SNS, *See* sympathetic nervous system
social behavior, 181
by mammals, 69–73
need for, 126
oxytocin release in, 88–89
resilience and, 101–2
trauma and, 113
vagal stimulation by, 45, 72–73
at work, 144–45
Social Engagement System
activation of, 33–34, 184
attachment and, 184

Social Engagement System
(*continued*)
    autonomic balance and, 184–85
    as condition for safety, 194
    in co-regulation, 79, 83, 85
    coupling autonomic state with,
        185–86
    defined, 196
    in fawning vs. appeasement, 43
    fight-or-flight system and, 189
    mammalian evolution of, 71–72
    prosody and, 151
    psychiatric disorders and, 200,
        201
    reciprocal, 186
    in therapeutic settings, 195
    ventral vagal complex and, 62
social interactions
    in COVID-19 pandemic, 129–30
    for mammals, 71
    need for, 77–81, 172, 173
    priming audiences for, 151
    for prisoners, 172
    vagal stimulation through, 52
    in work settings, 144–45
social isolation
    during COVID-19 pandemic,
        125–29
    for mammals, 31
    physical and mental effects of,
        80–81
    in prison settings, 81, 173
socialization, learning and, 156–57
social media, 29, 50, 51, 158
social monogamy, 87–88
Society for Psychophysiological
    Research, 68
solitary confinement, 81, 172–74
solitary tract, nucleus of, 193
somatic experiencing (SE), 118
somatomotor component of SES,
    196
somatomotor pathways, 196
Sopranos, The (TV show), 102
S–O–R (stimulus–organism–
    response) model, 13, 196–97
special visceral efferent pathways,
    196
Spencer, Herbert, 188
Spider-Sense metaphor for
    neuroception, 19
S–R model, *See* stimulus–response
    model
SSP (Safe and Sound Protocol),
    119–22
stage fright, 145–47
stimulus–organism–response
    (S–O–R) model, 13, 196–97

stimulus–response (S–R) model, 13,
    191, 196–97
Stockholm syndrome, 183
stress
    activation of SNS by, 12, 56–57
    addiction and, 105, 106
    commute as source of, 141–43
    in COVID-19 pandemic, 128, 131
    heart-rate variability and, 98–101
    pervasive, 12n*, 105, 112, 138
    in Polyvagal Theory, 98–99
    social isolation as source of, 125
    window of tolerance for, 97–99
    work and, 135, 136, 138
subdiaphragmatic vagus, 184–85,
    189, 197
substance misuse, 105–9, 168
supradiaphragmatic vagus, 197
survival
    face-to-face interactions for,
        79–80, 82
    pandemic-era emphasis on,
        132–33
survival instincts, 140, 148
survival of the fittest, 80
survival state, 11–12, 92
sympathetic nervous system (SNS);
    See also Yellow state
    balance between parasympathetic
        and, 11–12, 184–85
    coupling Social Engagement
        System and, 185–86
    defined, 197
    effects of activating, 8–10, 185
    and fight-or-flight system, 8, 10,
        189
    hearing during activation of, 21–22
    music that activates, 65
    neuroception and activation of,
        34–35
    psychiatric disorders and, 201
    in traditional model of ANS, 38,
        39, 56–57

teacher behaviors, 161–62
theater, 174–75
therapeutic settings, safety in, 118–
    22, 195
This American Life (radio show), 174
"This Nerve Influences Nearly
    Every Internal Organ. Can
    It Improve Our Mental State
    Too?," 50
threats to safety, 178–81
    addiction and, 109
    evolution of systems for detecting,
        24
    manufactured, 28–30

neuroception to gauge, 18–19
priming to detect, 20–22
in prison settings, 165–67, 169, 176
for students with behavioral issues, 156–57
for trauma survivors, 92–93
vagal transmission of signals related to, 46
TikTok, 50
traffic-light model of states, 32–38; *See also specific states*
evolution of components of, 35–38
fawning and appeasement in, 42–44
Green system in, 33–34, 44
hybrid states in, 38–44, 85–86
intimacy in, 41–42
play in, 38–41
Red system in, 35, 44
Yellow system in, 34–35, 44
transgenerational trauma, 103
trauma, 92–122
acknowledging, 102
addiction as response to, 105–10
bonding after, 104–5
bullying as source of, 158
and concept of stress in PVT, 98–99
during COVID-19 pandemic, 127, 132–34
described, 92–93
digestive issues and, 11n†
duration of, 113
and efficacy of safer-feeling treatment, 118–19
fawning and appeasement in response to, 42–43
health effects of, xx–xxi
immobilization response to, 14–17, 35, 94, 188
neuroception after, 25
physiological effects of, xvi–xvii, 23–25, 179
Polyvagal Theory on, 110–13
resilience in response to, 95–103
and Safe-and-Sound Protocol, 119–22
shared symptoms of, 116–18
transgenerational, 103
treatments for, 113–16
trauma history, 12n*, 130–31
Traumatic Stress Research Consortium, 114, 115
trigeminal nerve, 60
trigger warnings, 25
trust, 78, 86, 129, 194–95
turnover, 141

unconscious control, 5–6
Unyte Health, 122

vagal afferents, 197–98
vagal brake, 180
and ancient vs. modern vagal branch, 58
defined, 198
into Green vs. Red system, 55–56
intentional activation of, 46
vagal nerve stimulation (VNS) devices, 51
vagal paradox, 56–58, 198
vagal tone, 54, 57, 76, 198
vagus nerve, 45–67, 180; *See also* dorsal vagal complex (DVC); ventral vagal complex (VVC)
ancient motor branch of, 58–59, 66–67, 70–71
bidirectionality of, 47–48
charisma and activation of, 63–64
controlled breathing and, 48–50
defined, 199
destinations of, xv–xvi
and effect of music on emotion, 64–66
heart rate, breathing, and calm, 52–55
in mammalian evolution, 69–71
methods of stimulating, 50–52
modern motor branch of, 58–66
in parasympathetic nervous system, 8
signals transmitted by, 46–47
social behavior and, 45
stimulation of, 72–73
van der Kolk, Bessel, 23
vasopressin, 87, 89
vegetative vagus, *See* dorsal vagal complex (DVC)
ventral vagal complex (VVC), 60–62
charisma and, 63
co-regulation and, 79, 81–82
defined, 199
dorsal vagal complex vs., 66–67
and fight-or-flight defense system, 189
mammalian evolution of, 71
psychiatric disorders and, 199–200
safety in therapeutic settings and, 195
Social Engagement System and, 62, 185
vagal tone and, 198
video-conferencing apps, 84n*, 151n*
video games, 84–85

violence
   biological rudeness and, 83
   manufactured threats to safety
      and, 28
   in prison, 164–67, 176
   PTSD vs. resilience after exposure
      to, 95
visceromotor component of SES,
   196
visceromotor nerves, 199
visitation, in prison settings, 170–72
VNS (vagal nerve stimulation)
   devices, 51
vocal prosody, *See* prosody
vulnerability, 86
VVC, *See* ventral vagal complex

Warwick, R.I., 160
Washington State, 172
weakness, acknowledging trauma
   as, 102
weapons, 166
window of tolerance, 97–101, 194
Wisdom of the Body, The (Cannon),
   97
withdrawal, substance, 107, 110
working from home, 142–43
work settings, 135–53
   achieving peak performance in,
      148–52
   commuting to, 141–43
   as constant stressor, 135
   empathetic perspective on issues
      in, 138–39
   for hourly employees, 136–38
   office space design, 143–44
   performance monitoring in,
      139–41
   posture in, 153

public speaking in, 145–47
social interaction in, 144–45
wound healing, 89
Wright, Will, 77

Yellow state
   appeasement and, 43
   behavior associated with, 33–35,
      44
   breathing in, 45, 55, 152
   during commute, 142
   controlled breathing to shift out
      of, 48
   in COVID-19 pandemic, 126, 129
   dissolution process and, 37
   facial expression and voice in, 61,
      149
   fawning and, 43
   for hourly employees, 137
   middle-ear muscles in, 111, 120
   music to induce, 65
   negative view of, 57–58
   play and, 38–41, 101, 162, 175
   for prison inmates, 166
   public speaking and, 145, 147
   sensory experience in, 111
   Social Engagement System and,
      79
   students in, 156–57
   substance misuse to shift out of,
      106
   in substance withdrawal, 107
   trauma and, 93, 94
   vagal brake and, 46
   at work, 140, 144
yoga, 46–47, 49–50, 55

zombie face, 85
Zoom, 84n*, 151n*

About the Authors

Stephen W. Porges, PhD, is Distinguished University Scientist at Indiana University where he is the founding director of the Traumatic Stress Research Consortium in the Kinsey Institute. He is professor of psychiatry at the University of North Carolina, and professor emeritus at both the University of Illinois at Chicago and the University of Maryland. He served as president of the Society for Psychophysiological Research and the Federation of Associations in Behavioral & Brain Sciences and is a former recipient of a National Institute of Mental Health Research Scientist Development Award. He is the originator of the Polyvagal Theory, creator of a music-based intervention, the Safe and Sound Protocol, and a founder of the Polyvagal Institute.

Seth Porges is a journalist and filmmaker. He wrote, produced, and directed the hit film *Class Action Park*, which debuted at number one on HBO Max, was nominated for a Critics Choice Documentary Award, and won Best Documentary at the 2021 Hollywood Critics Association Film Awards. He is currently directing an upcoming film for a major streaming service, as well as a documentary about professional pickleball. Seth was previously a technology editor at *Popular Mechanics* magazine, a columnist for *Bloomberg Businessweek*, and has appeared in roughly 50 episodes of the Travel Channel's *Mysteries at the Museum*.